Islam in Urban America
Sunni Muslims in Chicago

ISLAM IN URBAN AMERICA

Sunni Muslims in Chicago

GARBI SCHMIDT

TEMPLE UNIVERSITY PRESS
Philadelphia

Temple University Press, Philadelphia 19122
Copyright © 2004 by Temple University
All rights reserved
Published 2004
Printed in the United States of America

⊛ The paper used in this publication meets the requirements of the
American National Standard for Information Sciences—Permanence
of Paper for Printed Library Materials, ANSI Z39.48-1984

Library of Congress Cataloging-in-Publication Data

Schmidt, Garbi.
    Islam in urban America : Sunni Muslims in Chicago / Garbi Schmidt.
    p.   cm.
    Includes bibliographical references and index.
    ISBN 1-59213-223-5 (cloth : alk. paper) — ISBN 1-59213-224-3 (pbk. :
alk. paper)
    1. Muslims—Illinois—Chicago—Social conditions.   2. Sunnites—
Illinois—Chicago—Social conditions.   3. Group identity—Illinois—
Chicago.   4. Immigrants—Illinois—Chicago—Social conditions.
    5. Chicago (Ill.)—Social conditions.   6. Chicago (Ill.)—Ethnic relations.
    7. Chicago (Ill.)—Religious life and customs.   I. Title.

F548.9.M88S36 2004
305.6'971–dc21   2003050788

2   4   6   8   9   7   5   3   1

Contents

Acknowledgments

ONE PERSON ALONE can write a book, but not without the support of many. To the following people and organizations that influenced the creation of this work, I offer my gratitude and respect.

A number of Muslim institutions in Chicago and the people involved in these deserve thanks for allowing me access to the community: the Arab American Community Center, the Al-Aqsa School, the Council for Muslim Organizations of Greater Chicago, the Inner City Muslim Action Network, the Institute for Islamic Information and Education, the Islamic Cultural Center of Chicago, the Downtown Islamic Center, IQRA International Foundation, the Mosque Foundation, the Muslim Students' Association (MSA) at the University of Chicago, the MSA at Loyola University, the MSA at De Paul University, the MSA at the University of Illinois in Chicago, the Naqshbandiyya *tariqa* (order), the Muslim Community Center, the Muslim Education Center, and the Universal School. Special thanks go to the Morsi family for taking me under their roof with astonishing hospitality.

Academically, I am indebted to a number of teachers and professors: in Denmark, Sven Frøkjær Jensen and Jørgen Podemann Sørensen; in Sweden, Jan Hjärpe (my Ph.D. adviser) and David Westerlund; and in the United States, John L. Esposito, Yvonne Y. Haddad, Asad Husain, Karen I. Leonard, Bruce Lincoln, Larry Poston, Harold Vogelaar, and John Voll.

I cordially thank the following friends and colleagues for their support, readings, and comments: Leslie Barnett, David Bunnage, Laurie Estes, Philip Halden, Torsten Jansson, Heike Peter, Jonas Otterbeck, Catharina Raudvere, Leif Stenberg, and Jonas Svensson. Thanks to Dorothy Anderson, who edited the manuscript in its first version as a dissertation, and to Natalie Reid, whose competence as an editor and enthusiasm as a kindred soul were indispensable in the process leading to the final version of the book. Warm thoughts also go to the late Inger Kirsten, who let me live in her house during the early months of my fieldwork in Chicago.

I wish to thank the Danish Fulbright Foundation, the Danish Research Academy, the Danish Research Council, and the Knud Højgaard Foundation for making my fieldwork possible. Sincere gratitude also goes to the Swedish National Bank for financing one year of writing, and to the Academy of Migration Studies in Denmark (AMID) and the Danish National Institute for Social Research for giving me the time and the funds to rewrite the dissertation into a book. Warm thanks also to editors Doris Braendel and Janet Francendese at Temple University Press for their patience, help, and encouragement.

I am grateful to my spouse, Jan T. Pedersen, whose support during my writing made stressful periods less stressful. Last, but far from least, I wish to thank our son, Johan Aske (who was born during the early phases of rewriting this work), for his smiles, curiosity, and zest for life.

A Note on Transliteration

TRANSLITERATING the Islamic vocabulary that Muslim Americans use became a major issue in the preparation of this book, because fixed standards for an "Islamic-American English" do not yet exist.

In North America, as elsewhere in the Western world, Arabic terms for aspects of Islamic practice and theology do not necessary follow the standards of Arabic spoken in the Middle East. For instance, American Muslims may use phrases such as *hijabis* (women who wear the Muslim head scarf) and *khatibs* (the people who deliver the sermon during Friday prayers). This Anglicization (that is, making plurals by adding *s*) makes the words look and sound very different from the standard Arabic plural forms (*muhajjabat, khutaba'*).

As both Isma'il Raji al-Faruqi in *Towards Islamic English* and Barbara Daly Metcalf in *Making Muslim Space in North America and Europe* have made clear, Islamic-American English is part of Islam as it is lived and practiced in the United States. Yet deciding how to deal with Islamic-American English was difficult. In this work, I have chosen to follow the standards that Metcalf suggests in her work note on transliteration. My hope is that this simplified standard for transliteration will prove useful for both experienced and less-experienced readers of works on Islam. One divergence from Metcalf's book is that I have chosen to italicize all Arabic terms.

However, when I quote writing or transliteration by other authors, I follow their preferences for both spelling and italics. In the instances where Muslim institutions have transliterated their names according to phonetics other than the system I use in this work, I likewise follow their usage. Plural forms of Arabic terms follow either standard Arabic or American colloquial forms.

A glossary of Arabic words and phrases in the text appears in the back matter.

Islam in Urban America

Sunni Muslims in Chicago

1   Introduction

ISLAM IN THE URBAN CONTEXT:
INTRODUCING THE MEDINA

Medina, in Arabic, means city. But *medina* also encompasses
community, familiarity, and people's sense of belonging. *Medina*
even has religious connotations for Muslims, because the city of
Yathrib changed its name to Medina when the Prophet Muhammad established his community there in 622 A.D. The "medina"
in this book is Chicago, a city in the heartland of the United
States where Muslims from all parts of the globe have settled. To
these immigrants, Chicago is an American *medina.* In this city,
they are creating a new home, combining habits of their homelands with an American way of life. In this city, they practice
Islam and establish mosques, schools, and colleges. And in this
city (and in the many other American medinas across the continent), they present Islam to their fellow citizens as a component
of American life. Muslims have lived in the United States for
more than a century, and, some argue, even longer than that.[1]
Muslims are pupils at American schools, students and professors
at American universities, doctors at American hospitals, reporters
at American newspapers, police officers, and soldiers in the U.S.
Army. Islam is part of the appearance of American cities, visible
in finely designed mosques with minarets and domes; in small
halal butcher shops with hand-painted signs in predominantly
Middle Eastern neighborhoods; and in the long robes of women
shopping in malls and grocery stores.

   Islam in Urban America offers its readers a deeper understanding of the Muslim-American community and Islam as a
faith in the American context by introducing the everyday lives
of Muslim Americans. Islam has grown into one of the country's
three largest religions. This book seeks to answer two questions
important for American society in the twenty-first century: First,

can Islam be considered an "American" religion, as opposed to one so far removed from American realities that it is simply a temporary but eventually impermanent resident? Second, can Muslims be considered a unified community, considering that Islam in the United States comprises more than sixty ethnic groups from such differing contexts as Bosnia, China, Egypt, Malaysia, Nigeria, and Pakistan?[2] *Islam in Urban America* will answer these and other questions through intense scrutiny of the details of Muslim life in one city, Chicago, in the 1990s. By focusing on one city, we see details and aspects of Muslim life in America that otherwise are easily overlooked. And by looking at Chicago, we encounter one of the largest, most vibrant, and most influential Muslim communities in the United States.

The non-Muslim world needs to understand the Muslim-American community for various reasons. As several studies show, Islam is on its way to becoming the second-largest religion in the United States,[3] despite numerous misconceptions (about the religion, its content, its people) that present Islam as both alien and hostile to everything American. After the terrorist attacks against America on September 11, 2001, it is more critical than ever to lay these misconceptions to rest. To this end, *Islam in Urban America* presents detailed descriptions—based largely on the author's long-term encounters with the community—of a population whose diverse and often conflicting beliefs and aspirations need wider understanding within the shifting demographics of American society.

THE MUSLIMS OF THE UNITED STATES

Before moving into the details of Muslim life in Chicago, some general facts about Muslims in North America will help set the scene. The community comprises a large number of ethnic groups, with significant consequences for both community organizing and religious interpretation. A survey by one of the country's largest Muslim lobbying organizations, the American Muslim Council, estimated in 1992 that the major groups are African Americans (42%), South Asians (24.4%), and Arabs (12.4%), with American whites representing 2 percent.[4] Other studies estimate that South Asians count for 29.3 percent, Arabs for 32.7 percent, and African Americans for 29.9 percent of the Muslim American population.[5] Either way, Arabs, South Asians, and African Americans are the largest ethnic groups representing Islam in the United States.

As for size, the most recent studies estimate that Muslims make up 2 million to 7 million—or 0.7 to 2.4 percent—of the U.S. population.[6] The majority represents Sunni Islam, with a small number of Shi'ites and others belonging to different Muslim sects, some of which are indigenous to America. The schism between Sunnis and Shi'ites took place within the first years after the death of the Prophet of Islam, Muhammad, in A.D. 632. Whereas some followers believed that the leadership (*khilafa*) of the believers should be decided by the leading companions of the Prophet, others claimed that the leadership belonged to Ali (d. A.D. 661), the Prophet's son-in-law, because of his familial relationship to the Prophet. Throughout Islamic history, relations between the two groups have often been hostile and violent, fueling the schism. The two groups disagree on a number of issues, ranging from ways to pray to determining religious leadership. Although Shi'ites form the majority in countries such as Iran and Bahrain,[7] most of the world's Muslims are Sunnis, including those in the United States.

The two main immigrant ethnic groups representing Sunni Islam in America come from the Middle East and the South Asian peninsula. Many South Asians came after congressional legislation in 1965 abolished the national-origin quota system.[8] The South Asian population in the United States mushroomed from 32,000 in 1970–71 to almost 910,000 by 1990.[9]

South Asians are among the country's most educated and prosperous immigrant groups. In 1990, immigrants from India had the highest median household income, the highest percentage of bachelor's degrees, and the highest percentage of professional employment.[10] That South Asians have been taught English since childhood is a significant factor in their success in the United States.[11] Not surprisingly, South Asians are usually the more socially advantaged of the Muslim immigrants. They also tend to fare better than Middle Eastern Muslims in the media and other forms of public representation, although discrimination against South Asian Americans continues—for example, in the job market.[12]

Arabs have lived for more than one hundred years in the United States. Before the Second World War, Arab immigrants to the United States were predominantly Christian, but after the war, both Christians and Muslims came from all over the Arab world. As with the South Asians, many Arabs who immigrated to the United States in the second half of the twentieth century were highly educated, with a firm understanding of the role of citizens in a democracy.[13] This understanding greatly affected the level of activism within the many organizations that the community later established.

After the 1967 war between Egypt and Israel, the community established organizations such as the Arab-American Anti-Discrimination Committee, and the Association of Arab-American University Graduates became a focal point for many Arab Americans. Despite the military defeat, ethnic pride grew, and efforts to change American attitudes toward the Middle East began.

In large part because of the political involvement of the United States in the Middle East, Arab Americans faced, and still face, many social obstacles related to their ethnicity. Negative stereotypes linking Arabs in the United States to terrorism and Islamism have, for example, motivated some presidential and senatorial nominees to refuse campaign money from Arab American donors.[14] Federal agencies have subjected Arab Americans to surveillance and generated plans for their internment during the late 1980s and the Gulf War.[15] In addition, the movie industry often depicts Arabs as villains, although more positive images have appeared in movies since the late 1990s (e.g., *The 13th Warrior*, starring Antonio Banderas).[16]

Although immigrants carry ethnicity and ethnic affiliation with them to their new homelands, the understanding of what such affiliations actually mean is very often created *within* these new settings. The same can be said for religion. Although Islam has a core component of rituals, practices, and texts, religious practices in China, Nigeria, and the United States, for example, differ greatly.

The most challenging aspect of Islam in the United States—and also one of the most important—is its ethnic diversity, an issue that *Islam in Urban America* will seek to deal with in detail. Is the community well coordinated or deeply fragmented? Why has Islam become such a powerful source of identification for some Muslim Americans?

There are undoubtedly numerous individual reasons for the strengthening of a Muslim identity. The immigration process in itself creates challenges that may spur a focus on religion. Some of my informants stressed that the experience of American democracy facilitated a stronger and more correct Islamic practice—a practice inhibited by more or less totalitarian regimes in their homelands. Others said that their strong focus on Islam was the only way that they could "survive" ethically and morally in what they regarded as a decadent society.

To many young Muslims born or raised in the United States, Islam has become an important source of identification. Islam to these young people provides a means of engaging in American societal processes. Although some are highly critical of, if not fully antagonistic toward, the norms of this country, they are aware of their identity as people who must relate to an American reality. Life in the United States, for them, is about reforming Islam. They believe that this reform will come about when Muslims from all over the world come together, set aside all emphasis on their native cultures, and work together to find a common understanding of Islam.[17]

The establishment of an Islamic community in the United States is highly influenced by thoughts and ideas from elsewhere in the world. Revivalist Islamic movements such as the Jama'at Islami and the Ikhwan al-Muslimun—established by the Pakistani Mawlana Abul Al'a Mawdudi (d. 1979) and the Egyptian Hassan al-Banna (d. 1949)—have gained wide influence on both individual and community levels.[18] Much of this revivalism aims at eliminating the divisive effects of ethnicity and nationalism and focuses on the Muslim *umma* (community of believers) as one unbreakable entity. Such ideas are important to Muslim Americans trying to create common ground among several ethnic groups. Inspired by revivalist Islamic concepts, as well as their own experiences, they are attempting to promote a trans-ethnic Islamic identity.

However, this revivalist process is not limited to Muslim Americans. Rather, it is a challenge that Islam faces on a global scale. As the world increasingly becomes a "single place,"[19] Islam and other world religions must seek ways to talk cohesively to increasingly diverse groups of followers.[20] To the early Islamic converts, the act of conversion marked "a passage from being only a member of a tribe to being also a member of a superior Community that has its justification in transcendence."[21] In today's world, tribal affiliation translates into divisions of nationality and ethnicity. Revivalist Islamic movements seek to activate Islam on societal and personal levels, furthering the conviction of a common identity and a common course among Muslims in all parts of the world.[22]

Although revivalist movements and ideas have greatly affected how Islam is interpreted in a modern and global world, the impact of ethnicity has not disappeared. Ethnicity marks people's faces. Regional affiliations are evident in the language spoken in the home and in the foods in home-cooked meals. Individuals may define themselves as being Pakistani *and* Muslim *and* American, with varying emphasis on each of these components according to context. In the Muslim students' associations, students define themselves predominantly as Muslim; with their families, they are predominantly, say, Pakistani; and with their basketball friends, they are predominantly American. These dynamics again and again show that Muslim identity is not entirely to be understood as "either–or" but, in most cases, as "both–and."

THE 1990S: YEARS OF MUSLIM-AMERICAN ACTIVISM

This book presents the religious, cultural, and political aspects of a local Muslim-American community in the late 1990s, a time of important community consolidation for Muslims in America. Much of this work was done by Muslims who were increasingly experiencing themselves as a part of the American tapestry—as citizens living, working, and raising their children in this country—and therefore wanting influence. To most Muslim

Americans, exercising their rights and duties as American citizens involved showing the American public that Islam and Muslims are neither foreign nor hostile to American norms.

But the community often faced the obstacle of a United States that was involved politically and militarily as a superpower in countries and regions with large Muslim groups (e.g., the Persian Gulf, the Middle East, and Central Asia). Because of this involvement and the country's stand on, for example, the conflict between Israel and the Palestinian territories, the United States became the main target for disfranchised and radical Muslims worldwide. Reactions ranging from burning the American flag in the streets of Baghdad to violent attacks on American property in the Middle East often fueled stereotypes of Islam and Muslim, with grave consequences for Muslims living in the United States. Muslims became a group that was easily linked to violence and terrorism, even when its members had not committed such acts.

One example was the aftermath of the terrorist attack on the Murrah Federal Building in Oklahoma City on April 19, 1995, killing 168 people and injuring more than 500. In spite of President Bill Clinton's and Attorney General Janet Reno's warnings against prejudging Arab Americans, the initial judgment took a toll on Muslim Americans, whom many assumed stood behind the incident. According to the Council on American Islamic Relations (CAIR), 222 hate crimes against Muslims nationwide were reported in the days immediately following the bombing.[23] Moreover, Muslims of Middle Eastern descent have been prone to FBI surveillance and interrogation during, for example, armed encounters between America and Iraq.[24]

The Anti-Terrorist and Affective Death Penalty Act, enacted in 1996, also highlights the conflict between some extremist Muslim groups on the international scene and the American political and military establishment, as well as the complicated "in-between" positions of Muslim-American citizens.[25] The events of September 11, 2001, in which nineteen Muslim extremists highjacked four planes and crashed them into the World Trade Center and the Pentagon, increased tensions between the Muslim minority and the non-Muslim majority. Although President George W. Bush assured the American public within days of the

attack that "the face of terror is not the true faith of Islam....
Islam is peace" and that "Muslims make an incredibly valuable
contribution to our country,"[26] much harm had already been
done. On university campuses, Muslim women were encouraged
to keep a low profile and to invest in pepper spray to protect
themselves.[27] CAIR reported that no fewer than 1,717 incidents
took place immediately after September 11.[28] In its civil-rights
report for 2002, CAIR concluded that "the status of Muslim civil
rights has deteriorated sharply" and complained that "the sweep-
ing actions of the government have disturbed the lives of individuals and ethnic and religious communities."[29]

In the wake of September 11, 2001, the importance of the successes achieved by Muslim-American immigrant communities in
the 1990s may come into question. But I believe that these successes matter even more now to a community emerging from the
ashes of its work to improve its image. Although the community
faces a tremendous task in regaining trust and civil rights as
American citizens, the achievements of the 1990s will prove
valuable sources for that struggle.

In the 1990s, Muslim civil-rights organizations grew strong,
developed effective tools for agitating against religious discrimination and harassment, and mastered communications technology (TV, radio, the Internet) and the arts of politicking and political lobbying.[30] The sophistication of organizations such as CAIR
demonstrated Muslim Americans' increasing knowledge of "the
system," as well as their desire to challenge negative images of
Islam and prove their worth as American citizens.[31] This agenda
gained support from a number of non-Muslim people and institutions, including academics and academic institutions,[32] religious denominations and organizations,[33] and the press.[34] All of
these will be important allies in the early 2000s, as the community slowly regains it footing and works hard to regain the confidence and social position it achieved in the late 1990s.

Political statements and actions during the 1990s underscored
the federal government's increased sensitivity to Muslims as a
group within American society.[35] In 1991, Imam Siraj Wahaj
became the first Muslim ever to offer prayer before the U.S. House
of Representatives; in 1992, the leader of the American Muslim

Mission, Imam Warith Deen Mohammad, gave an invocation before the U.S. Senate.[36] President Clinton annually addressed the global community of Muslims, including Muslim Americans, in a statement during Ramadan, the Islamic fasting month. *Iftar* dinners (meals eaten to break the fast) have been celebrated at the White House since 1996.[37] During the 1996 presidential election, candidates Bill Clinton and Bob Dole addressed the views of Muslim voters.[38] In 1998, a resolution submitted to the House of Representatives and the Committee of the Judiciary explicitly supported religious tolerance toward Muslims, stating: "Congress recognizes the contribution of Muslim Americans, who are followers of one of the three major monotheistic religions of the world and one of the fastest growing faiths in the United States."[39]

During the 1990s, America became aware of a vigorous and growing community of Muslims in its midst. What happened in the 1990s—the actions taken by Muslim organizations and the signs of acceptance and inclusion by the American political establishment—undoubtedly played a role in the Bush administration's handling of the community in the days and months immediately following September 11, 2001.

THE SUNNI MUSLIM IMMIGRANTS OF CHICAGO

Islam in Urban America offers an in-depth view of immigrant Sunni Muslims who were living in Chicago by the late 1990s, an important period of activism and community consolidation for Muslim Americans. But why choose Sunni Muslim immigrants in Chicago for a study of the Muslim community in the United States? First, focusing on Muslim Americans in one locality yields details of daily life that broader studies cannot offer. Second, such a concentrated study allows a close-up look at the inner workings of Muslim institutions in this country—of the activities and the people involved, as well as their motives, ideas, and life histories. Such a study gives a sharper impression of how these institutions work with and against one another, how they relate to American society, how Islam is practiced in an American context, and how Muslim Americans combine heritages of faith and ethnicity with the norms and values of the country in which they now live. An investigation of Islam in one local context, but within a broad variety of institutions, results in a microcosmic impression of the implications of this faith and its institutions nationwide. The end result is a clear impression of Islam in urban America.

Chicago is an excellent starting point for such a study because of the large variety of institutions that Muslims have established there.[40] The following chapters will include descriptions of Sunday schools, after-school projects, Qur'anic schools, student organizations, colleges, grassroots organizations, and mosques—all established and run by Muslims. The focus on institutions and organizations is important, because they are focal points for community activity. Although faith can be practiced at home, institutions are the key when it comes to describing how people practice faith together and how faith becomes a visible element in society.

One dimension of intra-community relationships that *Islam in Urban America* does not cover is that between African-American Muslims and immigrant Muslims (although Chapter 2 will give an overview). Given that about 40 percent of Chicago's estimated 285,000 Muslims are African Americans,[41] contacts and alliances between immigrant and indigenous Muslims theoretically ought to be numerous. But they are not.

My primary reason for centering on the Muslim immigrant community is that it still behaves very much as a separate (yet diverse) community. Although statistics show that the largest ethnic group representing Islam in the city is African-American, such numbers did not translate into everyday experience within the institutions that I studied. Instead, the participation of African Americans was small. During my fieldwork, I carried out interviews with some prominent spokespeople for the African-American Muslim community in the city, at one point visiting Minister Louis Farrakhan in his home in Hyde Park. But the differences between the two communities seemed too great to be encompassed in a single volume. Other researchers make similar distinctions (see Chapter 2).[42] For similar reasons I have not described the Shi'ite community. My visits to Shi'ite mosques and interviews with representatives of the Shi'ite community revealed minimal contacts with the Sunni community. The complicated relations between Sunni immigrants and other groups of Muslims further exemplify the complex dynamics of identity—ethnic, social, and religious—that are so prominent in American Islam.[43]

A brief history of Muslims in Chicago (in Chapter 2) will help frame the discussion necessary to understanding the community as it had developed by the late 1990s. The empirical data is organized into three large chapters, each presenting Chicago's Muslim institutions, the activities that take place within them, and the people who come there. The description is broken down and arranged according to the age group to which the institution is directed, because the roles of individuals within various Muslim institutions change according to their age. For young children in the Muslim Sunday school, Islam is part of their upbringing; they are taught by others and do not define faith for themselves. For young people in college, the issue of personal definition (or rejection) of religion becomes stronger; it has to do with the life they want, with style, with activism, with independence. For adults, religion may have to do with leadership, authority, and organized community representation. Focusing on age groups reveals the complexity of "lived Islam" on both individual and institutional levels.

Two distinctions become critical at this point. For processes of learning or representing Islam both within and outside of Muslim institutions, the key concept is knowledge. But for the issue of who, for example, takes the roles of teacher or student, the key concept is authority. Knowledge includes not only understanding complex philosophical concepts but also the simplest rules for conduct: how people interact, how they arrange spaces between themselves and others, how they decide what is socially acceptable. Although *Islam in Urban America* mainly covers the implications of Islamic religious knowledge, such knowledge is not an isolated entity. Religious knowledge and the practices that it entails always relate to something cultural or social, supported by the events, needs, and thoughts of particular phases of human history and the regions in which humans choose to settle. Therefore, religious knowledge and practices depend on complex intertwinings of community, conviction, and heritage; on the establishment and perspective of religious institutions; and on the people who take charge and authority within them.

How a Muslim American gains authority within and outside an institution varies. Access may be granted or limited on the basis of education, gender, moral character, and age.[44] In addition, beyond the qualification of having accumulated a certain level of Islamic knowledge, a leader's next important strengths are class and economic capability. Not surprisingly, the majority of the community leaders described in this book are from middle-class or upper-middle-class backgrounds. These are the people who can establish and maintain expensive institutions and who have the necessary educational background and self-assurance to take on the role of voicing their understanding of Islam to Muslims and non-Muslims alike. These are the people the community trusts.

However, claims to authority also depend on an individual's ability to gain an audience's permission and trust. Authority grants individuals, groups, and institutions the right to teach and speak on behalf of a community but not to do so freely.[45] In the United States, the level of authority of Muslim institutions and their staffs depends on their ability to manifest authority to both Muslims and non-Muslims. They have to be able to skillfully handle persuasive elements of speech and cultural norms within these audiences, and to speak convincingly within both. Chapters 3, 4, and 5 cover issues of authority and leadership across the spectrum of age, gender, education, and ethnicity.

A DANISH WOMAN IN CHICAGO

But what made me, a Danish woman, move to Chicago to do fieldwork among Muslims for a year and a half of my life? Why did I not stay at home and study Muslims in Denmark, a community that faces similar challenges? The answer lies in a combination of coincidence and interest. In the summer of 1994, I visited the United States for the first time. At that point, my academic life centered mainly on Islamic subjects of the past, and I had an undeveloped ambition to study the relationship between

Muslims and Manicheans (a now vanished Gnostic sect) in eighth-century Baghdad. I had been corresponding for some time with a researcher in New York and was pleased when he invited me to visit. What I had not expected was that my interest in Muslims living more than a thousand years ago would suddenly refocus on Muslims living in the United States today.

As the researcher and I sat in his kitchen, looking out at Harlem, we discussed not only the ancient conflict between Manicheans and Muslims but also living conditions among Muslims in the United States. Trained in the history of religions and Islamic studies and acquainted with anthropology and sociology, I knew that Islam in America was a topic that few researchers had yet investigated. The implications of such a study were fascinating. The United States was a superpower known to clash frequently with Middle Eastern countries and radical Islamic groups. What would it feel like to be a Muslim in this country? What role did Muslims play the United States, given that Islam was on its way to becoming one of the country's largest religious communities? And how, in turn, did the United States affect Islam? How was Islam interpreted, put into practice, and lived within this country? When I left New York three days later, my focus had deeply shifted. I returned to the United States a year later—this time, traveling to Chicago—to begin a study that ultimately took up several years of my life.

Did my being Danish have any impact on my decision or my research? On the one hand, for getting around the city, the answer is no. My appearance in no way signaled that I came from another country. On the other hand, to those informants who got to know me, my foreign heritage became an advantage. We shared the identity of not being entirely American, of having accents, and of having larger parts of our families living elsewhere in the world. In addition, my foreign identity increased my position as a safe person to talk to and be around. My informants were also less likely to view me as a possible agent of the U.S. government.

The one personal factor that may have affected my fieldwork more than my Danish nationality was my being female, because Muslim communities are segregated by gender. My being female influenced what spaces I entered and what spaces never became "mine," a dividing line that runs as a thread throughout the book. Whenever I entered the Muslim community, I followed its rules for interaction, not only because I believed this to be methodologically wise and culturally respectful, but also because it was impossible to do otherwise. Because I shared the space of the community's women, women made up a majority of my informants. They were the people with whom I chatted before *jum'a* (congregational prayers) in the prayer halls and whom I joined in study groups. Much of *Islam in Urban America*, therefore, comes from a woman's viewpoint, although I balance that perspective with taped interviews. Further, for every five women I interviewed, I also interviewed three men.[46]

Women's perspectives and lives therefore play a major role in *Islam in Urban America*. I might have told the story differently had I been identified according to other social roles—had I at that point been married, had I had children at the time, or had I been a man. But the conditions governing my role in no way invalidate the book's findings. Rather, the impact of gender underlines the complexity of the Muslim community. Because certain spaces and roles are assigned to men and others to women, positions and perspectives on religion are highly affected by gender, even when voiced inside a communal whole.

An essential element of my fieldwork was the cooperation of those people who are the subjects of this book. After all, I came as a stranger and a foreigner, and though I promised to use statements and observations solely for research, they had no guarantee that I would keep my word. As I mentioned earlier, Muslims in Chicago have been exposed considerably to federal investigations. Although people often spoke about these negative experiences, they seemed remarkably willing to grant me interviews and let me participate in meetings and study sessions. Only in two instances was I told politely that I could not participate in sessions—in one case because the meeting was for Muslims only, and, in the other, because the meeting was for men only.

People reacted positively to my presence, I believe, because of two factors. First, Chicago Muslims practice a traditionally high level of religiously dictated hospitality. And second, during the second half of the 1990s, negative images in the press (spurred by national and international political events) made the community want to be heard on its own terms. My informants undoubtedly understood that getting the chance to tell their story and have it recognizably retold was valuable to the community and its vision of a continued and peaceful existence in Chicago.

To protect privacy, I use pseudonyms for the people I quote and describe. Only in cases in which informants are known as the authors of books or booklets of significance in the community— and useful as references—did I find it necessary to use real names. I also use the names of prominent leaders of organizations and institutions because they are public figures whose identity is almost impossible to conceal. Finally, the choice to use pseudonyms is mine alone, based on my beliefs about the value of privacy. In no case did any of my informants ask for this privilege.

Now is the time to enter the American Medina, and encounter the many faces and voices of Muslims in Chicago. It is time to encounter the coolness of the mosque's prayer hall, the heat of theological discussions, the silence of those turned inward in prayer. It is time to encounter a part of America that frequently appears closed, even when it exists right next door. In the history that follows, it is my intention not to throw the door wide open but to offer a focused view of some vital aspects of Muslim-American life, such as institutions, practices, and formulations of Islam as they appear within one locality. These aspects are relevant both for further research of the subject and for a general understanding of a religious community that, in years to come, will be in the spotlight of public attention.

2   The History of Muslims in Chicago
An Overview

ISLAM IS NOT NEW to the United States. Stories of fortune and adventure drew people from the Middle East and Asia to the New World from the late nineteenth century on. Faces of these early immigrants appear in photographs from the Columbian Exposition in Chicago in 1893.[1] In Chicago, the Muslim community grew slowly, gaining prominence in certain neighborhoods and taking its first steps toward establishing institutions: the mosques, schools, and cultural centers so evident in the late twentieth century.

Who were these initial immigrants, and how did Chicago react to their creating mosques and schools? How did these institutions start? Which ethnic groups established them? What were the characteristics of these groups? Although Sunni Muslim immigrants form the majority within Chicago's Muslim tapestry, groups such as the Ahmadiyya Mission, the Nation of Islam, and the Moorish Science Temple all play important roles in the development and diversity of Muslims in Chicago. Because different groups understand and practice Islam differently, the interpretations from people within the institutions that this book describes are frequently challenged by other Muslims. These "others" have an influence, even when the majority of Sunni Muslims reject their ideas, and it is therefore useful to briefly introduce their history and activities, particularly in the Chicago area.

THE PIONEERS

Chicago's first recorded exposure to Islam took place during the Columbian Exposition of 1893. No fewer than seven nations with Muslim majorities were represented at the part of the exposition that took place at the Midway Plaisance in southern Chicago.[2]

Visitors to Cairo Street could acquaint themselves with the "strange" faith of the Orient. There, the muezzin Mohammad Abdullah called the faithful to prayers five times a day from the minaret of the prominent and centrally located mosque.[3] A number of Muslim festivals were celebrated during the exposition, including the birthday of the Prophet Muhammad (*Mawlid al-Nabi*) and Ramadan.

The public could also visit a *kuttab* (school for the memorization of the Qur'an). In the morning hours, Egyptian boys were seen sitting on the floor of the school, memorizing the scripture from copies of the Qur'an resting on bamboo stands. More dramatic were the Egyptian Sufis,[4] who performed what the public came to call the the "torture dance," because in their ecstasy the dancers ate cactus leaves and pierced their skin with skewers.[5] Although the audience found Muslim devotion enchanting, they still perceived it as childishly inferior to Christianity. As an American humorist stated, "You can't tell whether they're praying or in a dog fight, but I suppose it's all the same in Arabia."[6]

The exposition, above all, was an event of pleasure and imagination, keeping a safe distance between audience and performers. The more than one hundred Egyptians who lived in Chicago's Cairo Street could leave the exposition grounds only with difficulty to visit the city's attractions.[7] The boundary between the Occident and the Orient was broken, however, when a white American presented Islam to the audience during two talks at the Parliament of the World's Religions, an event affiliated with the Columbian Exposition. Although this parliament was highly driven by the aspirations of Christian missionary interests, Mohammad Alexander Webb—a convert to Islam—transcended lines of belonging. He was white, male, and Muslim:

I am an American of the Americans. I carried with me for years the same errors that thousands of Americans carry with them today. These errors have grown into history, false history has influenced your opinion of Islam. It influenced my opinion of Islam and when I began ten years ago, to study the Oriental religions, I threw Islam aside as altogether too corrupt for consideration. But when I came to go beneath the surface, to know what Islam really is, to know who and what the Prophet of Arabia was, I changed my belief very materially, and I am proud to say that I am now a Mussulman. . . . I have not returned to the United States to make you all Mussulmans in spite of yourselves. . . . But I have faith in the American intellect, in the American intelligence, and in American love of fair play, and will defy any intelligent man to understand Islam and not love it.[8]

To Mohammad Webb, Islamic and American discourses were compatible, and he declared this conviction in both words and action. Although Webb stated that he did not aim to win new converts to the faith (though he was not hesitant to say that every man of intellect would "understand and love it"), he encountered opposition all the same. Reverend George E. Post, visiting Chicago from his missionary post in Beirut, challenged Webb during his own speech at the Parliament. Although Webb was cautious to present Islam as a tolerant faith of reason and good morals, Post did his best to counter these arguments. With a copy of the Qur'an in his hand, "a book, which is never touched by 200,000,000 of the human race," Post pointed to statements in the Islamic Scripture that, according to him, urged the killing of the infidels, the practice of polygamy, and the permitting of divorce.[9] Pointing to polygamy was the strongest attack, as polygamy was then viewed as eroding the moral code on which the American nation prided itself.[10]

The Columbian Exposition is probably the earliest and best-documented example of early Muslim presence in Chicago. As a result, some Muslims decided to settle in the city soon afterward.[11] Although census reports from the late nineteenth century list migration from countries with a Muslim population, they do not indicate the immigrants' religions. By 1860, the census reported two immigrants from the Ottoman Empire (called "Turkey"); in 1880, fourteen Ottoman immigrants are listed. By 1900, the numbers had increased to 180—and to 2,244 by 1910.[12]

Muslim immigration depended largely on the immigration legislation of the period. Immigration escalated after the Homestead Act of 1862–70 and the 1865 Appomattox Court House opening of visas[13] but decreased when migration from areas other than Europe was restricted by the turn of the century. Many Middle Easterners were barred from entry because of trachoma, an infectious eye disease.[14] Migration from Middle Eastern countries was further restricted by the Act of 1917 (admittance on the basis of literacy) and the Act of 1921 (admittance on the basis of quotas).[15]

One of the first direct descriptions of Muslim settlement in Chicago dates to 1922, when Edith Stein, a student in social services at the University of Chicago, mentioned the community in her master's thesis: "Most of the Syrians in Chicago are from Lebanon, although there are also a number from Palestine. However, the last are said to be mainly Muhammedans. The two groups are quite separate, the first living around Ogden Avenue along about 2600 West, while the second group lives in the vicinity of 18th Street and State."[16]

In addition to describing the location of Muslim immigrants, Stein gave demographic data. Referring to U.S. Census reports, she mentioned that 732 persons of Syrian and Arabic decent lived in the city by 1910 (519 foreign born), compared with 883 (684 foreign born) by 1920.[17] However, Stein did not give any numbers according to religious practices.

About thirty years later, two students at the University of Chicago, Lawrence Oschinsky and Abdul Jalil al-Tahir, carried out independent studies.[18] They described early-twentieth-century Palestinian immigration to the city, which, according to al-Tahir, was mainly driven by the ambition to "amass all the wealth possible in the shortest time and then return to their homeland to enjoy it in peace and quietude."[19] In addition to introducing the early settlement, Oschinsky and al-Tahir concentrated on the appearance of the community at the time of their writing. Middle Eastern settlement was still located in the neighborhood of 18th Street and Michigan Avenue. Two-thirds of the settlers lived in furnished rooms in low-rent neighborhoods between 18th and 45th streets and between Cottage Grove and Lake, conveniently near the shops that a number of them had established in the area.[20]

Most immigrants were male peasants from the Palestinian village of Beituniya, with very few professional skills and very little or no English.[21] The majority made their living by peddling door to door, and those who were successful in this endeavor bought small shops in the blue-collar African-American neighborhoods. Contact with other Middle Eastern groups was limited.

Christians and Muslims from Greater Syria rarely interacted, notably because of differences in religion, kinship, village attachment, and perspectives on American society. In Chicago, interaction between the two groups was particularly troubled by a murder case in the first decade of the twentieth century, in which a Muslim Palestinian was accused of killing a Syrian Christian boy.[22]

Researchers on Muslims in America often mention that the first immigrants felt forced to assimilate.[23] But the historical sources suggest that such assumptions are not always accurate. It appears that although Chicago's Muslim immigrants lived near the center of the city, they kept very much to themselves, except in business matters. Language, village ties, and religion became factors in the preservation of tradition, emphasizing the group's reluctance to adapt to the host culture.[24] The immigrants founded their own restaurants—Mecca, Arabian Nights, and Sheherazad—and these became the centers of the community's interactions.[25] Once a month, an Arabic movie was shown in one of the downtown halls.[26]

In the period between the two world wars, the number of cultural clubs and societies grew. One club, the Children of Beituniya Society, was established before 1924. The society supported newcomers financially and made considerable contributions to improving living conditions in Beituniya: The society established a secondary school in the village and partly financed the building of a highway in the area.[27] Later in the century, the community founded organizations such as the Arab Progress Society, the Arab-American Aids Society, the Arab Club, and the Arab American Women's Club. These organizations aimed to preserve national and ethnic identity rather than religious practice. In the 1950s, however, the Arab Club started working toward building a mosque.[28]

The early community was not particularly engaged in the preservation of Muslim rituals (such as the five daily prayers), though its members continued to claim adherence to Islamic values and principles.[29] Among the first generations of immigrants, men's relationships with and marriages to non-Muslims were frequent. This practice was criticized by not only the community elders but also the Arab-American press, which had been in existence since 1892.[30] The newspaper *al-Hayat* stated clearly in 1947:

> What is the matter with us that we fight against our morals and our doctrines and we lose our last bit of dignity by our own hands? In our countries Arab and among others America we have left our holy religion and we have left our character *akhalag* and tradition adat. What did we get in return from the Western nations? Did we get their culture? Have we imitated them in good things? Have we won something that we have lost? The answer is no. We left noble things and we adopted evil. We must always think of our religion and our traditions, and must not repudiate anything because the European does so and so. We must think first of the benefits of a thing and so take that which is best and leave the worst.[31]

Beyond the Muslims who came from the Middle East—in particular, from Palestine (Greater Syria)—very little material exists on other ethnic groups representing Islam in the city. Their history can be pieced together only by referring to a number of articles and more general works.

From early on, Chicago has been the American urban area with the largest number of Yugoslav and Bosnian immigrants.[32] The Bosnian community was the first to establish a religious Muslim organization in Chicago. In 1906, Bosnians established the club Khaivat al-Ummah. In 1954, the Bosnian American Cultural Association founded one of the city's first Sunni mosques, on North Halsted Street; in 1976, the mosque moved to the suburb of Northbrook and became known as the Islamic Cultural Center of Greater Chicago.

Indian (South Asian) immigration to Chicago can be traced back to 1880, when the U.S. Census shows fourteen people from that country. By 1930, this number had risen to only 126, a low figure attributable to the same legislation that limited Middle Eastern immigration.[33] By 1947, the quota system (reaffirmed by the McCarren-Walter Act of 1952) allowed no more than one hundred Indian and one hundred Pakistani immigrants to enter the United States each year.[34] How many of the first Indian immigrants to Chicago were Muslims was not accounted for (Federal and State agencies categorized them as "Hindus"[35]), but studies of Indian immigration suggest that one-third were Muslims.[36]

In sum, 1893 to 1947 was a period in which Muslim immigrants in Chicago (as elsewhere in the United States) lived relatively unnoticed. As a predominantly small merchant class, they posed no direct challenge to powerful strata in American society, and the limited political interest of the U.S. government in Muslims internationally reinforced that general view. Although critical voices arose within the community from time to time, religion played a limited role, overshadowed by nostalgia for the countries to which the immigrants hoped to return.

MUSLIM IMMIGRATION AFTER WORLD WAR II

Soon after World War II, a new flow of immigrants, many of them refugees, entered the United States, despite the quota system's limits. Whereas pre–World War II migration from the Middle East consisted of single men, the postwar period saw an influx of family members and distant relatives of those who had already established themselves in the country. In particular, the number of immigrant women increased. Louise Cainkar mentions that "all of the foreign-born wives of these early immigrant men came to the United States between 1943 and 1953, either upon marriage or within a few years of it."[37] Housing patterns changed, because homes now had to provide space for women and children.

Cainkar states that male Palestinians immigrating to the United States in the 1950s and 1960s were more skilled and educated than those preceding them, even though the newcomers came from the same families and villages, particularly the Jerusalem–Ramallah area (which remained under Arab sovereignty until 1967). The better skills of these new immigrants in some cases could be traced to the Chicago settlers of earlier decades: Many had sent money home to secure for their sons a level of education that they themselves had been unable to attain.[38] Although many of the newcomers took the same jobs as the elder generation, some chose new fields, becoming gas-station owners, auto salesmen, taxi drivers, engineers, and accountants.[39]

Whereas most Palestinian Muslims came with the experience and status of refugees (the United States Refugee Relief Act of

1953 allowed 2,000 Palestinian refugees a year), reasons for immigration differed somewhat for other Muslims. In the postwar era, the United States became an attractive destination for doctoral and postdoctoral studies, partially after the introduction of the Fulbright Scholarship. During the 1950s, a considerable number of my informants of Indian, Pakistani, and Middle Eastern descent pursued degrees at schools such as Northwestern University, the Illinois Institute of Technology, and the University of Chicago, and then decided to stay.

Further, many professionals and skilled workers migrated to the United States after 1965. Many of Chicago's present-day South Asian Muslims came during and after that period, settling in suburban neighborhoods such as Forest Park, Oak Park, the Ravenswood area, and the city's North Side (particularly in the 1970s).[40] A part of Devon Avenue (6400 North) is called Mohammed Ali Jinnah Way, for the founder of Pakistan, highlighting the concentration of Pakistanis in that area.[41]

The first Sunni mosques in Chicago were founded by immigrants from the former Ottoman Empire. In 1954, the Bosnian American Cultural Association was established on North Halsted Street, with both a Sunday school and a mosque.[42] The Turkish American Cultural Alliance established its center in 1964, and the Albanian American Islamic Center was founded in 1971.[43] The South Asian community established its first mosque for Friday prayers in a basement at North Winthrop Avenue in 1970.[44] Some of the people who came to that mosque were among the original members of the Muslim Community Center (founded in 1969), the Islamic Foundation (founded in 1974), and the North Side Mosque Inc. (founded in 1975, with leanings toward the Tablighi Jama'at, an Islamic movement originating in the South Asian subcontinent[45]).

Although the Middle Eastern community registered the Mosque Foundation in 1954, a mosque was not built until the early 1980s. However, the first Sunday schools for Islamic education of the community's children were established in the early 1970s. The South Asians established theirs in the Muslim Community Center, while the Middle Eastern community established the Arabian Islamic School at the Clark School in Oak Lawn. Another Sunday school was established on 55th Street and Fairfield Avenue.[46]

As the Chicago Muslims' numbers and institutions increased, and as they became more visible, public response was sometimes hostile. Particularly after the Iranian revolution in January 1979 and the hostage crisis at the American Embassy in Tehran between November 1979 and January 1981, public opinion turned against Chicago's Muslims. In 1979, just after the Iranian revolution, Chicago residents prevented the founding of a mosque on North Pulaski Road. And in 1989, the Muslim Community Center's attempt to purchase a school building in Morton Grove for a Muslim full-time school met similar opposition.[47]

Responding to external threats and suspecting immigrant groups of harboring terrorists, the FBI in January 1991—the time of the Persian Gulf War—interviewed thirteen Arab-American leaders in Chicago about their political beliefs and their knowledge of future Arab terrorism in the United States.[48] Although the American Civil Liberties Union of Illinois later filed and won a petition against the FBI, claiming a violation of the First Amendment,[49] members of Chicago's Arab-Muslim community later came under investigation both inside and outside the country. Between 1993 and 1995, the local press reported that four Muslim-Palestinian residents of the city (one of them a director of the Islamic program at the Aqsa School for Girls in Bridgeview) were detained by the Israeli government during visits to the West Bank and Gaza and charged with supporting radical Islamist groups such as Hamas and Islamic Jihad.[50]

As a result of these charges, the FBI monitored groups of Muslims in Chicago, not only to map the extent of financial aid from such groups to Hamas but also to rule out Israeli allegations that the United States had become a planning center for Hamas's terrorist operations.[51] In 1997 and 1998, the local press reported that the FBI had contacted members of Chicago's Arab-Muslim community about their alleged affiliations with Hamas.[52] In the summer of 1998, one man had his home and assets seized by the FBI, which accused him of being a high-level military operative of Hamas.[53] A local Muslim nonprofit organization, the Qur'anic

Literacy Institute, came under federal investigation on similar charges and, among other things, was accused of channeling money through housing-development projects in Chicago's western and southwestern suburbs.

Such accusations, regardless of the outcome, deeply affected the Chicago Muslim community. Federal investigations fueled mistrust and feelings of social exclusion, especially because most of the community tended to see the investigations solely as products of prejudice. Although the FBI may have had serving American interests as its goal, one consequence of its actions was that an entire community found itself intimidated, misrepresented, and isolated.

Ironically, the tensions between Chicago's Muslims and non-Muslims sometimes produced stronger ties. The Morton Grove Muslim school, for example, was finally established with the support of a non-Muslim neighborhood organization, Citizens Advocating Responsible Education (CARE).[54] Although the Muslim Community Center did not get its mosque on Pulaski, it later established one on North Elston and promoted friendly relations with its neighbors through annual friendship dinners. Palestinians also enjoyed support from the Jerusalem Action Committee of Chicago (JACC). During the Second Parliament of the World's Religions (August 28–September 5, 1993), sixty-nine Muslims from Chicago and around the world were among the speakers.[55] Since then, prominent members of the Muslim community have been engaged in the local Council for a Parliament of the World's Religions, established with the ambition of furthering the ideals of the parliament within the Chicago area. In 1997, five of the fifty-four members of the Council's Board of Trustees were Muslims.[56]

THE COMPLEX PICTURE OF MUSLIMS IN CHICAGO

The Sunni Muslims who are the focus of this book are part of a larger, more complex picture of Muslim groups in Chicago. Among the Sunnis, for example, are Sufis representing various orders, and outside this circle lie communities of Shi'ites, the Ahmadiyya, and African-American Muslim sects. Although all groups claim adherence to the same religion, they are separated by conscious and unconscious barriers. By the late 1990s, the six-county Chicago metropolitan area had five Shi'ite centers, [57] serving mostly South Asians and Iranians. Before obtaining these properties, the Shi'ites had congregated at the Sunni Muslim Community Center on North Elston Avenue.[58] But variations in practices, along with an almost 1,400-year-old conflict over leadership, kept the two communities apart. At no point did I see the two communities officially holding joint events.

Another group of Muslims more directly involved in the Sunni Muslim community are the Sufis. Three Sufi orders (sing. *tariqa*; pl. *turuq*) exist in the Chicago area: the Tijaniyya, the Nimatullah, and the Naqshbandiyya-Haqqaniyya. The largest and most influential of these orders, the Naqshbandiyya-Haqqaniyya, is covered extensively in Chapters 4 and 5. Sufis attend Sunni mosques and are therefore an integrated part of Sunni community life. However, parts of the community strongly criticize core aspects of Sufism as heretical, particularly the idea of becoming close to God through spiritual guidance and the ritual of *dhikr* (meditative remembrance of Allah).[59] Most Sunnis are also opposed to the strong, authoritarian role of the *shaykh*, the leader of the Sufi order who guides the initiates on the mystical path.

Similarly, the immigrant Muslims' relations with African-American Muslims had been complicated by the appeal of some sectarian Muslim groups (founded outside the United States) to African Americans and the indigenous Muslim sects that have sprung from them. A number of these foreign and indigenous Muslim sects have established large centers or headquarters in Chicago. The Ahmadiyya Movement of Islam was the first to found a mosque in the city. In 1921, the first Ahmadiyya missionary, Mufti Muhammad Sadiq, established his headquarters in Chicago, and a *jami* (place to gather for prayer) was founded at South Wabash Avenue.[60] The mission is still located at the Wabash address and has 300 members (of whom fifty are African Americans).[61]

African-American Muslim groups have existed in Chicago almost since the beginning of the twentieth century. In 1923, Noble Drew Ali, founder of the Moorish Science Temple, moved his headquarters to the city. In 1926, the Unity Hall was established on Indiana Avenue, just south of the Loop (downtown Chicago).[62] By 1933, a considerable Moorish population lived in Chicago—notably, in colonies on the South Side and North Side.[63] Although the Moorish Science later split, the leader of one of the factions that emerged still lived in Chicago at the start of the twenty-first century.[64] As late as the 1970s, a branch of the Moorish Science Temple was formed when an African American street gang, the Black P Stone Nation, accepted the teachings of Noble Drew Ali, adding about 5,000 members to the sect's rolls.[65]

Both the Ahmadiyya Movement and the Moorish Science Temple are considered heretical sects by Sunni Muslims. The founder of the Ahmadiyya movement, Harzat Mirza Ghulam Ahmad (1835–1908), claimed to be the messiah foretold in many religions, including Islam (the *mahdi*). He further claimed to receive revelations and, according to these, preached a "purified Islam" that Sunni Muslims cannot accept (Sunnis see Muhammad as the last Prophet and therefore the last person in history to receive revelations from God).[66] Clashes between Sunni Muslims and Ahmadiyya sometimes have been violent (for example, in Pakistan). Sunni Muslims, among others, also reject the Islam of the Moorish Science Temple for two reasons: first, because the core scripture of the sect, called the Holy Koran, in no way resembles the Qu'ran; and, second, because the sect teaches that God is black, an anthropomorphism unacceptable to traditional Islam. Not surprisingly, Sunni relations with both groups are mainly antagonistic.[67]

The Nation of Islam, another sectarian Muslim movement indigenous to North America, also has its headquarters in Chicago.[68] The most notable leader of the movement, Elijah Muhammad, moved to the city in the early 1930s. After Elijah Muhammad's death in 1975, his son, Warith Deen Mohammad, pushed the movement toward Sunni Islam. Warith Deen Mohammad's ministry, highly active within the Chicago area, is well known for publishing the *Muslim Journal* (known under his father's leadership as *Muhammad Speaks*). In 1977, Louis Farrakhan Muhammad announced the re-establishment of the Nation of Islam according to the original doctrines. When Warith Deen went bankrupt in 1986 (after three of Elijah Muhammad's illegitimate children filed a lawsuit), Farrakhan was able to buy Elijah Muhammad's house (known as "the Palace") on South Woodlawn Avenue in Hyde Park.[69] He and his family have lived there ever since.[70]

Farrakhan is one of the most dynamic, provocative speakers within the African-American community. However, many Sunni Muslims in Chicago—and elsewhere—do not consider the Nation of Islam to be "Islamic" at all, and they blame Farrakhan for creating a negative public image of Muslim Americans. Some Sunnis add that they are often forced to defend their religious positions because of statements that Farrakhan has made to the press. Still, the beliefs of the Nation of Islam have to some extent caused a rift within the Sunni community. Although some Sunni Muslim organizations strongly criticize the Nation of Islam, calling it a "pseudo-Islamic cult,"[71] others proclaim Farrakhan to be the most influential Muslim leader in the African-American community today.[72]

The self-perception of the Muslim-American community is highly affected by the dichotomy between the ideals of its faith and the realities of ethnic differences. On the one hand, a religious ideal calls for transcendence of ethnicity; on the other hand, ethnic affiliations play a leading role in formulations of faith, and therefore cause friction. The status of African-American Sunni Muslims illustrates this problem. Even though African Americans are active in various immigrant mosques and organizations, Muslims of immigrant background often voice skepticism when African American Muslims independently interpret Islam according to their communal experiences and history—especially when that history involves the Nation of Islam.

Bruce Lawrence, a professor of Islamic studies at Duke University, says:

> This duality between indigenous and immigrant Muslim Americans is fundamental to the Muslim American future. Differences between them may persist or may attenuate, but they can never be eradicated. They will remain as distinctive markers of cultural disparities that,

despite creedal and ritual sympathies, separate African American from South Asian Muslims. Their basis is a racialized class prejudice against African Americans that predates the 20th century and circulates beyond the parameters of a Muslim American community, however broadly defined [by] its membership.[73]

Although this book does not deal in depth with the African-American Muslim community, Lawrence's statement emphasizes the fault lines between the differing communities. In the same way that ethnic groups are often defined according to sentiments of "inside–outside" (that is, who belongs and who does not), so may ethnic divisions affect the outlook of segments of a world religion such as Islam. For all that the Chicago Muslim community sought to be all-inclusive, in the tradition of Islam as its members understood it, religious and ethnic differences kept the community from truly unifying.

3 Between Michael Jordan and Muhammad

Muslim Children in Chicago

ACCORDING TO some of my informants, a Muslim identity is something that one is given at birth. To be a Muslim, therefore, is a natural part of one's human identity, because Islam is the religion given by Allah, who is also the creator of humans and all things. Such theological convictions notwithstanding, Muslim parents in the United States must deal with the realization that "Muslim-ness" within the American social reality calls for socialization, teaching, and discipline. Parents cannot be certain that their children will remain Muslim unless they as parents make an extra effort to lay the proper foundations.

Much of the socialization of Muslim children takes place at home as an integrated part of family life. It takes place in the rhythm of the day—for example, when a family prays together. It takes place in the rhythm of the year, in the month of fasting (Ramadan), and the religious feasts of 'Id al-Adha and 'Id al-Fitr. Islam is practiced in dress code, cuisine, and norms for conduct. Islam is a way of being together, inside and outside the family.

Places where the sphere of Islamic practice easily extends outside the home are Islamic institutions. Some of these institutions—Sunday schools, Muslim full-time schools, religious schools for the memorization of the Qur'an, Muslim after-school projects—specifically target Muslim children. These institutions combine the daily practice of Islam with education. Muslim children learn the "basics" of their faith, which center on texts and tradition. The daily practice of Islam, combined with a conscious evaluation of what this practice means, works to validate and reinforce Muslim identity. Such tools for validation form an important line of defense within a society in which Islam is a minority religion.

30

However, this is not to say that the knowledge conveyed within Muslim institutions for children is coherent or goes unchallenged. As this chapter will show, the ways in which Islamic knowledge is adapted to the American context, and to the lives of Muslim-American children, vary greatly. In some environments, the focus on text and tradition creates segregation from the surrounding society; in others, it creates a direct involvement in it. Conflict inevitably arises when children find the lessons either inapplicable to their present lives or inappropriate to the lives they hope to lead as adults.

This chapter will cover Muslim weekend schools, Muslim full-time schools, and *hafiz* schools where students learn to memorize the Qur'an. I will also take a very close look at one of these institutions, IMAN (Inner-City Muslim Action Network), a Muslim after-school program in the Chicago Lawn neighborhood on the city's South Side. Focusing on IMAN offers a perspective on how some Islamic institutions seek to answer the needs of recently immigrated or poor members of their community. The organization aims to help these children perform better in school and develop pride in their religious identity. IMAN's efforts also exemplify how Islamic institutions may work to prevent Muslim children from getting involved in street gangs, and how they deal with the suppression of women and intra-Muslim discrimination on the basis of ethnicity. Although such things do not necessarily relate to formal education, they teach Muslim children skills and ideas that make them more socially mobile and attached to their religious heritage.

Enrolling one's child in a Muslim institution is one way to ensure that the child is socialized as a Muslim. However, parental focus on religion is usually combined with something else: academic and social ambitions, economic abilities, and ethnic affiliation. For example, most parents choose a particular Sunday school for their children because most of the staff and students there share their ethnic background.

Economic class plays a very strong role in Muslim schooling. Both full-time schools and Qur'anic schools are private institutions, involving expenses that not all parents can afford. Some parents send their children to public schools, while either paying for instruction in the less costly Sunday schools or sending the children to free after-school programs. The result is a variation in the level at which Muslim children engage in dialogue and direct contact with the surrounding society. Children enrolled in Muslim full-time schools study in safe havens of ethnic and religious familiarity; Muslim children in public schools have a vastly different experience.

When Muslim parents enroll their children in Muslim institutions, they do so because they want to secure the children's Muslim identity. They want to make sure that the icons and role models that the children admire and try to imitate are teachers and other adults of the Muslim faith, not public personalities such as Michael Jordan. They want their children to remain and develop as Muslims, all the while fearing that American society will pull them in another direction.

In the first section of this chapter, I describe the experiences that Muslim children enrolled in public schools may encounter in this environment. Next I describe Muslim weekend schools, and the after-school program IMAN. The chapter closes with a description of Muslim full-time schools and *hafiz* schools, or schools for the memorization of the Qu'ran.

THE PUBLIC SCHOOL EXPERIENCE

Like most other children in America, many Muslims attend a public system of learning for more than ten years. In this environment, they study math, English literature, history, and biology—and the norms of the American "public." Although descriptions of public school experiences vary, most of my informants said that their religious affiliation negatively affected their school experience. This reaction was especially strong among girls who wore the *hijab* (head scarf). A woman in her late twenties recalled:

> I was born in '69, so it was basically in the mid-'70s that I started school. It was not hard. When I went up to fifth grade, it was no problem. They saw me the same.... Then, in sixth grade, that was where I started wearing *hijab*.... It was like night and day. Some of the friends that I had there totally refused to associate with me after that. And then there were some who tried to understand it. I think that

the friends that I maintain now are the ones that I [met] after wearing [the *hijab*].[1]

Even Muslim boys who seldom wore clothes that were different from those worn by other American children were subjected to discrimination. A mother said:

> My own boys have gone through rough times in school, especially during the Kuwait War.[2] My one son got slammed into a locker and his nose was broken, and almost his arms. People were saying mean, ignorant, dumb things. And they are just kids. . . . During the Oklahoma City bombing,[3] my son was in his world history class, I think. Two or three of the kids knew that my son was an Arab and a Muslim, and they started making smart comments about "send all those black Arabs back where they came from." . . . What happened here was that the teacher was sitting back enjoying the verbal attack on my son, and saying nothing to [stop] it. Then, the next day, when it was discovered that the bomber was not an Arab or a Muslim but an American, and my son got up and tried to give back what he got the day before, the teacher was reprimanding him. . . . My question is, as an educator, where were you when four or five kids were verbally assaulting this boy? My middle son can verbally and intellectually kind of absorb it. My youngest has some difficulties. He resorts to fighting. . . . [My sons] feel that they belong here more than some of the others who are here. They were born here, they were raised here, they contribute to this society. *We* contribute to this society.[4]

Like this mother, several of my informants said that Muslim boys reacted to name calling or physical assaults by concealing their background (that is, by changing their names or claiming another ethnic identity)[5] or answering violence with violence.

The mother's statement points to the link between increased harassment and national or international events that involve (or are assumed to involve) a clash between U.S. and Muslim interests. It also emphasizes the reaction of the authority figure, the teacher, who seemed to encourage aggression. Another female informant, now in college, described her experiences after the 1988 terrorist attack that brought down a Pan American airplane over the Scottish village of Lockerbie:[6]

> The teachers were instigating arguments in class. . . . Like my chemistry teacher. What does chemistry have to do with politics? I got kicked out of his class, too. He attacked me. He said, "Ms. Ahmed,

what do you think about this terrorist action that is going on? It is your people, isn't it?" [A] lot of times, the teacher . . . started the argument. And there were a lot of times where I found myself sick or another reason not to go to school. It was not that they were ignorant per se; it was just that they did not want to hear it. You were different—just stay there.[7]

Whereas the first informant created a link between an ethnic and a religious group (Arabs and Muslims), the second reflected the importance of public discourse in the creation of Muslim-ness as a primary element of group affiliation ("It is your people, isn't it?"). Both informants placed the teacher as the pivotal player in the harassment. Although on the surface the teachers' behavior reflected only their own opinions, these opinions took on greater significance because they came from teachers. Therefore, students doing the harassing gained support from the statements of an adult who, by implication, represented the educational system and the society at large. As a result, Muslim students and their parents came to view themselves as doubly rejected—first by a specific person, and second by the society in which they lived in and the institutions to which the parents had entrusted the education of their children.

But Muslim children do not always experience a lack of support from the educational system and their classmates. Some informants said that the non-Muslim environment had actually encouraged them to emphasize their religious identity. One Muslim girl recalled her high school days in one of Chicago's northern suburbs:

It turned out that a lot of my friends were Jewish, and we would sort of talk about religion. . . . We did not have a lot of knowledge to talk about it, but we talked about the Trinity or something that we could focus on that we had in common. So . . . I ended up in participating in a sort of *halaqa* [study circle] sort of thing. This is something that I really quite like. I am still a friend with all these people, and one of my close friends was a Jewish girl, and she was one of the first people that I told when I started to wear *hijab*. It was sort of an intimidating thing for me, and I wasn't really sure how she would respond. And, *al-hamdu li-llah* [thanks be to God], she was just absolutely amazing about it and she told me that was one of the greatest things that she had known anyone to do and . . . it was just like a very sweet reaction and . . . I am glad that I still remained friends with them.[8]

Some of my informants spoke about conflicts with their parents. Like many youngsters, they felt that their parents' views on how a young person should behave were overly restrictive. One girl told me that she "lived three different lives"—one in her school, one among her friends, and one with her parents.[9]

In some instances, young people clashed with their parents about religion, regarding their parents as too influenced by ethnic culture and therefore ignorant of "true" Islam's significance and essence. These young people saw themselves as more religious than their parents and as representing an Islamic ideal that they needed to "teach" their parents. Parents, by contrast, viewed these conflicts as arising either from their own failure to teach their children properly or from the negative influence of the public school. In their eyes, their offspring had become too "Americanized"; they had been swayed from "good Islamic morals" because of such influences as sex education, mixed-gender gym classes, and inaccurate depictions of Islam in school books. Young and adult alike placed their defense of religion against real or imagined elements of locality and culture. The young saw their interpretation of Islam as threatened by the cultural heritage of the regions that their parents had left behind, whereas adults regarded the locality and culture of the present country—the United States—as the threat.

Within the American context, therefore, public schools have become the primary symbols of a battle in which young Muslims either lose or emphasize the religion of their parents.[10] That the younger generations may be "lost" to the norms of the surrounding society has inspired the Muslim community to take a number of initiatives. The concept of Islamic education gained ground in the 1980s and 1990s,[11] resulting in the establishment of a variety of institutions (weekend schools, youth programs, full-time schools) in Chicago as well as in other major American cities.

Muslim Weekend Schools

While I was in Chicago, I visited three Muslim weekend schools. At one of these schools, located in the Muslim Community Center

(MCC) on the North Side, almost all the students and staff members were South Asian. The MCC had opened its first weekend school in 1972, with fifty students in four classes. Its academic council had since developed a set curriculum, and all books were available in the center's bookstore. Further, a considerable collection of books, for children and adults, was available in the MCC library. By the late 1990s, most of the teachers were college students and graduates of the very school in which they were teaching.

Some 350 students from first to tenth grade attended the MCC school each Sunday, in morning and afternoon shifts.[12] After seventh grade, the students were separated according to gender. All school activity took place in small classrooms on the second floor. Classes were overcrowded, especially in the lower grades, but every classroom was well equipped with tables and chairs. I was allowed to observe classes because I had personal connections with some of the teachers, whom I had come to know through the Muslim Students' Association (see Chapter 4).

The two other Sunday Schools that I visited were situated in a predominantly Palestinian neighborhood in the southwestern suburb of Bridgeview. One occupied the basement of the local mosque (Mosque Foundation), and the other was close by, within a Muslim full-time school (Universal School). Both were staffed and attended mainly by Arabs; most classes were taught in English, but classes taught in Arabic were also available. However, the Sunday school that I visited most frequently, and where I found most of my informants, was the MCC.

Muslim weekend-school activities took place during the weekend, when the whole family spent time on their religion. While children participated in weekend-school classes, parents, grandparents, and siblings often engaged in other activities at the mosque. On Saturdays and Sundays, the centers teemed with activity, such as classes for men and women, lectures, and lunch in the mosque's cafeteria. Dozens of MCC Sunday school children moved up and down the stairs to classrooms, later joining their parents in the prayer hall or the cafeteria. When school was over, the center moved into a tranquil period, with only a handful of men and women attending adult-education classes. Weekend schools involved the lives of Muslim parents, offering them an opportunity to socialize with friends and family, participate in discussions, and listen to religious lectures in English or Urdu in the prayer hall while their children were in class. The schools provided a helpful overlap of ethnic and religious interests for the parents, who could meet fellow immigrants from the home country while their children were instructed in religious subjects.

That part-time Islamic education of children took place on the weekend illustrates an integral element of American Islam: As with any other religion, Muslims in Chicago had to schedule religious schooling when children were not in regular school and when parents were free from work. No matter how committed they were to their religious heritage, most parents understood that the rhythm of the surrounding society dictated the scheduling of religious teaching. How teaching took place in the Muslim weekend-school environment is illustrated by the following example.

The Prophet Muhammad Is Our Model:
A Class on the Tribulations of His Life
It was Sunday afternoon. Fifteen eighth-grade girls were gathered in the classroom. Most of them were wearing the traditional brightly colored *shalwar kamiz* (wide trousers with a matching long, wide dress), with a twist of "Americana"—Nike tennis shoes and sweatshirts. Although the girls had covered their heads, they relaxed when the door was closed, letting their scarves glide back to reveal strands of shiny black hair. The absence of men made the dress code less severe. The teacher, an articulate college student in her early twenties, stepped in. Her clothing was typical of the "Islamic uniform"[13] worn by many women of the Muslim Students' Association (MSA): a solid-colored *jilbab* (long gown) with a solid-colored *hijab*. Only a few years separated the students from the teacher, but this separation was immediately apparent in their roles.

As the class had not done very well that semester, the teacher started the lesson by asking whether the students had any ideas about how they could earn extra credits. If they did not, she was certain that they would all flunk the course. Four of the girls still did not have their books. When the teacher asked why they attended the school but came without the required books, a couple of the girls answered straightforwardly: "Because of our parents." Despite her obvious frustration, the teacher appealed to the girls. If money was the reason that they came without books, she was willing to lend them the money. But she was unable to let them continue the class if they kept coming unprepared. Three of the girls promised to buy the books before the next class. The fourth girl said that she would probably get them within the next few weeks.

The teacher began to present the day's subject. She retold a story from the Prophet Muhammad's life, a story that the girls had supposedly read for homework. She tried to engage their interest by asking short questions. The girls answered hesitantly and often incorrectly. Thereafter, the teacher chose to read fragments of the story and retell it in her own words.

"In the early history of Islam," she said, "two people were very important to the Prophet." One of them was his uncle, Abu Talib, who protected Muhammad against the Quraysh (the tribe from which the Prophet originated), even though Abu Talib himself was not a Muslim. When Abu Talib died, Muhammad lost his political protection. That same year, the Prophet lost his other important support when his wife, Khadija, died. The Prophet was now alone.

"Khadija was the one who comforted the Prophet when he received his revelations," a student remarked. She received an accepting smile from the teacher.

"After the death of his uncle and wife," the teacher continued, now and then writing key words on the board, "Muhammad went to the city of Ta'if. Although he had already suffered much persecution, he later said that the persecution he suffered in Ta'if was the worst he had ever experienced. He felt alone, unprotected, and in great pain. The two most important people in his life were gone, so he had to carry the burden of Islam on his back. He complained about his own weakness. It was just like us when we ask ourselves, 'Why does this happen to us?' But when he realized that Allah was happy with him, he did not care about his misery. Even though he was such a special person, he was only concerned about God being pleased with him.

"That is why he is a model for all of us," the teacher concluded. "As he did, we should only be happy if Allah is happy with
us. Muhammad was never trying to be a leader, but only to do
the will of Allah."

The teaching of Islamic principles in this class depended not
only on what the teacher said but also on the role she modeled.
Particularly through her dress, she embodied a model of Islam
for the girls and for herself. Whereas her control over the class
(as the person who gave the grades and decided whether students
should pass the course) reinforced the model she represented, so
did her success in teaching. As much as she knew the stories she
told and the requirements for a Muslim life, her main claim to
trustworthiness—and the basis of her influence on her students—
lay in her choice of clothing, her personal dedication, her reflections on life experiences.

The life of the Prophet Muhammad was the subject taught
most often in the classes I attended. Muhammad was described
as a "special person," the last of the prophets, who not only came
with the final message but also lived it to the fullest. His life was
presented as the superior model for imitation. Although the children were taught that they could never reach Muhammad's level
of perfection, they were not disheartened. Instead, they were
encouraged by the presentation of the Prophet's all-too-human
and sometimes painful experiences, because they knew pain and
disappointment from their own experiences. That the students
could recognize themselves in this model made for successful
learning.

From a Focus on Memorization to a Focus on Friendship:
Changing Muslim School Strategies

The curriculum of Muslim weekend schools also included instruction in Islamic conduct, *salat* (ritual prayers), and memorization of the Qur'an. Teachers spent very little time on issues
that students struggled with in their daily lives; instead, they
focused strictly on teaching. They expected students to answer
questions and participate in dialogues that centered on the lesson. In most sessions, the students' answers closely resembled
those in the texts they were using. Teaching of *sira* (the life of the

Prophet) and Qur'an was based on knowing a story or a pattern of behavior or a piece of text so well that the students could recite or restate it. Teachers usually modeled their behavior on religious training in their home countries, their own weekend-school experiences, or what they considered "Islamic." They believed that knowledge could be attained through mere familiarity. To know the Qur'an is to remember the Qur'an precisely. To know *salat* means remembering the patterns of *salat*. In their context, knowledge had nothing to do with the needs and challenges of the present. Instead, it was something pointed toward that was believed to be beyond time and after time: divine will and the hereafter.

But teaching strategies within Muslim weekend schools are changing. The teachers are young people who are being raised in a society in which education involves not only relating well to students but also using knowledge to fulfill individual ambitions. In the future, Muslim weekend schools may well choose to follow the example of successful Muslim youth programs—that is, placing their activities within settings that Muslim youngsters know as integrated parts of their everyday lives, such as their schools, streets, and weekday lives. Role-playing and pizza parties may increasingly become part of class interactions, as suggested by a Sunday school manual from the mid-1990s.[14]

During my time in Chicago, Sunday school teachers at the MCC center began to visit high schools in the area to engage Muslim students there and to encourage them to participate in *jum'a* (congregational prayers) and *halaqas* (study circles) to discuss their religion. Teachers in charge of these discussion groups did their best to bridge the generation gap by presenting attractive role models. As a Sunday school teacher at the MCC, one of the initiators of these visits, said, "When I grew up, we did not have many older kids. We hardly speak to our parents because they are from back home. . . . We can make [the students who participate in the discussion groups] feel that they are not the only ones . . . to have those problems."[15] The image of an Islamic teacher has changed from a person who distributes knowledge unchallenged to someone who is a friend. Such friendships ideally give children and young people of Muslim background the sense of belonging to a peer group and a faith-based community. Although most teaching efforts attempt to preserve religious knowledge in ways that seem detached from the lives of Muslim children in America, parts of the community vigorously adapt Islamic knowledge to the social reality of their children. Like many large American cities, Chicago is segregated by a mixture of ethnicity, income, and immigration, and recent immigrants who lack professional skills, savings, and visas end up in run-down neighborhoods where housing is cheap and their country-men are neighbors. Gang violence, drug addiction, and domestic abuse are social problems that the Muslims immigrants living in many of these neighborhoods face daily, sometimes even within their own families.

THE IMAN PROJECT

The Kedzie/West 63rd Street area on the South Side is a major neighborhood for recently arrived Arab immigrants, mainly Pales-tinians.[16] According to a 1990 demographic report, 2,587 of 51,243 individuals in the Chicago Lawn area, where Kedzie Avenue and West 63rd Street are situated, claimed Arab first or single an-cestry.[17] The slow deterioration of the neighborhood is reflected in the stagnation of family income. Between 1979 and 1989, the median household income fell from $28,651 to $25,757 (com-pared with an increase in the city's median household income from $25,644 to $26,301).[18] By 1989, 63 percent of Arabs living on Chicago's southwestern side were living at or below the pov-erty level.[19]

The Arab community in Chicago Lawn is far from the major ethnic minority. About 50 percent of the neighborhood is His-panic. Signs on Kedzie Avenue grocery stores, restaurants, and hair salons are predominantly in Spanish. During the summer, the street is dusty and gray. The sun flickers on the walls of old build-ings, illuminating traces of once-bright paint. People drive by with rap songs blaring through their car windows. Roman Catholic ro-saries hang from most rearview mirrors, although occasionally a tasbiha (Muslim "rosary") is visible.

On 63rd Street, however, the stores and doctors advertise in three languages—English, Spanish, and Arabic—or in Arabic alone. A storefront mosque, Masjid al-Salam, sits several blocks to the right of the intersection, and less than half a block to the left is the Arab American Community Center (AACC). Established in 1974, the AACC is the nucleus of several community-oriented projects, including IMAN. (*Iman* is also the Arabic word for faith.)

A group of Muslim students at De Paul University established IMAN in 1994.[20] During my fieldwork, IMAN recruited volunteers from most of the MSA chapters in the area, especially from De Paul and the University of Chicago. Non-Muslim volunteers were also welcomed. In 1996, a few non-Muslim volunteers from the Quaker American Friends Service Committee supervised a video project with a group of adolescent girls attending IMAN. The result was a thirty-minute video titled *Benaat Chicago* (Daughters of Chicago), which received a considerable amount of attention within and outside the community.[21]

From October 1996 to June 1997, I worked as an IMAN volunteer. During that period, IMAN grew from a small project directed only by volunteers into a well-known community organization directed by professionals. Professional counselors and social workers structured the goals and met the needs of people who had spent their childhood in the neighborhood. They were qualified to help parents handle the problems of raising children in an unfamiliar environment. They also recruited volunteers, raised funds, and publicized the project among Muslims and non-Muslims. Although IMAN's goals did not always seem clearly defined, the organization had entered a phase of ideological stabilization by the end of my stay. By then, most of its volunteers were active and practicing Muslims.

IMAN's Struggle with Ethnicity

IMAN was affected by having its base at the AACC, where groups arguing over religious and ethnic identity continuously vied for internal power. A huge Palestinian flag hanging in the main room and Palestinian newspapers and magazines in the book stacks demonstrated a strong nationalist influence. The flag seemed to provoke those in IMAN, to whom Islam meant promoting the equality of all races and nations, not one ethnic group at the expense of the others.[22] A staff member commented during a taped interview:

> That is more the secular people, the non-practicing Muslims in the community, that [have] put up the Palestinian flag and really promote nationalism. The Muslims in the center don't do that. . . . So I kind of see that struggle within the community that the people who are more secular fight with the people who are religious here, and the conflict is inevitably that the Muslims won't support this kind of nationalistic focus on Palestine, for example—issues that the seculars focus on. I have talked with a couple of people who have put up Palestinian flags here, and I said, "You know, not everyone in this community is Palestinian. Can everybody walk into this center and feel comfortable? When you put up only Palestinian flags, you say something in a very subtle way." [The man I was talking to] got really nuts and complained about me to [another female employee at the center].[23]

In addition to these external stresses, IMAN was affected by an internal conflict between those who promoted an exclusively religious ideology and those who saw the objectives of the project as mainly social and therapeutic. Another employee, Jinan, said during an interview in 1995:

> For example, we have students who come in and do arts and crafts. To me, arts and crafts is kids developing the ability of creative expression, a way to express themselves, connect them with social change, and to be able to realize their full potential. This is the higher goal to me about what art and developing art in children is. But for a religious Muslim, the art has to be connected with God, so if the kids draw, they have to draw a mosque or they have to draw the name of Allah or something that is connected with Islam. If the kids want to draw a house with a flag, that is no good. If the kids just want to draw a tree or whatever, that serves no purpose. So the clash often does not happen over the "what" but the "how to." O.K., we agree that we want to do arts and crafts, or we agree that we want to do this video project. But how do we want to do it? That is where the difference in perspectives starts to emerge.[24]

The Call for Equality:
IMAN's Ideas on Gender and Ethnicity

Interpretations and opinions also differed according to gender. Although its president was male, the AAAC comprised a number of strong, assertive women. Barbara, the wife of the center's late founder, worked next door in another community initiative, the Southwest Youth Collaborative.[25] Jinan, the executive director of the Union of Palestinian Women's Association and Sanad (a counseling initiative for battered women), had her office at the back of the AACC. Maryam, a young Assyrian woman with certification in rape and sexual-assault counseling, got involved in IMAN through her friendship with Barbara and Jinan and was a staff member in August 1996. Originally a Christian, she converted to Islam in November of the same year.

The three women were strongly and vocally engaged in women's issues, with a sincere focus on educating the community's girls and mothers. All three were active in the Arab-American Action Network, which was established in 1995 and housed at the AACC.[26] But only Jinan and Maryam based their interpretations of gender issues on an Islamic ideal. Maryam related with some humor how Jinan had been an active element in her conversion by providing literature that challenged her "atheistic" search for answers and "broke it down scientifically." She further argued that the mythical images she encountered in Islam not only contradicted the general American understanding of the religion as oppressing women but had also answered a number of spiritual questions that she had raised in her atheist, feminist past:

> I think that once I started reading [the Qur'an], it really enlightened me. And then I think for a lot of women it really promotes a lot more aspects of yourself than I think Christianity does. I was always having a problem with [the idea] that Eve screwed up the world, basically, and the notion that Satan sought out Eve because she is the weaker sex—that God put a curse on all human beings because of Eve's mistake. . . . When I read the Qur'an, I saw that Adam was sleeping, and Satan just went to Eve because she was up. Adam had equal blame and responsibility— and, I think, even more responsibility than Eve. God did not put a curse on humankind after this. It was . . . really positive for me, because I really struggled with these images. [The Qur'an] really promoted motherhood and womanhood in a positive light, and it really, I think, promoted male responsibility. That is where I think that a lot of women connect to it—to get rid of these stereotypes that they have and understand the cultural versus the religious differences.[27]

As a counselor and program director, Jinan focused on the prevention of psychological stress and abuse. As a woman to whom women's issues were a major concern, she wanted to prevent the community's girls from becoming passive victims of domestic violence and of what she saw as cultural biases. Her ideas about Islam as a religion that promoted equality and brotherhood among ethnic groups further characterized the initiatives that she promoted. During Jinan's involvement, IMAN moved from concentrating on the neighborhood's Muslim and Arab children to including non-Muslim children of Hispanic and African-American background. In addition, the majority of new staff members hired during her time were neither Muslims nor Arabs. But despite these changes, Islam remained the dominant and persuasive marker of discussions within IMAN—the system of knowledge according to which teaching strategies and teaching roles were interpreted and defended.

Hussein, a Palestinian Muslim in his late twenties, added another perspective to the function of IMAN. He worked full-time on the project until Maryam took over. His focus was on the activation of socioreligious awareness both among the children and within the Chicago Muslim community as a whole. He often presented IMAN from this viewpoint at MSA meetings and community conferences. To Hussein, Islam as system, ideal, and knowledge constituted the perfect solution to the social illnesses of inner-city children and their families. Success and despair, according to Hussein, were determined by who was inside or outside of Islam. What was responsible for the depression of the neighborhood's Muslims was the *kufr*, unbelief, in American society. To him, any empowerment of the community had to come from a sincere unification and revitalization of the Muslim *umma* (community of believers) within a local setting.

Afternoons in the Markaz

The dogmatic goals of IMAN were not obvious to someone entering the center—or Markaz, as it was generally called. The first children arrived at 2:30 P.M., right after public school. Four tables stood in the middle of the main room, and the children were expected to take their seats and start doing their homework. Because many were recent immigrants, and their parents' proficiency in English was limited, most suffered from insufficient reading and writing skills. If the children finished early or claimed to have no assignments, photocopied worksheets were provided to keep them occupied. Between 3:00 and 4:00 P.M., the number of children rose to between thirty and forty. A handful of volunteers moved around the tables, helping individual children with their homework. This task was not easy. Most of the children quickly lost focus and started running around the room, although they were forbidden to do so. A pool table, standing at the far end of the room, was a perpetual temptation.

The Markaz had its own version of reward and punishment. A huge yellow poster with the children's names written across an image of the Ka'ba (Islam's holiest shrine) hung on one of the walls. When a child finished five worksheets, he or she was awarded a green sticker. A child who earned fifty stickers was honored for making the 'umra (little pilgrimage); those who earned 100 stickers were honored for making the hajj (great pilgrimage). But if a child received three warnings, he or she got a black sticker, which meant expulsion from attractive activities such as swimming or basketball. In spite of such disciplinary measures, however, the noise and chaos in the room often approached the unbearable. Children shouted, screamed, and fought, and volunteers and staff shouted even louder to make the violators return to their seats.

Most children finished their homework before 5:00 P.M., after which they entered the arts and crafts room. Supervised by a volunteer or staff member, they were allowed to draw, make collages, or play until IMAN closed its doors at 5:30 P.M. Some days the program was extended to provide visits to the local YMCA swimming pool or one of the South Side's mosques.

How did IMAN integrate and formulate Islam in this setting? How did teachers and staff use Islam to analyze, understand, and eventually demand a restructuring of existing relations of power between the minority and the majority in American society, between haves and have-nots, between young men and women? First, the staff used the daily, monthly, and yearly cycle of religious rituals and periods of celebration to help the children internalize an Islamic way of life. Second, IMAN used Jinan's "how to" teaching methods. Third, the staff helped students internalize their knowledge by creating a community based on religion. And fourth, IMAN used models and images found within Islamic history and among the staff members and volunteers who taught the children.

For the children, time in the Markaz was always fixed: when they did homework and when they did not, when they did arts and crafts and when they did not, when they behaved according to the rules and restrictions and when they did not. In addition, time in the Markaz was fixed for prayer and religious instruction. During prayer, all children (including non-Muslims who wanted to participate) were lined up behind Hussein or a male volunteer. From time to time, one of the older boys was allowed to lead the prayer. After *salat* (ritual prayers) and *du'a* (personal prayer), a short religious lesson was given focusing on aspects of the children's lives or on events that had taken place during the day. The instruction included an Islamic perspective on situations that the children encountered at school, in the neighborhood, or on television. Further, the instruction educated the children about how they were expected to behave in such situations according to an Islamic model.

For example, on one day in mid-December, when every street and store was decorated with colorful ornaments, Christmas was dominant in the homework of the children who attended the Markaz. One of the girls struggled to write a poem about Santa Claus, while another talked about her class's preparation of Christmas baskets. After prayers, Hussein told the children to stay seated in their lines and look at him. He began his *khutba* (sermon), telling them about the prophets in whom Muslims believe— that Muslims also believe in Abraham, or, "as we call him, Ibrahim," and in Jesus, or, "as we call him, Isa." Finally, Hussein said that the children, as Muslims, believed in the prophethood of Muhammad. He added that no matter which prophet they talked about, they had all encountered people who did not want to listen to the message: people who said that they were too busy, that they wanted to make money more than follow Islam. These people gave the prophets a really hard time.

"What we see," Hussein continued, "is that the same thing happens today. You look around, and people do not want to listen because they want to be cool and hang out with 'gang-bangers' and wear gold." He warned the children against such a future. The main thing was to think about what came after this life. Hussein instructed the children to imagine the fire, to imagine *Jahannam* (hell): "Don't get the idea that you have to spend all your time on getting gold and drugs like the gang-bangers. Don't think about getting some blond girl. Don't think about nice and fancy and expensive cars. Because neither gold nor BMWs can save you from the fire."

He told the children to close their eyes. In this darkness of the senses, where only his voice rang through, he asked the children to imagine *Janna* (paradise). "Imagine all the nice things there," he said. "You are never tired, never sad. There are beautiful mountains and valleys, and whenever you think about something or want something, it is right there. You will get it. You are together with the most beautiful people you may imagine. And even the best things you imagine are one hundred times better in reality." The children stayed silent and concentrated. "Then," Hussein continued, his voice changing from soft and cheerful to harsh and sinister, "imagine *Jahannam*. Think about the flames. People there are angry. Whenever they eat, they are torn up inside. They go through torture every day. When they drink, the water is so hot that they are burning themselves. Try to remember this. To get into *Janna*, it is important how you behave toward your parents, and that you do what they tell you to. It is important how you behave toward all your brothers and sisters. *Amin* [amen]."

In his *khutba*, Hussein used images of Islamic historiography and mythology to create a new perspective on issues that his young listeners encountered daily. Describing prophets of Islam, he conveyed a message countering the feeling of being different that the children might experience in the outside world of Christmas ornaments. But the children were not expected to totally deny the image of Jesus. Jesus was a prophet, and they could honor him as such, just like Muhammad. In this way, through the veneration of a person important to Islam, the outside world became religiously familiar. Hussein also used persuasive Islamic images of heaven and hell to instill fear and expectation and—through those responses—self-discipline, control, and moral behavior. He stressed that eternal pleasures were connected to community and authority, to the "brothers and sisters" who shared the conviction of the hereafter, and to honoring the family structure. Both explicitly and implicitly, the message was clear: Children should not defy their parents.

In the Markaz, a certain amount of time was spent on arts and crafts or games, which teachers often used to impart interpretations of Islam. On one afternoon while Hussein was in charge, I entered the room when the children had just finished their collages and drawings. Hussein encouraged them to describe their work. One girl presented her drawing, explaining that she had used the colors that her mother liked the most. Hussein smiled and said that it was nice that she had done so, reinforcing the importance of honoring and respecting one's parents.

Another girl said her artwork was a collage of a mosque. In one corner of the picture, she had drawn the image of the Qur'an and written a short poem about fasting. She had made the top of the mosque green, because green, she said, reminded her of the pleasures of paradise. Under the mosque she had written, "*Allahu akbar* [God is great]," because to her Allah was the best in the whole, wide world. The bottom of the mosque was red, because that was the color of those who had suffered for Islam. Finally, she had painted the Qur'an blue, because, she explained, that color reminded her of how much *hasanat* (God's positive rewards for the good deeds of humans) she got for telling other people about Islam. When she finished her description, Hussein shouted, "*Takbir* [Give praise]!," and the children answered, "*Allahu akbar!*"

Gathering in the Markaz every day created a sense of community among the children, with numerous friendships established, lots of hugs given, and secrets shared. Hanging out with "gang-bangers" no longer seemed attractive, partly because the people in the Markaz would know about it. Because the outside world could observe the frequency of the children's visits to the center, the attractiveness or possibility of changing identity (for example, by using a Hispanic name or denying ethnic and religious background among non-Muslim, non-Arab peers) also declined. Being Muslim and Arab in the Markaz involved no risks—only the safety and comfort of being in the majority. Hussein's ideological determination reinforced the sense of community and power when he called the children "brothers and sisters." They were "knights of Islam."

The Call for Respect:
IMAN's Efforts Outside the Markaz

This small community slowly but forcefully communicated its activities and its message to the surrounding neighborhood. An example was the annual '*Id* dinner, marking the end of Ramadan, held at the Marquette School, one of the area's public schools. In early 1997, IMAN was given permission to arrange the dinner, with some support from the Universal School in Bridgeview, a Muslim full-time school. The Marquette School's new gymnasium was decorated with balloons and signs conveying the message, "Happy Eid—Eid Mubarak." The air vibrated with taped recitations of the Qur'an and Arab music played over a loudspeaker. Middle Eastern food was served free in the school cafeteria. The children could win candy at games arranged in the gym. The climax of the celebration was the evening prayers. For those who were not Muslim, the prayers were translated into English and Spanish and distributed on a sheet of paper. After *sura al-Fatiha* (the opening chapter of the Qur'an), parts of two other *suras* were recited, conveying a message of both tolerance and warning:

> And dispute ye not/ with the people of the book (Christians and Jews) / except in the best way, unless/ it will be those of them/ who do wrong. / But say "We believe/ in the revelation which has/ come down to us and in that/ which has come down to you."/ Our God and your God/ is One, and it is to Him/ We submit (Sura 29:46–47)/ . . . / If any do wish/ for the transitory things/ (of life) we readily/ grant them such things/ as we will, to such persons/ and we will: In the end/ Have we provided Hell/ for them: they will burn/ therein, disgraced and rejected. (Sura 17:18)[28]

In this situation, the children attending IMAN, their parents, their teachers, their fellow students, and the local press received the message of a strong community and a strong community effort. The invitation to one of the Muslim community's major religious celebrations communicated a sense of tolerance that only a group in power could allow itself to claim openly.

But the South Side children did not always experience that kind of empowerment in their collective encounter with the surrounding society. One instance showing the risk of crossing the border to public spaces was a field trip that the group took to downtown Chicago in May 1997. A museum was showing an exhibition of Arabic calligraphy, which IMAN's staff saw as an opportunity to teach the children about their cultural heritage. Two docents showed the children to the second floor, where the exhibition was located, and quickly explained what the abstract paintings were about. Then the children were allowed to explore on their own. Most of the children showed disappointment in what they saw around them. Some laughed when they saw a painting of a naked woman. A number of the boys detected the security system in the window and spent the rest of the visit discussing its efficiency.

Suddenly, everyone focused attention on Maryam and one of the docents, who were engaged in a heated discussion in the middle of the room. The docent firmly told the group to leave the room, because she had a dinner appointment and could not let the group stay unattended. Maryam objected, saying that the group had been promised much more time. But the group had to leave. As the children returned to the lobby, security guards followed them to the door, all the way to the outside stairs. Although the volunteers told the children to sit down on the steps, within a couple of minutes a security guard came out and told them to move. The children were discouraged; the staff and volunteers were furious. Why were they not allowed to stay longer? Why were they not allowed to sit on public stairs? Because the children were poor? Because they were Arabs? Because the accompanying mothers wore the *hijab*? Why did the security guards treat the group as if it was a threat? After all, these children were only children, weren't they?

The Call for Diginity: IMAN's Efforts for Women

Issues of the body (ranging from dress code to male and female sexuality) were an integral part of IMAN's ongoing discussions. These issues were also intrinsic to IMAN's way of communicating, interacting, and negotiating with the outside world. Consequently, gender issues became subjects of debate.

Both sets of issues received more attention after Maryam joined the staff. Arguing for a definition of womanhood that allowed women more right of action (thus rejecting standards prevalent in her Middle Eastern upbringing), Maryam wanted to teach boys and girls to interact with and respect each other. She clearly wanted to change some of the children's habits and norms—and, ideally, to change those of their families, their community, their culture, and the images dominating American public life.

Raised in an Assyrian Christian family in Chicago, and a convert to Islam, Maryam had internalized the images of more than one culture. Suppression, violence, and harassment of women, she asserted, were not found only among Muslims or Arabs. Such behavior, in her eyes, was not even Islamic but "cultural." As she observed, "This stuff with domestic violence, you know, these are people who say that they are Muslim. So I see that as similar to some of the practice in the Middle East: '[I am] oppressing women, but I am a Muslim, and this is what I am doing for Islam.' This abuse of religion [is] to achieve their personal gain, which has nothing to do with religion."[29] Maryam claimed that domestic violence was the most pervasive issue in the center. Children told her about their mothers being beaten up at home and their fathers drinking heavily. This phenomenon, she asserted, resulted from cultural misperceptions coupled with the impotence that many men felt in the new environment. This violence, she told me, was silent: The community had neglected it and refused to challenge it. Maryam saw it as her mission to initiate discussion about the silence surrounding family violence.[30] Her strategy was both therapeutically and religiously determined, involving parents and children, boys and girls. In this pursuit she gained support from other strong figures in the center, such as Jinan, who shared her views.

That both the AACC and IMAN had female staff members to whom the fight against the suppression of women stood high on the agenda strongly affected the activities and interpretations of Islam that took place in the Markaz. Through my interaction with the group and my discussions with Maryam, the volunteers, and the children, I learned that factors of mobility, space, and speech determined how women in the community were defined, how they lived, and—in case of abuse—how they were enfeebled. IMAN's staff saw the mothers as being physically and psychologically isolated. As Maryam told me:

What we see, basically, is that the moms stay at home. A lot of them
don't have an education because they were raised in the Middle East. . . .
So when they come here, they really feel *displaced.* [my emphasis][31]

The displacement resulted not from a dismissal from the outside world but from the isolation of women from the surrounding world, caused by both the immigration experience and the
expectations of men. According to Maryam, space in the community was most often male-dominated, adding to the vulnerability, insecurity, and silencing of women:

Sometimes I walk in somewhere and just feel these eyes staring at me.
It is really unsafe, so to speak, because it is just—it is not necessarily
meaning something physical will happen. I mean, just your being is
questioned. Just the virtue of being a woman walking in there and it
is kind of a "What are you doing here?" look. And it is really an unsafe
place for women to be, because, you know, what is that saying about
women? What is that saying about who you are as a woman if you walk
in and people think that you shouldn't even be there? So I mean unsafe
in terms of feeling secure and positive about yourself as a woman. If
you are not in an environment that supports that, you are in trouble,
I think. And that is, I think, what a lot of women struggle with religiously. [It] is finding those places where they can feel comfortable.[32]

IMAN and the Arab American Action Network attempted to
create a space of safety for these women.[33] A women's group was
formed, creating a network for the mothers of children who attended IMAN and for the other Arab Muslim women in the neighborhood. Apart from sharing experiences with one another, the
mothers were encouraged to strengthen themselves through education and involvement in the wider neighborhood. Some pursued
high school diplomas, while others studied English as a second
language or became active in the PTA at their children's schools.
   Working with the mothers was one step; working with the
daughters was the next. Many girls, just like their parents, viewed
restrictions on women's mobility as "protection," even while
they complained that they were given less freedom and shown
less trust than their brothers. Why was it, they asked, that the
boys were allowed to go to the mall and see their friends or return
late from the movie theater, their friends' houses, or parties when
they as girls could not? Like their parents, the girls tended to

interpret female sexuality as involving a risk: Premarital sexual relations might harm the family's honor.

The IMAN staff disagreed with these restrictions, and they did so from a religiously determined standpoint. They therefore established a group for girls age twelve and older that met every Monday to play basketball. Initially, the group focused on creating a sisterhood among the girls and encouraging them to talk, thereby giving the staff a more direct understanding of the issues that were most important to them. Later, the group developed into a study group, in which the girls discussed cultural issues and biases and ways to handle them from a religious point of view. Maryam described her teaching in the group:

> The way that I addressed [situations in which parents treat daughters and sons differently] was that, if their parents are trying to base this on religion, then you have to let your sons be at home, too. Because if you let your sons out to a party, this opposes everything religiously. You let them go out where there is drinking, and there is, you know, interaction with men and women who are of age, so to speak. This opposes everything religiously. . . . So when I talk to the girls, I say: "You need to talk to your parents seriously about these things. If you argue with your parents about 'Let me go to a party, too,' you should be smart enough actually to say, "In the Qur'an . . ." and get the *sura* and find the *aya* where it talks about this, and say, "Why is he going? I thought that you were Muslims." And then bring up those issues that reverse this. That "he needs to be home, too, like I am."[34]

The girls in the group learned to use Islam—to refer to indisputable quotes from an authoritative text—to lessen the discrepancies in mobility between them and their brothers. Nevertheless, IMAN in no way encouraged the girls to claim the same spaces or the same level of experimentation with partying and sex that their brothers had. Rather, the strategy for equality called for both genders to limit their public interactions and control their sexuality.

IMAN's teaching was highly based on the children's encounters with, and potential imitation of, the models they met in the Markaz. The girls interacted with practicing Muslim women such as Maryam and Jinan, who were unmarried and lived alone. They were taught by women who resisted gender segregation (but stressed sexual control) by being articulate and visible, whether in the mosque or at community meetings. For example, Maryam once sat down in the men's area in a North Side mosque, claiming that she had come to listen to the *khatib* (the person giving the sermon), not to sit behind a curtain. In the Markaz, girls were taught by volunteers who wore the *hijab* but went to college and who wanted to become doctors and lawyers in addition to mothers and wives.

As the girls were learning the Islamic model for womanhood that IMAN advocated, the boys were learning an Islamic model for manhood. Because the boys sometimes came from homes with abusive alcoholic fathers, IMAN saw its mission as conveying an alternative model, to prepare the boys for adulthood, marriage, and fatherhood—and, ideally, to help them educate their fathers. Again, the behavior and professionalism of the volunteers and staff (notably Hussein) were the primary tools for conveying this model. The boys were exposed to the male volunteers' respectful interactions with the girls, behavior they were expected to imitate. They were exposed to the volunteers' successes (always attributed to their pursuit of education and submission to Islamic standards) when they were allowed to ride around the parking lot in one of their cars. Imitating the "gangbangers" was no longer the only way to achieve prestige.

Maryam claimed to see some progress in the statements and assertiveness of mothers and their daughters. But though the progress was noticeable when the women visited the center, she remarked that the influence of the fathers and the patriarchal system that supported their claim to dominance was still in power outside the center. When I asked Maryam to share the experiences that she had had with girls' using the Qur'an as a means of persuasion in gender and family disputes, she admitted:

> I haven't heard any feedback yet about trouble at home, so I'm not sure if there is a conflict.... My problem is that I am teaching the girls these things—this is great. But if they're going to go back home and the dad is really abusive, he is still going to dictate what is going to happen to them.[35]

Although domestic violence and alcoholism are prevalent problems in many of Chicago's low-income neighborhoods, regardless of ethnicity or religion, addiction and abuse are not general trends within Arab Muslim households on the South Side. What is specific to any community, of course, is how the abuser and abused defend the behavior and how it is silenced or discussed by the community. Within the overall South Side Muslim community, all arguments and actions were part of the ongoing debate over what Islam is, what it permits and forbids, and how adults should convey Islam to the younger generation. The IMAN staff viewed this struggle as a result of a clash between cultural traditions (what is "ignorant") and Islamic knowledge (what is "authentic" and "educated"). Within IMAN, then, the struggle was far more substantive than intellectual, involving people more than symbols.

Calls for Understanding: IMAN's Efforts on Ethnicity

Ethnicity, and the attempt to redress or transcend the personal inequalities that it often created, was another theme discussed within IMAN, mainly because of IMAN's transethnic perspective. Both the composition of the staff and the ethnic diversity of the surrounding neighborhood contributed to the transethnic preference. Volunteers recruited from Chicago campuses came from many ethnic backgrounds. To many of them, a transethnic definition of identity validated their personal experience and underscored a move toward the ideal of the *umma*.

Furthermore, Arabs were far from the majority outside the center, and as time went by a number of non-Arab, non-Muslim children got involved in the after-school program. IMAN's task was therefore to develop strategies to help the children respect one another across ethnicities and to transfer this respect to their lives in the neighborhood. As always, this task was formulated Islamically.

During a planning meeting involving staff and volunteers, Hussein commented on the interethnic neighborhood struggles that affected IMAN. What he found unacceptable was that the two ethnic groups most represented in the center, Arabs and Hispanics, had joined forces against the African Americans who lived in or around the neighborhood. Among Arabs, African Americans had become known as *'abid* (slaves). Children brought the negative vocabulary with them to the center and used it partially for fun and partially to claim superiority. Some volunteers and staff members commented that a number of children of non-Arabic origin had started rejecting their ethnic background in an attempt to become a part of the group.

Neither Hussein, Maryam, nor any of the other Muslims at the meeting could accept that one ethnic group found itself superior to others. "Islam," Hussein stated, "proclaims a utopia, an idea of equality between the nations"; this was what those in both the Markaz and the neighborhood outside should be taught. From then on, the group decided, the children were to be confronted with their own perceptions and misperceptions of others, through either religious instruction or arts and crafts. They should come to realize that Islam was all-inclusive.

Taking It to the Streets

Hussein went further. After a gang fight on the South Side in February 1997 in which two Muslim youths were reportedly killed, he posted an e-mail through the MSA-Chicago Net, an Internet list for members of the MSA in the Chicago area. It was now time, he said, to make a public statement about the status quo in the inner city:

> IMAN's primary objective throughout the years has been to generate enough support and interest from the broader Muslim community in the Chicago land area to deal [with] and confront many of the problems endemic to the inner-city. We have a number of programs and services currently in operation and are looking for the human and material resources to initiate many more. We are convinced that the deadly life for youths growing up in Americas inner-cities can only be solved by Islam, but this means Muslims everywhere must work towards this end. It is in this spirit that we invite all Muslims in the Chicago land area to a planning meeting for an event entitled "Taking It to the Streets." "Taking it to the Streets" will be an all day type Islamic festival held in the heart of a diverse community on the Southwest Side of Chicago. . . . We need everyone to be involved in some way or another, so bring yourself and several friends to the planning meeting this Sunday.[36]

The first planning meeting for "Taking It to the Streets" was held at the University of Chicago on March 9, 1997. Most participants at the meeting were active student members of the local MSAs. A number of committees were formed and put in charge

of different tasks: What activities should the festival facilitate?
What about food? What about security? What about fundraising?
What about *dáwa* (informing non-Muslims about Islam, or proselytizing)? Over the next few months, several meetings were held,
until a June 21 date for the festival was set. During this time, the
goals of Hussein and the festival's appointed *shura* (council, leadership) became firmer. Having started as a reaction to a tragic
event, the project developed into a forceful propagation of Islam.
"Taking It to the Streets," now subtitled "Nurturing Unity, Revitalization, and Success," was to articulate the need for, and the
move toward, unity among Muslims. It should generate an image
of Islam as a social movement. Islam was to be known as a religion that transcends borders of ethnicity and opposes violence.
At the end of March, another e-mail was sent from Hussein and
the *shura*:

> ["Taking It to the Streets"] is IMAN's first attempt to create a unified
> vision towards community growth and empowerment within the indi-
> viduals of Marquette Park (63rd & Kedzie community). IMAN hopes
> that this citywide initiative amongst Muslims of all walks of life will
> reinvigorate inner-city denizens with a clear and feasible alternative
> to all the social ills plaguing poor and disenfranchised communities
> throughout the Chicago land area. In addition to the aims and goals
> listed above, IMAN wants to use this event to inform Muslims and
> non-Muslims alike, of the needs of this and other similar communi-
> ties. By involving Muslims who are not familiar with the dynamics
> and needs of people living within the inner-city, IMAN hopes to gen-
> erate a collective spirit of consciousness and concern that will Inshal-
> lah [God willing] result in a desire to get involved.[37]

Although "Taking It to the Streets" was successful in engaging college students (who were mostly IMAN volunteers), festival organizers found it harder to connect to Muslims in the suburbs and on Chicago's North Side. Much help came from the
African-American-Muslim community, which shared the South
Side Muslims' experience of economic deprivation and of being
a target of social violence. Although "Taking It to the Streets" was
announced in the mosques, and flyers could be seen hanging in
the windows of stores in Arab and South Asian neighborhoods,
volunteers from these neighborhoods were absent until the very

end.[38] This absence was probably not coincidental. It underscored the sense of alliance (expressed, for example, through financial support) as primarily directed toward one's own ethnic group and only to a lesser extent toward those who shared one's religion. Ethnic affiliation within the Chicago Muslim community was clearly still running strong.

Further, the absence of Arab-Muslim volunteers from the suburbs illustrated that Muslims who represented one ethnic group or social class might devalue the needs and activities of other Muslims by claiming that they did not practice Islam correctly. An interview that I carried out in the southwestern suburbs, shortly before "Taking It to the Streets" took place, reflected the suburban position toward the Muslims living in the Chicago Lawn area. The informant (an Arab Muslim) claimed that Arab Muslims in Chicago Lawn lived according to poor moral standards, selling liquor and food coupons, and even donated some of this *haram* (forbidden) money to the mosque. Therefore, their unfortunate social situation was their own fault. Because their morals were bad, so were their family values, which he claimed were illustrated by a high divorce rate and domestic violence in the neighborhood.

The informant did not deny that the people in question were Arabs or that they were Muslims. But his statements demonstrated the barrier between the better-off Arab Muslims in the suburbs and those in the city. From his point of view, the behavior of Chicago Lawn's Muslims posed a subtle threat to the well-educated middle- and upper-middle-class Arabs and other Muslims in the suburbs. The behavior and low social status of the inner-city Muslims degraded the suburbanites' image of what Islam was about and what a Muslim was supposed to be. Any strong affiliation between the two groups could cause a negative judgment from non-Muslim neighbors and colleagues, challenging the suburban Muslims' claim that Islam fulfilled the requirements of the American middle-class ideal: a well-defined family structure, a respectful husband and a devoted wife, and above-board business ethics and religious morals.

But among college students, African-American Muslims, and the IMAN volunteers, "Taking It to the Streets" took root, moving quickly from idea to action. Although Chicago had been drenched in rain for several days (Hussein's June 20 e-mail encouraged everybody to make *du'a* that no rain would fall),[39] game booths, tents, and even a huge air-filled plastic castle were erected in Marquette Park during the early-morning hours of June 21. Participation in the festival was free, but meal tickets were sold at the entrance for a dollar each. A number of girls were busy in one of the tents, packing food: *zabiha* (food considered to be *halal*, or permitted) hamburgers, chips, cookies, and soft drinks. A larger tent offered a job fair, a health clinic, and legal counseling. The children were engaged at the games, and most of them soon collected a fair number of prizes.

Here and there, signs were posted: "Do you know that Islam is the fastest growing religion in America?" "Did you know that only 15% of Muslims are Arab?" A *da'wa* booth distributed pamphlets from the Institute of Islamic Information and Education (described in Chapter 5). Messages for change were further reinforced by the black T-shirts worn by a number of young men, on which "What do you choose—Good or Evil? Islam, a way of life" was written with white letters around the image of a mosque. From a stage raised in the middle of the park, Hussein announced the purpose of the fair: "Islam encompasses many cultures. That is what we celebrate and mark here. In a moment, when you see us pray together, you will see African Americans, Latinos, Arabs, and South Asians standing side by side." And as the call to prayer sounded through the loudspeakers, most of the crowd moved toward the prayer rugs that were spread out in back of the park. Their prayers were watched and studied by non-Muslims attending the festival.

This collective action seemed to be the culmination of the ambition of IMAN and "Taking It to the Streets": to be seen and known by Muslims and non-Muslims alike as a strong, united community. The festival's subtitle, "Nurturing Unity, Revitalization, and Success," verbalized IMAN's desire for collective and assertive action that offered the larger community what it saw as a divinely constituted knowledge. Islam was presented as the solution to problems of race and class, thus highlighting IMAN's egalitarian interpretation—an Islam that criticized American society while simultaneously taking an engaged, social-activist position within it.

Muslims who participated in "Taking It to the Streets" described it as a success. As a member of the *shura* committee stated in an e-mail a few days after the event:

> Throughout the day of the festival, I heard countless praises applauding the event: "ma shaa Allah [according to God's will] . . . very organized", "what a great idea . . .", ". . . the first of its kind". . . . But aside from the encouraging compliments, and much more importantly, by the powerful will and permission of our Almighty Creator, your hard work has enabled us to accomplish the deeper purpose behind this. Through this event, we have been able to portray Islam as a religion that advocates justice and condemns any form of oppression, particularly that of the victimized residents of the inner-city. We have also been able to bring Muslims of diverse ethnic and racial backgrounds together to strengthen bonds of sister/brotherhood in a community where Islam is generally associated with a particular ethnic background (by both Muslims and non-Muslims). We were able to remind Muslims of the universality of this Deen [religion], and to demonstrate an absolutely essential aspect of da'awa.[40]

This e-mail message encompasses the elements and ambitions that marked "Taking It to the Streets" as a whole: the act of communicating Islam as a solution to social injustice, the act of transcending ethnic and national borders among Muslims, the act of presenting Islam as universal and all-encompassing. "Taking It to the Streets" was viewed as a launching pad for IMAN, formulating the ideas and ideals that future Muslim social work in the inner city should follow. Not surprisingly, the festival has been repeated in subsequent years, and the tradition seems to continue. As a whole, IMAN and "Taking It to the Streets" highlighted an important aspect of contemporary and future formulations of Islam in America: social activism.

MUSLIM FULL-TIME SCHOOLS

Many Muslim parents see the education offered in public schools as contrary to the religiously defined norms that they want their offspring to learn and honor. At the same time, they are aware that secular knowledge is important to a child's eventual life and career. Some have responded to the dilemma by enrolling their children in Muslim full-time schools that integrate the Islamic perspective with the secular subjects that hold the key to a successful life in America. Islamic schools constitute an environment in which parents control what and how their children learn. Because these schools depend on parents for financial support, they are keenly sensitive to those parents' demands and perceptions of what the children are required to know.

Chicago is home to five Muslim full-time schools established since the late 1980s. All of the schools are certified by the State of Illinois and teach an accredited curriculum along with Islamic studies and Arabic. Most of the schools are located in the suburbs—one in a northern suburb (the Muslim Education Center), two in western suburbs (the College Preparatory School of America and the Islamic Foundation School),[41] and two in a southwestern suburb (the Universal School and the al-Aqsa School). Four of the five are open to both boys and girls; the al-Aqsa School is for girls only.[42] During my stay in Chicago, I visited all but the Islamic Foundation School and became especially well acquainted with the Universal School and the Muslim Education Center. These two schools allowed me to interview teachers and students and to observe classroom teaching. I also participated in extracurricular activities such as fund-raising and *iftar* dinners, PTA field trips, and staff-development programs.

The Universal School is located in the southwestern suburb of Bridgeview. The building is gray concrete with occasional horizontal strips of window marking the entrance and classrooms. The school is not the only sign of Muslim influence in the neighborhood. Across the parking lot is a mosque, and farther down the street are a Muslim youth center and an Arab grocery store. The Muslim community in the area started building the school in 1988; classes started on September 4, 1990.[43] The school contains thirteen classrooms, two laboratories, a library, large preschool and kindergarten rooms, a lunchroom in the basement, a large gymnasium, and a number of offices. In 1995–96, 338 students were enrolled in preschool through twelfth grade.[44] The majority of students were Arabs, mainly Palestinians and Syrians, although some were South Asians and African Americans.

The Muslim Education Center (MEC) is located in the northern suburb of Morton Grove. The Muslim Community Center purchased the building, a former public elementary school, in 1989. Initially, members of the local non-Muslim community resented the establishment of a Muslim school and formed an organization to keep the building as city property. These opponents argued that the public school system needed more classrooms in the area. A concern voiced at a less official level was that the school would house members of the Nation of Islam. However, the Muslim buyers found support in another local community group and the Council for a Parliament of the World's Religions. In the end, a local vote became necessary. The voters approved the sale, and the MEC opened its doors in 1990.[45]

The MEC sits in a residential area characterized by green gardens and small, middle-class houses. It has eight classrooms, a library, a large gymnasium, a cafeteria with a kitchen, and a number of offices. In contrast to the Universal School, the MEC is not part of a closely knit Muslim community, because it was established by an Islamic center situated several miles away. In 1996–97, 220 students were enrolled in the MEC, from preschool to eighth grade. Although it was establishing a high school program during that period, the MEC was doubtful that the upper grades would use the same location, because the high school classes would probably be held at the MCC. Most of the MEC's students were South Asians, but some came from Bosnia and the Middle East.

Why Choose a Muslim Full-Time School?

The most prominent parental demand for these schools was religious. People wanted their children to learn Islamic standards and get acquainted with the normative scriptures, traditions, and language of the Qur'an. But although the Islamic dimension of the schools was a decisive requirement, it was not the only one. Muslim parents also sent their children to Muslim schools because they expected the institutions to provide an environment marked by other goals as well. One principal remarked that, for some of the parents, the "main goal is academic. Some, their main goal is religious. And some, their main goal is a safe environment.

And it doesn't really matter to them even if [the students] graduate. They just want to know that when they are in the school, they are in a safe place."[46]

Although none of the parents I interviewed described their ambitions for the school quite as categorically, they left no doubt that safety was a primary concern. As parents sent their children to Sunday schools, and as the staff of IMAN used Islam to keep the children away from the streets, the Muslim full-time schools were viewed as small islands of harmony within a sea of apparent chaos. The aspiration of providing a safe environment was evident in the advertising material that some of the schools distributed:

> Agreed by all, the greatest quality Universal School offers its students *a school free of the West's social-ills.* Our school maintains an environment that reinforces and supplements the Islamic values that the parents teach at home. We believe that through the teamwork of parents and teachers alike, each student can reach an understanding of Islam unequaled by other environments. [my emphasis][47]

> The primary aim of this school is to offer students an excellent academic curriculum in *an Islamic environment free of drugs,* where children are empowered by their Islamic faith to participate as effective and responsible citizens in this society, and contribute to its enhancement in accordance with their Islamic values. [my emphasis][48]

In Muslim full-time schools, the surrounding society was often described as inherently violent. Although this description is somewhat true, its emphasis validated the need for Muslim schools. Ironically, the violence of American society played a dominant role among parents, because it highlighted what the parents saw as the wrongness and failure of the prevalent public norms. The violence justified enrolling their children in Muslim schools, because removing them from non-Muslim-American influence would ensure their physical and mental well-being. Reference to violence became a tool by which Muslim schools could sell their products—their teaching strategies and curricula—and a powerful argument for their existence.

This argument stressed the schools' minimal interaction with the outside world. Whereas a project such as IMAN saw the social ills in the nearby neighborhood as a challenge and therefore developed into a social-activist institution, Muslim full-time schools actively promoted exclusionalism from American society on the basis of religion or chose to interact with that society on *their* terms. As one teacher stated, "What I have noticed with the students here in this school is that they are . . . very isolated, at least school-wise, from contact with non-Muslims, other than the non-Muslim teachers. Even the non-Muslim teachers, when they are hired, have some knowledge about Islamic rule."[49]

"I Say Salam; They Say Hi":
Understanding Muslim Students' Attitudes
toward American Society

American social norms, however, were not absent from the world of the students. As another teacher told me, some students might know Michael Jordan, the Chicago Bulls basketball star, better than Muhammad.[50] The students returned to homes that usually had TVs and radios and, like many other American children, often spent Saturdays strolling through the local mall with their families. But whereas children living in the Chicago Lawn area constantly faced the tougher side of American society, students who went to Muslim full-time schools were kept "safe" from such experiences. Moreover, outside the school setting, their family's social status cushioned them from much of the consequence of religious and ethnic background—questioning and harassment—that Muslim families on the South Side often faced.

Most suburban Muslim parents were professionals who had secured for themselves and their family a good amount of social status by American standards. A solid, stable income allowed them to pay the tuition that Muslim schools required and to keep their offspring away from those elements of society that they considered harmful. In this setting, social class—ironically based on the parents' involvement in the non-Muslim society—segregated their children from that society. While IMAN used Islam to counter social despair in the Chicago Lawn neighborhood, Muslim full-time schools and their students did not have to consider despair at all. Instead, they valued keeping the status quo of religious discourse unchallenged and unchanged. Children were supposed to learn to be "good Muslims," strictly according to the norms of their parents.

To gain a clearer impression of how students understood and encountered American society, I conducted interviews with nineteen students in Muslim full-time schools, focusing on their lives inside and outside the school. In their free time, they engaged in activities such as baseball, soccer, computer games, and visits to family and friends (only a few mentioned routinely reading the Qur'an outside school). The students' contact with American society and norms mostly consisted of interactions with non-Muslim peers. Almost all of them had non-Muslim friends. Those friends either lived in the same neighborhood or were the children of their parents' friends.

What the interviews reflected was that friendship could not conquer the feeling of difference. As one child said, "I can't talk to them about the same things that I talk about to my Muslim friends. I don't know if they will understand, 'cause I have a different point of view than them. . . . I say my greetings different to them. And so sometimes when I pick up the phone, I will say my Islamic greeting. And then they will pick up the phone and they will say 'hello' or whatever."[51]

Relations with non-Muslim peers very often were seen as a risk of ridicule or outright rejection. Boys and girls alike expressed these emotions, most often as a consequence of dress code and ritual. As one boy said:

> If I am going to, like, a party—some of my cousins are not Muslims—I go there and I have to wear the *topi* [a small, round and soft hat worn by some Muslim men]. . . . Sometimes when I have to wear my *topi*, my friend will laugh at me. . . . If I am wearing a *topi*, I just try to ignore everybody, except people that I know are Muslims.[52]

Most of my informants were girls, who elaborated on the *hijab* and its importance to them within and outside the school. In every case, the school requirement that girls wear the head covering was described as positive and protective. Within the school, the girls felt safe from the judgment and harassment by non-Muslims. The outside world's reactions were generally presumed to be negative. As two of the students explained:

> At least I am glad that I am in an Islamic school, because I feel more comfortable. Because if I go to another school, maybe some people

would get bothered if I wore my scarf. Some people would discriminate. So I would want to be in this school; it is better than being somewhere different from myself.[53]

The feeling of risk when encountering American society outside the school might also have resulted from experiences that
students had with their parents:

> Like, my mom, when she goes out and she wears the *hijab*. She drives
> in the car. Some people are nice. One time we were driving, and so
> she turns. And then the guy in front of her is turning, too. But he is
> doing it on purpose, real slow. And so when he turns, he is on our side
> here, he sticks his finger at us. So my mother, I said to her, "What are
> you going to do?" And she said, "Just forget it." Like one time we are
> driving, and people want to get through. And I said to my mom, "Just
> go!" And she said, "No! Because people should have a good impres-
> sion of a Muslim." She tries to make people think that we are good,
> not bad.[54]

Although some students complained about their teachers, discipline, or boring subjects, most appreciated being in a Muslim
school. They experienced a sense of community and comfort that
they often described as contrasting with what they expected to
encounter among non-Muslims. They also considered it important that the school taught them to defend their identity:

> I just want to say that going to a Muslim school sort of enhances your
> personality, because at the end of last year I went to a camp—it was
> a leadership camp—where there were different schools from the
> Chicago area. . . . Because I came from such a unique school, I think
> that I had, like, a background, and I was firm in my beliefs, and I
> learned about other cultures and stuff. And I think that because I went
> to this school, I was able to teach other people more about Islam than
> if I had gone to a public school. I would not have known as much as
> I know now, and I wouldn't know how to teach it.[55]

One way or another, most of these statements relate to aspects
of American society and social norms. Most students viewed outside encounters either as threatening and hurtful or as having the
potential to be so. They therefore felt that they had to accumu-
late Islamic knowledge to defend themselves against verbal attacks.
In that sense, the students' interpretations dovetailed with those
of their parents. Just as the Muslim schools tried to minimize the

effect of the outside world, so the students' statements implied that encounters with non-Muslims required non-involvement, detachment, and a move to "the other side of the road." Separation helped enforce their undisturbed "firmness of belief."

You Cannot Live by Religion Alone:
The Double Expectations of Parents

Parents enrolled their children in Muslim full-time schools because they either felt excluded by society at large or did not want their children to participate in some of its customs for religious reasons. At the same time, parents recognized that if their children were to do well in America, then knowing the Qu'ran was not enough; they also had to do well academically. The schools attempted in numerous ways to fulfill parents' academic expectations. School advertisements presented students' academic achievements (awards and scholarships) as much as they described their Islamic profile. In the late 1990s, three of the schools were expanding their buildings and, in some cases, severely straining their budgets. This expansion was usually an attempt to satisfy parents' desires for smaller classes, better interaction between teachers and students, and a broader curriculum. Parents wanted their children to do more than memorize parts of the Qur'an or know the life story of the Prophet, because none of these skills would secure financial prosperity. Parents sent their children to Muslim schools not only to raise them as "Muslims" but also to prepare them for admission to well-established universities.[56]

The obvious clash between partial rejection of and partial inclusion in the norms of the surrounding society indirectly called into question the schools' very reason for existence. Although none of the school principals stated that any tension existed, some complained that parents pushed their children toward certain professions—such as medicine and engineering—while giving lower priority to subjects such as journalism and education. These complaints had their basis in the community's proclaimed need for professionals who could communicate a positive image of Islam to the broader American public. But whereas the principals (who were largely responsible for the image of the schools) stressed the absence of conflict between Islamic and secular subjects, some teachers expressed other views.

In particular, Islamic studies teachers mentioned that the double pursuit of a successful Islamic and a successful academic curriculum clashed. During a staff meeting at the MEC in October 1995, involving three of Chicago's Muslim schools, eleven teachers of Arabic and Islamic studies discussed the prospects for their field. A common complaint was that Islamic studies were given the lowest priority. According to these teachers, the board of education that set up the curriculum had no experience with, and no education in, Islamic studies. Whereas board members held positions in academic fields that the Muslim community—and the society at large—considered prestigious, they had little formal knowledge of Islam. The Islamic curriculum was therefore limited to the mere basics, a situation that these teachers interpreted as eroding the very purpose of the schools. The essential question raised in such discussions was why an Islamic educational system should be kept alive if there was no fundamental difference between Islamic schools and the public schools.[57]

All the schools that I visited had a number of non-Muslim teachers who taught subjects from physical education to biology. Although American social reality entered the schools with these people, it did so with the control and agreement of the school. No one ever mentioned to me that employment of non-Muslims was an obstacle to the development of a school's Islamic character. That two of the schools had non-Muslim principals came up for discussion, but mostly as an example of the community's twisted educational priorities. One of those principals had held her position for several years, and even though the community had tried to find a qualified Muslim person to replace her, it had so far been unsuccessful. The other non-Muslim principal was hired by the MEC during the summer of 1996. With a Ph.D. in school leadership, and working on her second Ph.D. in curriculum, she was undoubtedly the best-educated principal of any Muslim school in the area. She told me that the school had given her a couple of "religious advisers," one of whom was a faculty member at the American Islamic College (see Chapter 3).

During a PTA field trip in the fall of 1996, I discussed the choice of principal at the MEC with some of the parents. One mother told me that the school had tried to find a qualified Muslim for the position for three years but had finally given up. Either the applicants did not have sufficient education, or the education they had received was from "back home" and usually not adaptable to this country. The board knew of only one other qualified person—a former principal at another Muslim school in the area. But that person did not get the job, the mother speculated, because she was "very self-sufficient, and she would probably scare off some of the men."

The Role of Teachers

Although Islamic studies teachers complained about the schools' priorities, they still played the dominant role as transmitters of the norms that students were expected to live by, both in school and outside. While all of the teachers served as Islamic models through their behavior, dress code, and public knowledge of their private lives, the Islamic studies teacher was the only person to present and shape Islamic knowledge directly. Islamic studies lessons were given about five times a week. Teachers might use books from the local IQRA Publications (one of the largest distributors of Muslim schoolbooks in the United States) or revivalist Muslim works such as Abul A'la Mawdudi's *Let Us Be Muslims.*[58] The Qur'an and collections of *hadith* (the narrated tradition of the Prophet) were also used or referred to in all lessons that I attended. Some Islamic studies teachers also used videos and computer programs. Reinforcing their authority through reward and punishment, they assigned homework, determined when behavior was out of control, and decided when to order a student to the principal's office for a reprimand.

In my interviews with teachers and during observations in the classrooms, I noticed that the authority of the teacher was often associated with, stressed, or dismissed according to the models of authority that the students knew in their lives outside the school. When a teacher's behavior resembled that of a parent, for example, some children listened, but others would not. Teachers mentioned that students who had limited contact with their hardworking parents often caused disciplinary problems in class and outside. Some of the disrespect that female teachers were shown by male students was attributed to gender roles learned at home.[59]

The teachers' authority also seemed to depend on their familiarity with standards of teaching in American society at large. Teachers who spoke English with a strong accent or who taught the students according to pedagogic skills learned in the Middle East or Asia had a hard time disciplining their classes. In one Islamic studies class I observed, the students verbally attacked a Syrian-educated teacher because they were infuriated by her teaching methods. "We cannot learn unless it is done in a pleasant way!" voices shouted. "Why is it that you come in every morning and there is never a smile on your face? If you tried to smile, we might learn more."

"Why Should We Stay at Home?"

Although refusal to accept a teacher's authority obviously caused chaos, it also suggested new ways that Islam could be interpreted and taught. Students did not necessarily question Islam as a basic principle; rather, they questioned those who represented it, seeing their questions as a modern dialogue within the community's institutions. Whenever the authority of the teacher slipped, the students often seized the power of the moment to argue with his or her presentation of their religious heritage. In these instances, the students framed the discussion, as illustrated in the following situation:

A number of eleventh-grade girls had taken seats in the classroom. Each was dressed in a wide, blue *jilbab* and had her head covered with a black *hijab*. One girl was putting on lipstick. Some girls were discussing a subject from another class and ignored the female teacher who had entered the classroom. The teacher asked the students to be quiet and respect the rules of the school, after which the girls calmed down a little. One of them successfully hid her chewing gum under her desk. As conversation ceased, the teacher called one of the girls to the blackboard to read an essay on women and Islam that she had turned in the previous day. In her paper, the student had compared Muslim women's attitudes with those of non-Muslim women.

Facing the class, the student read her paper with calm certainty. Non-Muslim women, she began, cared about their children, but they cared about their careers even more. Children in America saw their parents on drugs or in gangs, and that was why so many girls became pregnant so early. But, she continued, Islam taught something different. First of all, Islam said that you must respect your mother above all. Islam secured women's ownership of property. Islam secured the equality of men and women. If we looked at the life of the Prophet, his wife, Khadija, owned her own business. The Prophet had respected her for that and helped her.

"It is true that Islam has never forbidden women to work," the teacher commented as the student returned to her seat. "But you have to remember that when you get married, your husband has the right to tell you not to."

The students' reaction was swift. Most girls objected loudly, and although the teacher tried to calm them down by softening her statement, she was unsuccessful. "But listen," she said. "It is really a luxury to stay at home nowadays."

"But that's so boring," one of the students replied. "I really can't see the excitement in just sitting at home, in spending your life cleaning the house and waiting for your husband to come home."

"Wait," the teacher objected. "Islam does not tell you that. Your husband can provide house care if you want it. But you must remember that the basic, biological purpose of woman is to give birth to children, to raise children, to provide for the next generation. Remember the saying, 'Whoever rocks the cradle with one hand shakes the world with the other.' Remember that the Prophet told us that 'heaven lies at the feet of the mother.' You are really stereotyping, the way the Western world is doing. The problem of the society we have around us is exactly the lack of the mother."

"But what does the man sacrifice?" one girl asked. "We let go of our jobs, we sacrifice our jobs—what does he let go of?"

"You do not know the hardships of the real world," the teacher replied. "You have no idea about how it is out there. You do not know what men have to go through."

"But couldn't the husband raise the children?" another girl asked.

"It is possible, but I wouldn't recommend it. People would make fun of a man who stays at home."

"But what then if your husband, before you marry him, agrees that you can finish high school, but after you've got married says you can't?"

"A thing like that you have to put in your marriage contract. It is a religious duty to obey your husband, so if he tells you not to finish your education, you must do what he tells you to do. It is, of course, a different matter if he is abusing your children or things like that. Then it is really your obligation to get away. If he abuses you, you must go out and seek help."

Instead of accepting the picture of Islamic womanhood that the teacher presented, the girls countered it with another that they found more attractive. In their arguments, they referred to concepts of female mobility, of women's access to work and careers, of their "right" to live a life equal to that of their husbands. These images were and are strong ideals in the society surrounding the school; they represent the American notion that individual value is produced more outside the home than within it. It was therefore no coincidence that the teacher's counter-argument was that the girls "stereotyped the way the Western world is doing."

To the teacher, the students' beliefs challenged the core of her belief in what Islam said about womanhood and what public spaces of interaction Islam granted to women. But to the girls, religious ideals were useless if they did not relate to their daily lives, especially their ambitions for the future. These ambitions were nurtured equally by the Muslim school environment and by the students' encounter with the majority norms outside it—what they saw, read, or heard on TV, in shopping centers, in magazines, and among non-Muslim peers.

Muslim Full-Time Schools and Gender Roles

One central aspect of learning within Muslim full-time schools was that of gender interaction and segregation. Girls were taught with girls, and boys were taught with boys, in junior high and high school. Girls were required to wear the *jilbab* and *hijab* when they reached puberty, and boys were required to wear long pants and, in one school, the *topi* (also known as *kufi*). Both students and parents agreed that the segregation of boys and girls in the school environment was an essential part of the "safety" that the school offered. The lack of segregation between girls and boys in public schools was perceived as a major threat to the children's— especially the girls'—sexual innocence. Islamic education was supposed to teach the children "good morals" and to prepare them for (and keep them chaste until) marriage.

Some adolescent girls did not have to wait long for a suitable husband. Although an earlier study of the Muslim Palestinian community in Chicago claimed that arranged teenage marriages had become rare in the late 1980s,[60] teenage marriages were widespread in the 1990s, especially among Arab Muslims on the Southwest Side.[61] Some of the college students I met mentioned that, for some of the girls with whom they had attended high school on the Southwest Side, the goal had been engagement before graduation. These girls found the attention, prestige, and gifts that a girl received at her initiation to life as a married woman very tempting. In that part of the city, engagement and marriage among teenagers was described as the "Arab prom," resembling the glamorous initiation to adult life that non-Muslim-American girls experienced at their high school prom.

Through my acquaintance with girls in Muslim full-time schools I was also exposed to examples of teenage marriage. These marriages were not generally accepted in the community and were especially rejected by the teachers, who saw it as their duty to protect their students' academic future. Teachers often objected when a student broke the news, and some even encouraged parents to let their gifted daughters finish high school and continue on to college—a tactic that sometimes worked. These marriages were often discussed by principals in presentations of what happened to female students when they left the school, by former students looking back on their high school days, and even by community leaders.

Boys were generally more trusted than girls. In their interactions within and outside the school, they were not expected to show Islamic standards as strictly as girls were (for example, through their clothing). While observing both boys' and girls' classes, I noticed that the subject of women's behavior received significantly more discussion. Still, just as girls prepared themselves for particular social roles, so did boys. As the future heads of families, they prepared themselves to become able providers, although such preparations had no effect on how hard boys and girls worked academically. The reason might be that some boys did not view academic skills as necessary for material success. Especially in southwestern Chicago, boys saw their fathers doing well in their grocery stores without even high school diplomas.

The most obvious area in which boys seemed to face higher expectations than girls was religious leadership. Within the school setting, boys were allowed to give the call for prayers, to recite parts of the Qur'an in congregation, and, in some cases, to give the khutba. Through the attention that the audience granted him in such short moments, a boy tasted the responsibility that he later would embody in his family unit: the leader of prayer, the head of the family.

Facilitators of Strongly Knit Community Bonds

Within Muslim full-time schools, the conveying of Islamic knowledge included the creation of community. The school setting was essential to this process. Community within the schools existed in common habits. People dressed alike. People ate the same kinds of foods. People prayed at the same time and fasted at the same time. People were aware of the significance of specific time-bound celebrations. People shared certain views on gender and interactions between genders and very often shared an ethnic commonality of language and cuisine. People shared the feeling of being challenged by the outside society. Similarly to IMAN's approach, the teaching in Islamic schools showed a utopian hope for the future, where competing voices of doubt and hypocrisy, both inside and outside of Islam's ideological borders, were to be silenced through the unification of the umma. The following story illustrates these hopes:

A number of teenage boys in their early teens hurried into the classroom, one of them buttoning his shirt. Gym class had just ended, and time to get properly dressed had obviously been short.

The teacher, an African-American convert in his fifties, shouted at the boy that he was supposed to do that kind of thing outside the classroom. The rest of the students laughed and joked a little until the teacher ordered them to take their seats. The teacher distributed Qur'ans and asked the teenage boys to find the first *aya* of *Sura al-Munafiqun* (*sura* 63). One student was told to recite the *sura* while another translated: "Knoweth that you art indeed His messenger, and Allah beareth witness that the Hypocrites are indeed liars."

When the teacher asked what the *sura* was about, the students hesitated a little. The teacher sat down in the corner of the room and let his chin rest in the palm of his hand as he presented his interpretation. Making a parallel to the days of the Prophet, he stated that hypocrites have been known within the *umma* from the very beginning and still exist today. "If we look at the world around us," he said, "we can take the example of Bosnia. No Muslim nation took action against the genocide that happened there. Muslims let other Muslims die."

"That is because we are not Muslims anymore," a student interrupted. "We have stopped practicing Islam the right way."

The teacher paused briefly, then turned the student's argument on its head by asking, "So are we all guilty, then?"

Another student replied, "I would not put it that way. We are all Muslims, as long as we stay within the boundaries of Islam."

"But is that really enough?" the teacher demanded. "Try to think about Saddam. Try to think about Qaddafi. Do you consider them Muslim? Are these people really Muslims?"

Silence ruled for a few seconds, giving the teacher a chance to turn the discussion to problems and issues that were closer to the students than abstract images on TV. "You know, I see a challenge for us," he said. "I see an opportunity here—in this country. Many see the United States as the new center for Islam. And it can be so if we take the challenge and move above culture—above the culture we came from—and when we live according to Islamic culture. How would you, by the way, describe Islamic culture?"

"Islamic culture is the *shari'a* [Islamic law]!" someone shouted.

Suddenly the room was full of discussion. The teacher jumped from his chair again. His voice and gestures cut through the verbal crossfire. "Listen," he said, "listen! Islam takes a uniform version in every culture. In all Muslim cultures, people follow the same thing. They follow Islam, but they do it according to their own culture. And what we see here, in this country, is that all these cultures come together, and something comes out which is universal. Opportunity is created not only by African Americans who redefine their West-African heritage. We have converts. We have people who come from abroad. There is this multiplicity of ideas that can create something unique. And we can use all those elements of America that are beneficial, while at the same time using that element that says that we are all linked together: That we are all Muslims. There is something in Islam that transcends differences and ethnicity. And we may get a whole new way of understanding Islam in this country due to the circumstances that we live under here."

The teacher neatly connected the fulfillment of an Islamic utopia to American society. Evil and hypocrisy, the misrepresentations and exploitations of Islam, were seen as consequences not of norms or actors standing outside the *umma* but as those of Muslim dictators who were receiving a great deal of media attention in those years. America, at the same time, was presented as the facilitator of good. When Muslims gathered in this country, they were exposed not only to one another's cultural differences but also to their commonalities: the principles of Islam. Community was thus created on the rightful principles of divine decree, not the disruptive and humanly created classification of ethnicity.

This teacher's interpretation of Islam, including his belief in the constructive process that Islam could undergo from taking root in American soil, possibly resulted from his status as a convert to Islam. Although some converts reject their past, others choose to integrate an Islamic worldview with a positive view of their American cultural heritage. Although they interpret their past in light of the Muslim identities they have chosen, the results are not black and white. Both this teacher and Maryam, the director of IMAN, emphasized the pursuit of an ideal future place for Islam in America. They believed that America would benefit from—and therefore promote—an Islamic renaissance among its Muslim citizens.

Converts, however, are not the only Muslims who hold the conviction that Islamic and American lifestyles can combine and flourish. Among both immigrant Muslims and Muslims born and raised in the United States (for example, African Americans), similar trends are strong. As Chapter 4 shows, many of my college-student informants were certain that, by encountering other Muslims from other cultural backgrounds in the United States, they would arrive at an authentic understanding and practice of their common faith. These young people saw America as a midwife in this process, not an opponent.

A *HAFIZ* SCHOOL

A final academic avenue Chicago's Muslims use to preserve Islam and Islamic identity among children is the *hafiz* school. *Hafiz* means that one has memorized the Qur'an. The *hafiz* school does not follow the traditions of semesters, exams, and degrees characteristic of the surrounding society; further, students graduate only when they are ready, and that may take from eight months to three years.

The *hafiz* school is situated in one of Chicago's western suburbs. It was established in 1989 by one of the city's major Islamic authorities, an 'alim (Islamic scholar) who was educated at Deoband Islamic University in India.[62] The school was originally located in the basement of the 'alim's home.[63] But by 1995 the number of students had grown so great that a former storage building was purchased and reshaped into a school. When I visited, the *hafiz* school housed twenty-five male students between the ages of seven and fifteen. Most of the students were South Asian, but six were Middle Eastern and two were African American. According to the 'alim, all of the students came from Chicago and the surrounding suburbs.

The students lived at the school five days a week, fifty-two weeks a year. They were sent to the school to memorize the Qur'an and to become *hafizes* (Arabic pl. *huffaz*). The school did not offer subjects similar to those of a required state curriculum. The boys later had to re-enroll at the grade level they had reached when they left public or Muslim full-time school. To become a *hafiz* required considerable hard work and sacrifice. Students were allowed to visit their families only between Saturday and Monday mornings. Tuition at the time of my visit was $250 a month; it covered teaching, food, and lodging. The staff consisted of three teachers—the *'alim* and two of his sons, who also had been educated at Deoband. One teacher always stayed with the students overnight.

The activity of the school was not visible from the outside. All one saw was a blue storage building in a gray parking lot. That the place actually housed children was noticeable only in the basketball hoop out front. Inside the building, however, the purpose was clear. In front, on the right-hand side, was a *wudu'* (ablution) area decorated with blue and green tiles. Just before it lay a small *masjid* (mosque) used by the students, teachers, and a handful of members of the local Muslim community. Depending on the hour, a visitor might hear an incoherent choir of voices, some shouting, some singing, continuously repeating fragments of Qur'anic *suras*. Classrooms and dormitories lay through a corridor to the right. The boys, mostly dressed according to South Asian interpretations of appropriate Islamic dress, sat on the gray carpets. They moved from side to side, back and forth, their eyes fixed on the Qur'an in front of them, repeating line after line, phrase after phrase.

The school day followed fixed patterns: The children woke up before dawn for *fajr* (morning prayers). After prayers, they returned to bed until 7:00 A.M. Education began at 8:15 A.M. and continued until noon, when the students were given a twenty-minute break for lunch. The afternoon began with a forty-five-minute lesson in Islamic studies. After a fifteen-minute break, the students returned to Qur'anic memorization, which continues until 6:00 P.M. When this last session ended, the students were allowed to go outside to play basketball. One of the teachers remarked jokingly that basketball was the boys' favorite spare-time activity. The studies at the school were very "dry," he said, especially because most of the students did not understand what they were memorizing.

It is tempting to say that time stood still in this setting. The focus on memorization as the sole means of learning, together

with the object chosen—the Qur'an—created a temporal and spatial vacuum recognizable in any part of the Muslim world, in
almost any time period, with the content the same. This feeling
of a timeless vacuum was reinforced by the 'alim's answer to my
question about the purpose and content of knowledge: "Knowledge is the blessing of Allah," he said. "When we start getting the
knowledge, we should not say: 'What is the use of this?' Right?
We do not in our minds have the details of use."[64] Because revealed knowledge (the Qur'an) was perceived as absolute, as well
as incomprehensible to humans, it was pointless to expect a
young student to understand it or adapt it to his daily life. Learning was therefore restricted to a process in which the student
imprinted each letter of the Scripture on his mind, without expecting any explanation of its meaning. Flawless memorization,
not scrutiny, held the key to status and "success."

Becoming a hafiz was associated with authority, with preserv-
ing knowledge seen as important for the boys' future roles as
heads of family and active members of the community. But
becoming a hafiz was not the final goal of those running the
school. According to the 'alim, the hafiz education was merely
the first step in establishing an institution for the training of
'ulama' (Islamic scholars) in the United States. According to the
'alim, as the Muslim community in the United States grows
it becomes important to educate people with the authority to address social issues from an Islamic point of view. As Chapter 5
will show, religious authority is a frequently debated issue among
Muslims that sometimes causes rifts in the community. It was
this situation that the 'alim hoped to change by establishing a core
of traditional Islamic experts who know Scripture and ritual
behavior well.

Discussion

Age often determines an individual's claim to knowledge and
clear understanding. Children and young teenagers are mostly
seen as dependent on others (for instance, on parents, family, and
teachers) who teach them the life skills they need. However, the
risk remains that the young will behave contrary to the teachings

of the older generations. Within the setting of Muslim institutions for children, teachers tried carefully to prepare the students for the roles that they were expected to take in the community later in life, and to ensure that the students did not rebel against the teachings that their families and teachers held dear.

Not surprisingly, expectation and worry accompanied all teachers, principals, and staff in Chicago's Muslim community. All of the institutions for transmitting Islamic knowledge to children used both spatial and ideological strategies to prevent children from internalizing other ideas and values from the outside society. For educators and parents alike, the greatest fear in this context was that such ideas would entice their youngsters away from their intended roles.

Among these educational institutions, the Muslim full-time schools and the *hafiz* school created the strongest Muslim environment. The goal of Muslim full-time schools was to create environments "free of the West's social-ills," as one advertisement stated. Reaction against the American surroundings showed in the staffs' teaching strategies, as well as in the self-reflections of interviewed students. In the *hafiz* school, resistance to American society lay in the unrelenting emphasis on memorizing a text, the absolute knowledge and truth of which was believed to nullify all competing interpretations and temptations. That the children lived at the school and had very little interaction with the outside world ensured that the teaching of Islam took place undisturbed and unchallenged. In this school, nonreligious aspects of life were seen as distractions.

Ideologically, Muslim full-time schools use the rejection of American society to legitimize their existence. In practice, however, they are forced to include aspects of American society, because the curriculum must satisfy parents' academic ambitions for their children as much as parental desires for an "Islamic" environment. Muslim schools, therefore, become American institutions. They follow the shape of other private religious schools and even compete with them. They are required to include a curriculum recognized by authorities, representing the norms of a state, not of a religion. Like other American schools, they include kindergarten, elementary school, middle school, and high school.

Their leadership includes academically trained principals and teachers, and their aim is to produce academically qualified students as much as to produce individuals who are socially recognizable as "good" Muslims.

The institution that best presented Islam within the conditions of American social reality was IMAN. As a social movement, IMAN related to the deprived neighborhood outside its doors and tried to offer attractive solutions to crime, violence, abuse, and ethnic fragmentation. Although IMAN was critical of certain facets of American society, it sought its solutions in inclusiveness, not exclusiveness. IMAN envisioned and formulated, in Islamic terms, an urge for tolerance, equality, and justice that would empower not only Muslims but an entire neighborhood.

As IMAN's projects sought answers to a particular social reality, so did that social reality force IMAN's leaders and volunteers into social-activist formulations of their religion. First, because ethnic fragmentation and fighting created a major obstacle to neighborhood empowerment, IMAN, to legitimize its existence and the relevance of its ideology, had to handle this situation credibly. Thus, Islam was "legitimized" in this environment as a religion that promotes local (and global) equality and tolerance. Second, because gender kept a group of Muslim women and girls in the area from the decision-making process, IMAN saw its purpose as liberating them within an Islamic context. Again, both liberation and education took place not only to free these women's potential for community empowerment but also to prove the justness of Islam.

Although this definition of Muslim-ness took shape within the realities and challenges of American society, it was also influenced by global realities. The idea of the *umma*, interpreted as the global community of believers, played a prominent role in IMAN's philosophy. Transethnic ideals showed in its teaching styles, in its constellation of volunteers and students, and in its preparations for "Taking It to the Streets." These ideals were also verbalized in Muslim full-time school settings—for example, by the teacher who lauded the coming together of Muslims from all parts of the world and framed the content of an "ideal Islam."

Within these institutions, the idea of Islam as transcending ethnic boundaries became a mobilizing ethical force and legitimizing motive, no matter how strong the actual impact of ethnicity.

The encounter with secular American society, however, changed concepts of authority within these institutions. Most notable was that children and teenagers did not always accept as true the interpretations of Islam presented by their parents and teachers. The reasons these young people gave when disagreeing with their elders were likewise "American." This shift in community dynamics contains the potential for discrediting the religious system and for religious reformulation.

Those young Muslims who disregard the faith of their parents are not the focus of this book. But the young Muslims who held closely to their religion were highly verbal about the possibility of religious reformulation. Whether their background was that of public and Sunday schools, Muslim full-time schools, or *hafiz* schools, they identified themselves as Muslims, and they did so according to powerful interpretations of the socially activating potential of Islam that made sense in their lives. Whereas their parents feared losing their faith and offspring to the secular norms of American society, the young people were integrating both American and Islamic worldviews.

4   The Circle and the Cutting Edge

Muslim Colleges and
Students' Associations

I AM DRIVING SOUTH on the expressway along Lake Michigan on a Wednesday afternoon. The car accelerates beyond 55 miles per hour, and the wind from the waterfront becomes more noticeable as it pushes toward the body of the car. I can only feel the wind, however, because all sound is drowned out by the loud music on the radio and the voices of the two young women sitting in the front seat. A high-pitched riff on a guitar from an alternative rock song blares from the speakers behind me. The women joke and laugh as they discuss their schoolwork, their teachers, and the inadequacy of the university library. The scene would seem stereotypical of American college students hanging out after school if the women did not have their hair covered to show their religious identity. They were identifiable not only as young women and college students but also as Muslims.

For most students, college is a time of self-definition and self-realization. Strong bonds of friendship, formed according to common interests and convictions, sometimes last for life. College days are also days of independence, the first major steps away from parents and family, often in a strange city. Such heady changes noticeably affect Muslim college students as they practice religion and define their Muslim identity, community, and tradition, and as they prepare to become the caretakers and shapers of tomorrow's "American Islam" and the future activism of their community.

What is the content and expression of a Muslim identity molded within college environments? How does this identity relate to the norms and expectations of the students' parents and the surrounding society? And, finally, how does Muslim youth identity relate to ethnicity? Is the issue of ethnicity—which can divide Muslim Americans and their institutions—equally important to Muslim young people, or are they able to integrate ethnicity and religion into a cohesive whole?

For young adults, the focus of my study shifts to activities that take place within local chapters of the Muslim Students' Association (MSA), an organization represented in all parts of the United States.[1] MSA chapters exist within institutions of higher learning, thriving on the changing Muslim student body that such institutions provide. The organization has a tremendous impact on raising Islamic consciousness and activism nationwide, thereby creating another framework for the definition of a Muslim-American community.

Most Muslim undergraduate students are enrolled in secular or Christian colleges or universities. Over the years, however, the Chicago Muslim community has established two Islamic colleges: the American Islamic College and East–West University. Important contrasts exist in how the MSA chapters and the Muslim colleges relate to and benefit from their surroundings. MSA activities highlight a primarily beneficial symbiosis between American institutions and Muslim-American activism; the conditions of Muslim colleges in the United States are far more complicated. Whereas MSA chapters enjoy economic safety nets provided by colleges and universities, the success and failure of Muslim colleges is determined solely by their ability to attract students. In that sense, the conditions of American society affect the formation of Islamic institutions and their ability to represent the Muslim community over time.

In this chapter, I present a number of institutions and initiatives that target young Muslims. Central to the discussion are these young people's influence on and interaction with American society, as well as the formation of their Muslim identities. The first section presents the two Muslim colleges in the Chicago area; the second section describes the activities and ideology of local MSA chapters. The third section considers the way in which Muslim university students interact with, and present Islam to, non-Muslim classmates and friends—for example, during the Islamic Awareness Week. Finally, I describe Muslim *halaqas* (study circles) and the aspects of Islam that are often discussed within them, including the relationship of Islam to ethnicity, science, and the role of women.

THE AMERICAN ISLAMIC COLLEGE AND EAST–WEST UNIVERSITY

In the early 1980s, the Muslim-American community in Chicago established the American Islamic College (AIC) and East–West University (EWU). Both schools are located close to the downtown area—AIC to the north and EWU to the south.

Struggling to Survive: The AIC

The AIC, which more distinctively manifests its Islamic mission, was incorporated on September 15, 1981. Its academic program began in September 1983.[2] Financial support came from large international Muslim organizations, including the Islamic Conference Organization (OIC) and the Muslim World League (Rabitat al-ʿAlam al-Islamiyya).[3] The first chairman of the college was a prominent spokesman in the Muslim-American community, Ismaʿil Raji al-Faruqi.[4]

By the late 1990s, the AIC offered two bachelor of arts degrees, one in Arabic and one in Islamic studies. Other academic disciplines included computer science, sociology, world history, and political science.[5] Although the AIC's primary purpose is to educate Muslims with permanent U.S. residence, degrees are also offered to students from Muslim countries, and a dormitory houses students from other states and countries. Although for some years the AIC was a candidate for accreditation by the North Central Association of Colleges and Schools, it lost its standing, according to a staff member, because of "financial difficulties."

That the AIC suffered from a deteriorating economy was obvious during my visits to the school. A large portion of the 3.3-acre campus was rented out to a non-Muslim institution for children. The faculty were employed part time, supporting themselves by teaching at other colleges in the area, such as Loyola and Northeastern Illinois universities. But the AIC's future had once seemed bright, and earlier visions of success echoed during my interviews with staff members. This was the only college on American soil offering a bachelor's degree in Islamic studies, using a scientific methodology that was simultaneously "Western" and "Islamic."

The AIC's dire economic situation showed in my interviews with students and contacts. One freshman in the Islamic studies program said that she was one of no more than six students participating in the first-year course at the AIC and that, although the school had auditoriums, classes were so small that they were held in the professors' offices. But the student had no doubts about the aspirations of the AIC or the qualifications of its teachers.[6] Rather, she criticized the Muslim community in Chicago for its lack of support: "It surprises me that in the third-largest city of the United States there are so few people interested in learning about Islam from an academic point of view."[7]

Yet the heads of the community showed interest in the AIC. They came to the school's *iftar* dinners, and some even donated to the school's academic activities.[8] But their children and grandchildren were absent from the classrooms, leaving the AIC looking like an empty monument to an unaccomplished dream. Many parents I spoke with during my research at the AIC stated that they were concerned about the school's economic viability and therefore did not send their children there. Some attributed the draining of the school's funds to the founders' lack of planning and to their failure to consult with specialists in American education. Further, they said, the school's academic level was not comparable to that of the many excellent universities in the Chicago area. No matter how highly parents regarded their faith, they held in higher esteem diplomas from prestigious universities. Although an AIC degree might be significant for someone pursuing a deeper understanding of his or her faith, they felt that the degree had very little market value in a country in which Islam was a minority religion.

Attempting New Strategies: The AIC Works with the Lutheran Church

In what may have been a survival strategy, by the late 1990s the AIC was directing many of its activities toward institutions outside its walls. Islamic teaching became an activity of teaching non-Muslims about Islam and of teaching Islam to non-Muslims, as much as it was an activity through which American and other Muslims could learn about their faith and history. Ironically, such activities were primarily carried out among members of a faith posing an ideological challenge to "American Islam": the Lutheran community. In particular, Dr. Ghulam Haider Aasi, associate professor of Islamic studies at the AIC, was active in dialogue and academic exchange with the Lutherans, who were represented institutionally by the Lutheran School of Theology at Chicago (LSTC). Together with Dr. Harold Vogelaar, professor of world religions at LSTC, Dr. Aasi regularly taught classes in Muslim–Christian understanding. Both professors were active in the local Conference for Improved Muslim–Christian Relations that met at the AIC.[9] In the summer of 1996, the AIC and the LSTC worked together to train the second Muslim chaplain for the U.S. Navy.[10]

Keeping the Door Open: The EWU

Whereas the AIC had moved slowly toward dialogue with the broader American society and academic institutions, cross-cultural dialogue marked the aspirations of the EWU from the very beginning. As I rode the El, Chicago's mass-transit system, around the city, I saw ads in the train cars encouraging those interested in an academic career to contact the EWU. Nowhere did the ads state that the EWU was founded on a particular religious creed. Instead, they presented the school with neutral but appealing concepts such as "individual development," "diversity in knowledge and culture," and "academic success."

The Muslim influence at the EWU was not proclaimed directly in advertisements or in the general informational material that the school distributed. The religious objective was briefly but subtly stated in the course catalogue's initial remarks on the school's philosophy: "The University is established primarily to preserve and extend and to integrate and transmit knowledge of human beings concerning themselves, the universe, and their Creator."[11] A more thorough study of the catalogue revealed a Muslim influence in the board of directors and the board of trustees (named on the last pages). But because the titles and affiliations of these prominent individuals were not mentioned, the international Muslim support showed only in the many Arabic-sounding names on the list. Among these were Dr. Abdullah Omar Naseef, secretary-general of the Muslim World League; Anwar Ibrahim, deputy prime minister and finance minister of Malaysia; and Dr. Mahmoud Safar, the Saudi minister of *hajj* (great pilgrimage).[12] In addition, the EWU's hiring in the 1980s of Muslim intellectual Ziauddin Sardar as director of its Center for Policy and Future Studies indicated an Islamic influence.[13]

The EWU's religious ideology also appeared in the stated objectives of the Institute of Islamic Studies that the university housed. The course description of the core Islamic studies program stated:

As contemporary Muslim societies and institutions come under study, the strains generated by Western colonialism and modern technology and the Islamic response to their impact form the content of these courses. Recent emphasis on Islam as an ideology and way of life is related to the actual sociocultural, political, and economic conditions in countries with Muslim majority and minority populations.... In the area of research the Institute of Islamic Studies plans to focus on state-of-the-art surveys of each discipline of knowledge from the *Islamic point of view.* [my emphasis][14]

American universities offering the study of Islam as a part of their coursework generally approach the religion as a social and historical phenomenon. The approach within the EWU's Islamic studies program was special in that, rather than interpreting Islam on the basis of (and even as the result of) social, scientific, historical, or economic conditions, it presented Islam as the standard according to which academic disciplines were to be understood. Thus, Islam gained an authority absent from mainstream American education. That an Islamic approach was held in high esteem was emphasized by the EWU's decision that only Muslims could teach courses in Islamic studies. Moreover, Islamic subjects were given higher priority than other academic subjects; students who chose to enroll full time in Islamic studies (twelve or more credit hours) were given a considerable tuition reduction through an international academic scholarship.[15] The program's first session began on June 29, 1992, taught by Dr. Abdullah Omar Naseef.[16]

Extracurricular activities at the EWU also reflected the Islamic ideological approach and its coupling with an American-style academic environment and scientific approach. The school funded and published the *East–West Review*, a periodical focusing on the political, historical, and social state of Muslim minority and majority communities and countries. In 1986, the EWU published an illustrated compilation of *ahadith* (the narrated traditions of the Prophet Muhammad), presented as the sayings of the "Prophet Muhammad, the last of God's prophets to mankind."[17] Further, the EWU's affiliation with the Muslim community and intelligentsia was underscored by the Muslim conferences that the school hosted. For example, both the Association of Muslim Social Scientists and the Association of Muslim Scientists and Engineers held their annual conferences at the EWU in November 1995.

Although the EWU—like the AIC—had received funding from international Muslim organizations and countries, and probably still did, its income no longer depended entirely on donors. According to a 1994 summary of the college's audited financial statement, between 1980 and 1994, $13,858,655 of the EWU's income came from tuition, fees, and grants from the Illinois Board of Higher Education, and donations and "other income" added up to $1,478,007.[18] Adopting North American academic standards promoted the school's economic independence and academic progress. Although the EWU's core ideology was Islamic, its leadership was evidently aware that the institution's existence could not be secured through an excessive focus on a minority religion. Success was more likely if ideology were coupled with social and academic standards recognized by the broader public, such as offering knowledge that got jobs for its graduates. Like the AIC, the EWU faced competition from Chicago's prestigious universities, but it stood up to the challenge by addressing the large group of lower- and lower-middle-class Americans (often ethnic minorities) who were unable to pay the high tuitions that the other universities charged. The chancellor justified the approach according to Islam's tenet of helping the poor and needy.

Although the approach did not land the EWU a position in the city's "Ivy League," it proved academically successful. In May 1980, two years after the school's founding, it received approval and operating authority from the Illinois Board of Higher Education, and classes started in mid-September of that year.[19] In 1983, the North Central Association of Colleges and Schools granted the EWU accreditation at the bachelor's degree level, and the school has kept this accreditation ever since.

By the late 1990s, the EWU offered bachelor of arts degrees in behavioral and social sciences, English, communications, and mathematics, and bachelor of science degrees in computer and information science, electronics engineering technology, and business administration. Associate of arts and of applied science degrees were also offered. The school's progress was reflected in its increasing number of students. In the fall of 1995, the EWU had 351 students. By the fall of 1996, according to the chancellor, the number had risen to 951.[20] This dramatic increase facilitated the $1.8 million reconstruction of the school's first floor and basement in 1997. Although the chancellor predicted that the EWU would limit the 1997 fall enrollment to 750, he believed that the economy and future of the institution was stable.[21]

Comparing the Two Colleges

Although the president of the AIC and the chancellor of the EWU were friends, the schools had no common coursework or exchange of staff, probably because their strategies for interaction with the surrounding society were quite different. What was remarkable was the lack of support for either college—other than donations—from the local and national Muslim community. The AIC's classes were close to empty, and the EWU's chancellor acknowledged that only one-quarter to one-third of his school's students were Muslims. Both schools depended for their survival on support and attention from non-Muslim institutions and individuals. For the EWU, in particular, the ambition to attract students resulted in a toning down of its Islamic profile and leadership. For the AIC, its emphasis on Islam notwithstanding, ecumenical co-work with other faiths proved necessary.

Therefore, despite the levels of success, failure, and Islamic focus that separated the two schools, they had two similarities. First, both were established with the goal of creating institutions of Islamic knowledge within the American context. The result of this ambition was new institutional and educational styles formulated according to models of higher education specific to the United States. Second, neither college was established as a theological academy; rather, they were founded as academies inspired by religious ideology. This crucial distinction was an obvious consequence of two concurrent pressures: the norms of the surrounding society and the educational priorities of the Muslim-American community.

THE CAMPUS COMMUNITY: THE MUSLIM STUDENTS' ASSOCIATION

Young Muslim adults, like members of other religions, often choose colleges and universities where years of study—and the draining of even the best-equipped parental bank account—will likely lead to the best job offers, salaries, and professional status. In a statistical survey conducted in the early 1990s, Muslims ranked thirteen out of thirty religious groups in the United States when it came to getting college degrees.[22] Although pursuing an academic career is a time-consuming endeavor, leaving little time for extracurricular activities, engagement in Muslim activities on campus for some young Muslims may bring about a religious "revival." This renewed interest in Islam is usually induced by the experience of a "young" Muslim identity and newly acceptable religious responsibilities. In this revival process, the Muslim Students' Association (MSA) plays a leading role.

By the late 1990s, the MSA had more than 500 chapters nationwide. In the Chicago area alone, the MSA was represented on at least fifteen campuses.[23] From the organization's establishment in 1963, its primary objective has been the call to individual and collective action and commitment, initially according to Islamic ideas promoted by revivalist Muslim movements such as the Jama'at-i Islami and the Jama'at al-Ikhwan al-Muslimun. (Both movements are revivalist in the sense that they work to promote a genuine Islamic identity and to further the importance of Islam in social and political life.)[24] The activist influence from such movements showed in the chapters' da'wa efforts among non-Muslims and in their persistent attempts to mobilize Muslims on campus, including those who had lost interest in their religion.

But the MSA's motives and ideas are not only imitations of the revivalist Muslim movements. Among the generations of young Muslim Americans from which the organization gains its members, religious inspiration and interpretations are no longer imported from abroad. Rather, Islamic perspectives develop through the members' interactions with one another and with the non-Muslim majority surrounding them.

MSA Coordinating Activities

During the nineteen months I spent in Chicago, I developed close contact with four local MSA chapters: at the University of Chicago (MSA/UC), at the University of Illinois at Chicago (MSA/UIC), at DePaul University, and at Loyola University. I had additional but less frequent contacts with the MSA Chicago, a coordinating board for the various MSA activities in the area, and with the MSAs at the Illinois Institute of Technology (MSA/IIT) and Northwestern University (MSA/NW). Although the geographical distance between these MSAs and the campus communities that they represent is considerable, they kept in contact with one another in three ways: through the MSA Chicago, the Internet list MSA-Chicago Net, and IMAN.

The MSA Chicago was a medium through which activities and experiences could be discussed and collective action taken. Meetings of the MSA Chicago were inconsistent, however, and at the meetings that I attended, only ten to fifteen people were ever present. The most successful event that the MSA Chicago coordinated was the annual "College Bowl," in which teams representing their local chapters competed in Islamic knowledge (focusing on such subjects as the life of the Prophet, Islamic conduct, and knowledge of the Qur'an).

A more immediate medium for contact was the Internet list MSA-Chicago Net. Daily postings from the various chapters kept all members informed about activities such as meetings, speeches, dinners, and campus arrangements, including the Islamic Awareness Week/Month. Significantly, information distributed on the Internet not only linked these small groups but also exposed them—through newsgroups, home pages, and distribution lists—to national and even international groups of fellow believers. This wealth of information, coming from all corners of the world, undoubtedly gave Chicago-area Muslim students the sense of belonging to a globally active community, even though they were living as a local minority.

A third support for the feeling of community among the MSA chapters was that a fair proportion of MSA members were involved in the IMAN project. As students turned up to do volunteer work on the South Side, assisting children with their homework and religious schooling, they got to know one another as practicing Muslims and fellow MSA members. As contact through various communication media fostered their awareness of belonging to a larger community, the discussions of various issues—ranging from reflections on ritual practices to da'wa strategies within the chapters—created a consensus of religious and social beliefs among the young adults involved.

The History and Characteristics of Five Local MSA Chapters

Collecting information on the early history of the MSA chapters with which I interacted proved difficult. Some of my informants, who were in their forties, fifties, or sixties, said that they had been active in the MSA in their youth, but only a few had participated in chapters in the Chicago area. In most cases, they were former members of the MSA at the Illinois Institute of Technology.[25] To this group of informants, the MSA was primarily a starting point for the establishment of mosques in the Chicago area, where they were now engaged as leaders or active members. The history of the MSA, for them, was framed in memories and of little current relevance.

Archival material at Muslim centers and city libraries did not extend the picture of this period much. A listing of national chapters by the MSA National in the late 1960s mentioned only one Chicago chapter—the MSA of Greater Chicago (the IIT/MSA)[26]—and a list from the late 1970s mentioned three MSAs, two of which were affiliated with a mosque.[27] Those of my informants who were currently engaged in the MSA knew very little about their chapters' past beyond their membership experience. The MSAs, then, behaved like ad hoc associations, defining their goals not according to any historical precedent but according to the conceptions, needs, and aspirations of a present and continually changing student body.

From interviews with present members, however, some historical lines can be drawn for the MSA chapters in this study.[28] The MSA/UC, according to the president and vice-president in the academic year 1995–96, was established in the late 1980s. Its structure appears to have remained stable ever since. The MSA/UC was granted its own carrel in the basement of the student center, and Friday prayers were held weekly in one of the campus ministry chapels.

One conflict in the history of the MSA/UC exemplifies the limitations that the MSA may put on Islamic practices taking place in its midst. In the early 1990s, a faction of the MSA/UC split off and established the Muslim Students Forum, later existing as an independent Naqshbandiyya-inspired student association on the University of Chicago campus.[29] Naqshbandiyya Sufis had for several years been active at the University of Chicago campus, using the main chapel, the Rockefeller Chapel, for *dhikr* (meditative remembrance of Allah). Sufism is often called the "mystical path" in Islam, because its adherents attempt to develop a deep, personal relationship with God. Central to Sufism is the idea of the spiritual journey through which the Sufi initiate moves toward God in this life, using various techniques—fasting, *dhikr*—and the guidance of a Sufi *shaykh*. The break between the two student groups was attributed to general skepticism among MSA members about Sufi practices.

When interviewed, the MSA's vice-president explained that *dhikr* "sounded more like singing," which was why it could not be accepted as "Islamic."[30] But when I later spoke with the president of the Muslim Students Forum, he expressed skepticism about the MSA because, he said, it was not a traditional Muslim institution and was established without any precedent in Muslim history.[31] Nonetheless, in spite of ideological and institutional disagreements, the MSA and the Muslim Students Forum worked together on various occasions. (For example, the Muslim Students Forum co-sponsored the MSA's Islamic Awareness Month in the spring of 1997.)

The history of the MSA at the University of Illinois at Chicago came to light through a former president of the organization and his wife.[32] According to these informants, the MSA/UIC started in the 1970s. It remained small until the mid-1980s, when the population of Muslims on campus increased, presumably because a large group of second-generation Muslims had reached college age. During that period (around 1988), the Muslim Women's Association (MWA) was established. The MWA was formed not in opposition to the structure or ideology of the MSA but, instead, as a gender-specific faction. Because some of the female Muslim students felt uncomfortable around men, my informants explained, they created the MWA as a "safe" alternative for studying their religion and socializing on their own terms.

Although the two associations worked successfully on the same projects, the men and women worked separately. By establishing two interrelated organizations on campus, Muslim students were granted extra space by the campus administration. The MSA had a large room on the fifth floor in the student center, and the MWA used a small room on the third floor. *Jum'a* (congregational prayer) was held twice every Friday in one of the student center's large meeting rooms, attracting both MSA members and a number of Muslims working in or near the downtown business area.

The MSA/UIC experienced one major ideological conflict. In the early 1990s, it refused to support the General Association of Palestinian Students (GAPS) after determining that a number of GAPS activities were un-Islamic. Although MSA/UIC members might be sympathetic to certain claims on behalf of the Palestinian people, they did not accept the means by which those claims were articulated, such as the ethnic dances and fashion shows that were a part of GAPS publicity events. This decision was important to the MSA/UIC, because it followed clear ideological guidelines. From then on, the MSA/UIC limited its cooperation with other political and cultural groups. Although it might occasionally work with—and seek support from—ethnic student groups, it did so only to the extent that the activities were acceptable from what it considered an Islamic point of view.

The MSA at DePaul University came into being between 1991 and 1993, when a number of students broke away from the campus chapter of North-American Middle Eastern Students and formed United Muslims Moving Ahead (UMMA).[33] Documentation about the reason for the split was not available. What is known is that the Middle Eastern association focused on the upholding and honoring of an ethnic identity and community, while UMMA had other aspirations. UMMA's goal was the ideal of the Muslim *umma*, the transethnic community of believers, but here applied to a local context. UMMA, like the other MSA chapters I visited, was granted its own room for activities. Friday prayers were celebrated either there or in the campus chapel.

By the early 1990s, the Loyola campus administration had handed over to the Muslim students a large basement in a campus building, which they turned into a mosque and meeting rooms. In the mosque, the students could pray the five daily prayers in two separate rooms (one for men, one for women) and use the other two rooms for meetings and study circles. In 1994, the Bait ul-Salaam, as the MSA was soon to be called, changed its leadership, and almost autonomous leadership was given to an *amir* (leader), a young man regarded as very knowledgeable in Islam. By choosing this kind of leadership, the chapter hoped to base its community on a true Islamic model, as practiced and dictated by the Prophet Muhammad. In the end, however, the experiment failed, both as a consequence of internal disputes (for example, many of the female members felt isolated and overlooked by the *amir*) and disputes with the campus administration (over leadership and financial issues). By 1996, the chapter once again embraced the structure of the MSA.

The history of these chapters shows how "Islam as knowledge" was articulated within the MSA, as well as the arguments and activities that were accepted and those that were not. Disputes over ideological motives and aspirations centered on (1) whether to accept Sufi practices, and (2) whether and how to support ethnic and political claims on behalf of groups loyal to geographic zones or countries with Muslim majorities. My visits to the chapters revealed that, although disagreement on such issues sometimes caused conflicts or expulsion, most chapters allowed a certain variation in views and ideas among their members.

For example, when some of the female students from Loyola University participated in the Naqshbandiyya *dhikr* held at the Muslim publishing company Kazi Publications on Belmont Avenue, their dedication to the Bait ul-Salaam was not questioned.

On occasion, one of the most active young women in the group enthusiastically proclaimed her Sufi commitment and identity (although she never presented herself as a *murid*, or initiate), especially in the summer of 1996, when she announced her engagement to a Sufi at a Naqshbandiyya-led conference in California.[34] The woman was not expelled from the Bait ul-Salaam, and she kept her role as one of the chapter's strongest and most respected members.

However, within other MSA chapters, direct action was taken against Sufi practices, mainly when Sufis were gaining prominence within the group. This, for example, was the reason for the expulsion of the University of Chicago Sufis, who were widely known for their weekly *dhikrs*. The expulsion indicated that most of the MSA members saw Sufism as incompatible with Islam and feared that strong Sufi tendencies within the chapter would affect the practices of other members. A further concern was how Islam would be presented to the campus community at large.

Ideological reaction and group fragmentation on the basis of ethnicity and politics followed similar lines. People proclaimed themselves to be Muslims dedicated to a tranethnic *umma* but also showed attachment to their ethnic past in the way they dressed or in their affiliation with ethnic minority organizations on campus. Such behavior was accepted, as long as the chapter did not see it as incompatible with Islamic behavior. The MSA/UIC dismissed the GAPS demonstrations and fashion shows not because the chapter opposed the Palestinian cause but because the dancing and focus on the female body in those events were not "Islamic."

All MSAs were democratically structured, with annual elections of personnel responsible for activities considered vital. The MSA/UIC, for example, had—apart from the usual president, vice-president, secretary, and treasurer—also appointed a *da'wa* chair, a publicity chair, a chair responsible for political awareness, and a chair for community service. The *shura* (council, leadership) did not have religious authority in the scholarly sense. Although all elected officials whom I met during my fieldwork were well versed in the tenets of their faith, their authority seemed primarily rooted in their outspokenness, their activism, and in their commitment to Islam as "a way of life." None of them had gone through a high level of Islamic schooling, even though some were known to be *hafiz*.

THE POWER OF VISIBILITY: MUSLIM STUDENTS ON CAMPUS

Muslim action on campus begins in the establishment of a "Muslim space." The MSAs in the Chicago area received the space for their activities from their colleges. A familiar physical framework was created within these walls: Prayer rugs were placed on the floor, pictures of the Ka'ba hung on the walls, and copies of the Qur'an and other Islamic literature placed on the bookshelves. The space was converted into Muslim land framed by signs on doors and walls: This was the "UMMA room" (or, better, the room of the *umma*), the Bait ul-Salaam (house of Peace), or just the "MSA." Doors were seldom closed. Their openness demonstrated strength, as when the tiny MWA room during prayer time became so packed that some people had to kneel in the hallway in front of the open door, or when the shrill sound of a mosque-shaped clock marked the time to break the fast during Ramadan and people had to stand in the doorway, eating their dates and sipping their glasses of water.

Muslims on Chicago campuses did not hide. Rather, they used their space to be seen, encountered, and known. From these rooms, flyers were distributed, activities planned, posters hung on bulletin boards in student centers and department hallways, marking Muslim presence with proud insistence. As much as such activities were the results of Muslim student commitment, they were also supported by non-Muslim school administrations that allowed Muslim activities to take place on their campuses and provided funds for that purpose. American secular society, therefore, was not only an element against which Muslim identity was formulated but also an indispensable element for expressing this identity.[35]

"We Hunt Down Muslims":
Getting Other Muslims Involved

To expose the campus community to Islam, the MSAs had to increase their numbers. Because members predictably graduated and left, constant proselytizing was necessary for the survival of the MSAs. As older students took jobs in other parts of the city or out of state, the remaining members began to look for their replacements. Therefore, massive recruiting among freshmen took place at the beginning of every school year. As one student said:

> We actually try to hunt down Muslims. That is what we have to do in order to get them to participate and, like, become members. We actually get lists of new freshmen coming to the school, and we find out about who are Muslims on the list or we try to guess who are Muslims. Actually, this year we got a list of people who had checked that they were Muslims on their applications. We, like, call them, inform them about all the activities taking place, send them letters [and] e-mail, and just, like, really try to get them to the activities. We advertise all over the place. You see our flyers everywhere: "Come to *jum'a* prayer," and about the *halaqas* and about any other kind of seminars that we have. A lot of it has to do with interacting, talking to other Muslims, you know. I think that is a really large component of it, just—when you see peers, like—when you see other students your age going into these things and they are telling you that it can be really fun and there are people your age there.[36]

Although active Muslim students interact and create bonds of friendship with people of other faiths, borders between "us" and "them" are clearly marked by how Muslims may defend or reject the nature of such relationships. My student informants did not commonly allow themselves to participate in partying because of the dancing and drinking. Neither did they participate in the ritual of dating, which was widespread among their non-Muslim classmates. Such "temptations of the world," as MSA members often described them, pointed to what they were convinced that Muslims were not and what Muslims should avoid. Those "temptations" also created the necessity for a supportive network of like-minded students, who in this milieu were fellow members of the MSA.

While some young Muslims used the MSA to proclaim their dedication to Islam, many of my informants stated that belonging to the MSA actually changed their view on Islam from a nonengaging part of their family heritage to a conscious, individual choice. A female student in her early twenties noted:

When I first came in my freshman year—I am a senior now—my concept of Islam was, "Oh, Islam is a great religion, it is my religion, I am Muslim. That's cool." . . . Of course, I had feelings, like, [I should] defend Islam and all that. But since being here at De Paul and working at UMMA and just meeting other Muslims, my strength, my faith in my religion, has just grown more than 500 percent. Before, I did not wear the head covering, the *hijab*. After a little while, I started wearing it, and I just educated myself so much more. I know so much more about Islam, my rights within the context of Islam. I am just really, really proud to be a Muslim. I am ready to shout it from the top of— what do we have . . . [laughter]. Before, I would have been more hesitant and I was not as sure of myself.[37]

As space was converted into "Muslim space" and students became motivated to use it and mark their Muslim-ness through activism and changes in dress and behavior, the MSA strove to keep the structure intact. One step was to elect a leadership council—a *shura*. The *shura* was generally responsible for meetings and activities and for making sure that all members were contacted and motivated. Planning meetings took place every week or every other week. Because such meetings were extracurricular, attracting new members was a constant challenge. However dedicated young Muslims might be, they still faced the requirements of homework and papers; to take an afternoon or evening off for a meeting was not always easy. Some MSA chapters never attracted more than a handful of members to their meetings.

A Session of "Spiritual Discourse"

In the late 1990s, the MSA/UC developed a successful strategy for attracting members, and it became common for thirty to forty people to show up at meetings. At the beginning of each meeting, a member of the *shura* would present and discuss every point on the agenda. These points were mostly activist, such as planning *da'wa* efforts and Muslim study circles. When the debate had reached a satisfactory end, another member of the *shura* would offer a "spiritual discourse," discussing religious issues in the light of personal experience. Finally, refreshments—Coca-Cola, pizza, or pastry—were served, allowing people to socialize informally. The success of the MSA/UC in gathering its members had little to do with the topics on the agenda, because subjects such as

Islamic Awareness Weeks, the conditions for Friday prayers, and annual fund-raising dinners were discussed by all the MSAs. What attracted people to the MSA/UC meetings seemed to be the learning and sharing that the meeting included. Central to these was the spiritual discourse, which the following story exemplifies:

At the first MSA/UC meeting of the school year, one of the *shura* members, a pale but charismatic young woman, got up to speak. Alia, who had started college the previous year, began her discourse by reflecting on her freshman experience. During the orientation week, she said, the newcomers were continually told how great the university was, and it was difficult to keep a sense of modesty in that arrogant environment.

Alia encouraged her listeners to remember that even two points on an academic record were God-given. Human life was perishable, and nothing was accomplished except by the will of Allah. There would always be someone smarter than you, and however hard you studied and however well you did academically, it would all be gone if you got a brain tumor. Certainly, it was an Islamic virtue to seek knowledge—that, indeed, as stated in a *hadith*, it was an asset on your way to paradise. But if knowledge made you arrogant, it hindered your entrance to that blissful place.

There was, though, another side of the coin, because the effect of arrogance depended on what you were arrogant about. There was one reason for this group to be arrogant, and that was because they were Muslims. Alia said that she had felt intimidated in her beliefs when she started at the the University of Chicago, even though she had studied at a Muslim high school. But as time passed, she had regained her confidence that Islam was the correct way of life. She was proud that she did not drink or party. Drinking made people act like animals, and partying kept them away from sleeping at the ordained times. Islam was a choice— not for the sake of God, but for peoples' own benefit.

"So," Alia concluded, "do not be arrogant, but be arrogant. Be arrogant about your way of life—that you have chosen to live as you *should* live."

The spiritual discourse was a central element of the MSA/UC meetings because it created identity and community between speaker and audience on three levels. On the first, or "familiar," level, the speaker emphasized community by reflecting on a set of experiences that she and her listeners had in common: the beginning of college. This initiation also included a dilemma connected to the second, or "confessional," level of the spiritual discourse. This level usually suggested the student's having to choose between two powerful sets of behavior: the Muslim and the secular–academic. The struggle between the two was presented as a mental drama. In this instance, Alia described the intimidation she had experienced because she had felt it difficult to stay religiously modest. She had, at that point, almost lost what her childhood had taught her was true.

However, the third level, the "redemptive," promoted a firmer commitment to her faith. In the end, she found a renewed faith in Islam, which granted her the arrogance of what she saw as correct and natural. Whereas the habits of secular America left its participants "victimized," as animals, her choice had given her the grace of a human being, of being what her God wanted her to be. Islam was the primary element around which identity was formed.

Apart from presenting a personal and communal life drama, the three levels of the discourse—the familiar, confessional, and redemptive—helped solidify a Muslim position within and against the campus milieu. Although Muslims attended American colleges to obtain secular knowledge that they (like their non-Muslim peers) wanted, the secular environment, in Alia's words, lacked the recognition of divine authority and intent. In such an environment, people came to see themselves as gods, forgetting their own fragility and accepting a false knowledge that was both unnatural and demonically tempting. Pitted against the secular was the spiritual or Islamic, where people saw themselves as dependent on God for everything. This position allowed individuals to fulfill their potentials by recognizing God as the sustainer of knowledge and the path to knowledge. It was this last position that the MSA had chosen and with which its members identified. It was the reason that Muslim students gathered, and the reason that they could accept the mantle of Muslim "arrogance." Similar to a Christian revival meeting, the "spiritual discourse" helped the students dedicate themselves to Muslim activism.

In addition to demonstrating how Muslim students position and identify themselves in a campus milieu, Alia's talk exemplifies how authority and the right to distribute knowledge was understood in MSA chapters. True knowledge was not so much scholarly as experiential—that the individual proved strong enough to resist the temptations of the world. In this setting, students understood Islam and the roles they took in its name as defying the larger American society.

Communality in Language, Prayer, and Appearance

Muslim student groups were held together by more than their meetings. At the MSA/UC, as on other Chicago campuses, the e-mails students received from the *shura* had a motivating force. As the entire MSA community in the Chicago area was connected by the MSA Chicago network, so were local campus communities bound together by internal e-mail lists that distributed notices for meetings, lectures, and study groups. The messages came in an informal style that gave the impression of a direct personal response.

Not only meetings—virtual and real—but also shared terminology reinforced the sense of belonging to a group. As was common in much of the Chicago Muslim community, MSA members combined American English with Arabic and Islamic terminology. For example, a young woman expressing her satisfaction with the group's plans might say, "That will, *in sha'a Allah*, be cool." Expressions such as *"in sha'a Allah"* (God willing), *"ma sha'a Allah"* (whatever God wants), *"al-hamdu li-llah"* (thanks be to God), *shura* (council, leadership), and *halaqa* (study circle), as well as ritual terms such as *jum'a* (congregational prayers), *khutba* (sermon), and *salat* (ritual prayers) were common. Many students used Islamic terms only among their Muslim peers, either leaving out, explaining, or translating them in the presence of a non-Muslim. MSA members also used titles such as "brother" and "sister" when they addressed one another. Terminology thus became a means of creating borders between those who were inside and outside the community.

Just as occupying a certain space, meeting regularly, and sharing a particular language helped bond the community, so did rituals, dress codes, and collective propagation of ideas. Although rituals were avowedly a means to honor God, they also marked space and solidified identity within the colorful American tapestry. For example, every Friday a large group of Muslim students and teachers gathered on the prayer rugs in the Bond Chapel at the University of Chicago in the early afternoon. Beyond the public act of praying to the God of Muhammad, Musa (Moses), and Isa (Jesus) in a way unfamiliar to most Americans, this Muslim student action took place in a setting where Christian images of Jesus and archangels looked down from stained-glass windows: Muslim "space" was set within a room marked by the icons of America's largest religion.

But because the MSA used the chapel for only thirty minutes, the gathering was hidden from most of the campus community. People sitting outside may have been eating their lunches without any idea of what was going on inside. To make Islam known, to empower the group through persuasive presence, Muslim students therefore had to move beyond walls. To some, that move included the adoption of a specific model for behavior and dress— a model they claimed came from divine decree.

One such religious signifier was the *hijab*. In the United States, among other places, Muslim women's clothing and behavior among men takes on heightened significance. The reason is that those individuals and groups discussing and defining women's behavior are not merely Muslims but also non-Muslims. Because the stereotypical—and highly visible—*hijab* publicly goes against the American "melting pot" ethos, wearing it proclaims a refusal to bow to the norms of the majority. By so doing, of course, the wearer reinforces cohesion within the community of religious observers.

This is not to say that men refrain from Islamic standards of clothing. During my summers in Chicago, I never saw any of the young men who attended the MSA wear shorts (Islamic tradition tells men to cover themselves from the waist to their knees). The most religiously conscious of the men grew beards, and a few of them wore the traditional *jalabiyya* (robe). But even though some students presented the beard as a religious requirement (and a statement of Muslim identity), few actually took the step of wearing one.

The situation among Muslim women students was different. To them, their style of clothing made them exactly "what they were expected to be" to Muslims and non-Muslims alike. Wearing the *hijab* marked not only gender, religion, and community but also specific public statements of their overall identity. It marked the individual's choice to become "more" than gender— the choice to *be* a specific model for her gender and her faith. For many, the decision to wear the *hijab* was a rite of passage into authentic Muslim womanhood.

Not all female students, however, chose to wear what might be called the Islamic "uniform"—a solid-colored *hijab* over a solid-colored *jilbab*. Some saw it as unnecessarily public and therefore countering the Islamic precepts on modesty. As a Muslim girl on Chicago's North Side said:

> I don't wear [the *hijab*] because I think I want to de-emphasize what is on the outside. I think that Islam is really stressing the inside. It talks about modesty. People look on modesty as, like, clothing on the outside. But what about modesty on the inside? Humility and, like, you know, loving other people and kindness and stuff? That is all on the inside. So, I mean, you wear a *hijab* so that you detract attention from your physical attributes. In America, if you wear *hijab* you are an exception, you draw attention, because people are, like, "Oh, what does she wear on her head?" when it is eighty degrees out in the summer. I don't know if that is necessarily modest.[38]

Antagonism was not visible between the girls who wore the *hijab* and those who did not. Non-*hijabis* often sat in the *shura* and represented the MSA in various campus forums. Wearing loose-fitting long clothes, they were still accepted as practicing Muslims.

Despite this acceptance, however, a number of the MSA women with whom I interacted began wearing the *hijab* during our acquaintaince. Three explanations for this transition are possible. First, the increase in *hijab*-wearing MSA women followed similar trends in and beyond the Chicago community. Second, wearing the *hijab* often signified the transition from the safe, controlled family environment to the less controlled and even "sexually disturbing" campus environment. Many of the girls chose to wear the *hijab* in their freshman year, when they moved into the dorms or began engaging in campus activities removed from family influence.[39] Third, wearing the *hijab* accentuated the individual's authority within the community, because her choice labeled her as willing to embody the traditions of the community. She was no longer "just" a girl or a woman. She was a "Muslim woman," representing an ideal.

Women within the MSA stressed the increased authority that followed the choice to wear the *hijab*. Whereas female Muslim students who did not wear the *hijab* seldom gave religious justifications for their Islamic choices, women who wore the *hijab* always spoke of their choice as an expression of divine command. Most non-*hijabis* supported this claim, although they had not taken the step to wear the head scarf themselves. Although I never observed any direct pressure on the non-*hijabis*, the expectation that they would one day wear the head scarf was definitely present.

In one case, I watched the transition from non-*hijabi* to *hijabi* became an institutionalized, communal ritual. In early March 1996, the MWA/UIC held a potluck dinner for its members. Following the meal, congregational prayer, and a lot of cheerful talking and singing, one of the women walked to the central podium. She explained that the women's group wanted to pay tribute to the sisters who had either converted or started wearing the *hijab* during the previous year. One by one, she introduced the young women and asked them to join her on stage, where she gave each a small decorated bag containing a head scarf, chocolate, and audio tapes with religious speeches and recitations from the Qur'an. She then encouraged each woman to give a short speech about why and how she had decided to wear the *hijab*.

Most of the new *hijabis*, nervous and shy in front of a microphone and an audience, emphasized that their choice came about through MSA/MWA meetings. They had started college that year, and the friendships and activities with other young Muslims had inspired them to take this major step. After each presentation, the young speaker was applauded with a *"takbir! Allahu akbar!"* (give praise! God is great!) before returning to her seat.

What these young women experienced can easily be seen as a "rebirth," a remodeling, an experienced re-creation of the individual. The audience emphasized, validated, and authorized the power of the experience by allowing each young woman to present her experience from the stage, by giving her gifts (which accompany rites of passage in many cultures), and by elevating her in space, honor, and experience before the community. To some degree, these actions took place at the cost of those in the group who did not wear the *hijab*, because the applause and attention now differentiated all *hijabis* from those who still let their hair show to Muslims and non-Muslims alike. As this tiny community celebrated itself, it also expressed the expectation that the rest of the MWA community inevitably would truly become "sisters."

Young Muslim women's self-image often included a reaction against certain representations of Islam, whether in the press or among non-Muslim peers. Muslim women particularly pointed to books and films that portrayed women of their faith as suppressed. Instead, they argued, they saw themselves as free and liberated because of Islam. Whereas the media and popular literature, when focused on the international scene, often emphasized the image of Muslim women as uneducated and ignorant,[40] Muslim-American women pointed to their presence at esteemed universities and counterargued that they were pursuing an education because Islam required the individual pursuit of knowledge. During interviews and conversations, these women revealed the dichotomies among how secular American society portrayed young Muslim women, how they portrayed themselves, and how those they saw as their critics and opponents portrayed them within the context of how "Western women" behaved.

Here are two of their voices:

> [In] the [past few] years, I am realizing how women in Islam are not ... stereotypical, ... [the] submissive, subordinate, abused, Middle Eastern, "slash," Islamic women that the West seems to portray. I never knew how much toward the opposite it really was. I think women in Islam are so liberated. When I wear my scarf and my *hijab* and go out, I feel that I demand respect from other people. I do not have to be anyone besides myself, besides my personality to be appreciated, to be liked, to get ahead in my education or career or whatever, as you see so many women do. I don't have to spend hours looking in the mirror. I am just myself, coming out the way that God created me. I feel

that he is giving us this protection. If I go out, get a job, apply for a job, I know it is for my skills, not for what I was wearing or how I looked, how my eye shadow matched my lipstick.[41]

What we see here in this country, and perhaps in the West in general, [is that] there is an extreme emphasis on how you look. That is why so many girls have eating disorders; because they are really insecure, because their whole value is driven from what they look like. That is a really hard thing, because if you don't conform to the societal standards or whatever, then it is very difficult position to be in. So that was to me a very empowering thing to say, and now [since I started wearing the *hijab*] I find that people cannot just judge me on how I look. It is impossible. So you are necessarily evaluated in terms of yourself as a person and your mind and your actions, and that is a very beautiful thing.[42]

These statements express what is known as an "apologetic pitfall"[43]—that is, the speakers have adopted the vocabulary and preferences of a powerful "other" (in this case, American society) and used them to promote their own conceptions of truth and reality. At the same time, they are arguing that the norms of this "other" are flawed. Ironically, these young women's portrayals of the value of Islamic womanhood sounds strikingly like the fulfillment of American secular ideals. Muslim women see themselves as "liberated"; they are to be hired on the basis of their skills and evaluated in terms of their personality, intelligence, and behavior. At the same time that the informants felt wrongly judged by stereotypes, their statements reflected other stereotypes: For example, they saw themselves as judged by the exaggerated de-sexualization of the body and in turn judged their non-Muslim counterparts as suffering the exaggerated sexualization of the body. In their words, non-Muslim-American women spent hours in front of the mirror, thinking about lipstick and eye shadow and dieting to fulfill the "extreme [Western] emphasis" on how women look. This common use of powerful stereotypes—by Muslim and non-Muslim women—shows that cultural battles over the definition of womanhood often are still fought by women against other women.

To many Muslim women, wearing the *hijab* also involved choosing specific patterns, colors, and styles. The Islamic uniform of the MSA/MWA slowly became the signifier of cohesion and consistency in a community seen even by Muslims as "fragmented" and "ethnic." As the larger community of Muslims pursued unification across cultural and national lines (because religious Scripture and tradition mandate that unification), a "true" Islamic dress code eventually had to express itself in only one style. However, because wearing the *jilbab* and *hijab* on American campuses is a dress code without any direct stylistic precedent, the women who wear the Islamic uniform claim that it follows divine commands in the Qur'an.[44] To be sure, religious female Muslim students still wear the *shalwar khamiz* (wide trousers with a matching long, wide dress) and other traditional clothing— or simply jeans and sweatshirts with the *hijab*. But the aspiration to act as a unified community shows itself in the growing prominence of the solid-colored *jilbab* under a solid-colored *hijab*.

Choosing a dress code based on the claim that it represents the order of God and his community of believers certainly required assertiveness, debating skills, and the accumulation of knowledge. Muslim women on and off campuses often said that they found it necessary to know their religion well, not only for their individual growth and that of their future children, but also as a means of defense. Being so visible, they were frequently questioned about their faith by everyone from classmates and teachers to shoppers in the supermarket. They saw it as an honor to be able to answer these questions as correctly—and with as little chance of counterargument—as possible. As a female student at the University of Illinois at Chicago said:

> When you know about yourself, your background, you are able to tell others. . . . So if anyone has something bad to say about you, you can say, "No, it is not really like this." When I was in elementary school, I had—specifically because I didn't wear *hijab* and I was from India— a lot of the people assumed that I was Hindu. And they always told me, "You are Hindu." And when I was in elementary school that was considered to be so bad. . . . And I [said], "No, I'm not. I'm a Muslim." And they [said], "Oh, yeah? Prove it!" Then I kind of said, "How can I prove it?" Then I would see this Arabian girl wear *hijab* and I would be like, "Why don't you dress like her? Why is she wearing it, and you aren't wearing it?" So if you are educated about your religion, you are able to respond to that.[45]

Muslim college students also expressed community through collective participation in rituals, such as Friday prayers, where they reaffirmed both submission to divine command and their bond to one another. But, however important this gathering appeared, it took place only once a week. By contrast, during Ramadan, the month of fasting, students shared their restless anticipation as the clock moved slowly toward the time when the fast could be broken, when plastic containers with dates were passed around. They shared the seriousness of prayer, standing shoulder to shoulder, foot to foot, facing in one direction as if nothing else existed. They shared the delicious aromas of potluck Middle Eastern and Indian food, covered and warm, in huge pots and pans. They shared stories of Ramadan fatigue and Ramadan hunger. This sharing gave their lives as humans a higher purpose.

Although Ramadan seemed intimately devoted to the spiritual development of the groups, the students did not exclude the larger, non-Muslim world. Ramadan offered another chance to present Islam to the broader campus community. On most of the Chicago campuses, an 'Id dinner, open to Muslims and non-Muslims alike, marked the end of Ramadan. During these dinners, non-Muslims met their Muslim classmates (often conspicuous because of their particularly colorful and stylistically distinctive clothing) and heard the message of Islam. Popular Muslim speakers from Chicago and beyond presented their community and their religion. Often these talks aimed at countering negative images of Islam—political and gender-specific. Ramadan dinners therefore signified defense as much as empowerment: Muslim students used the events to counter questions raised frequently about their religion in American society and to do so in their own way, showing their community as hospitable and colorful, and with a human face.

Islamic Awareness Week

MSA members presented Muslim identity and knowledge to the larger campus community through other publicly celebrated occasions as well, especially by participating in inter-religious dialogues on campus. Through such events, generally initiated by the student administration or the campus ministry, Muslim students were able to point out their ideological similarities and contrasts to the other religions represented on campus. From time to time, the MSAs also arranged so-called study breaks in student centers, serving free meals while promoting Islam from *da'wa* booths or video screens. But none of these activities had the power of the yearly Islamic Awareness Week (IAW) through which the MSA introduced the majority of Chicago campuses to Islam as a message and Islam as an active community of believers. The MSA National presented the objectives of the event as follows:

> During this week, various activities will be held in order to promote Islamic principles and ideas and spread the message of Islam. Activities and lectures will be held with the idea of educating students, faculty, staff, and other members of the university community on the basic teachings of Islam as well as clearing up the misconceptions that have formed due to existing political issues and the often irresponsible and insensitive mass-media. IAW may also be used by the MSA to focus on current events or breaking stories in the media and better represent the Islamic and Muslim perspective on the issues. . . . IAW must also be used to work towards helping the Muslim students on campus. It must serve both as identity supporter and unifier, as well as an effective form of *da'wa* to all Muslims on campus which is something often overlooked. IAW should be a time when the MSA brings in the inactive Muslims and activates them Islamically on campus.[46]

The goal of the IAW, therefore, was to address three audiences: non-Muslims (staff and fellow students), "inactive" Muslims on campus, and the media. The first two audiences—non-Muslims and "inactive" Muslims—were a predictable target of this campus event. The focus on the third group, the media, however, exposed an internal conflict: If the media were "irresponsible and insensitive" (as some members insisted), then why did the MSAs choose them as a primary target for promoting their views?

Targeting the media points to larger issues of having power over the shaper of a public opinion that was often unfavorable to Muslims. On various occasions during the 1990s, Muslim youngsters, together with their friends and family, had faced the negative impact of radio and television—from the reporting of international events such as the Gulf War to national events such as the Oklahoma City bombing. A wide range of Muslim-American organizations and community initiatives, including the MSA, reacted directly against such media images.

Within the Chicago area, students often talked about the efforts of the Council on American Islamic Relations (CAIR). Apart from its numerous press releases, CAIR had published the *Media Relations Handbook for Muslim Activists*, focusing on how Muslim Americans could deal with the press both locally and nationally.[47] During the First Annual Islam in America Conference, held at the DePaul Center in downtown Chicago in September 1995, a panel comprising Muslim and non-Muslim reporters and intellectuals stressed the importance of media relations for Muslims who wanted to change the status quo.[48] The IAW's targeting of the local media was therefore in harmony with general activist trends in the Muslim-American community as a whole.

The strong will to change "negative" media images of Muslims implies motives that are just as legitimizing and motivating as they are defensive. Publicizing one's group as victimized and misunderstood while demanding public recognition and empowerment actually highlights a group's vulnerability. A further reason that Muslims pay the media a high level of attention is the mobilizing effect that this act has within the group: Emphasizing collective suffering as a consequence of truth claims provides a way to uphold group cohesion. This is a process common to many immigrant groups in America. The result is frequently—as seen among Muslims—an increased focus on how to state the community's voice within the society at large, whether through the media, social activism, or politics.

By the late 1990s, however, intentions to engage in media relations were seldom put into action on Chicago's campuses. Although IAW lectures often presented images of the media as the source of misconceptions of Islam, only once during an IAW did I observe an MSA chapter (the MSA/UC) devote an entire lecture to the issue of media representation of Islam and Muslims.[49] I never saw any MSAs make direct contact with local newspapers or radio stations (apart from campus stations) to create attention for Muslim views and events. For the most part, announcements of activities, lectures, and film screenings took place on bulletin boards. The gap between ambition and action may reveal Muslims' unease with, and distrust of, the public media. By the end of the 1990s, Muslim-American students by and large lacked the social power and position to use the media to get their voices heard.

The MSA used the IAW primarily to make contact with non-Muslim and "inactive" Muslim students and staff and to gain visibility in public spaces. Beyond the goal of informing and transforming individuals and groups through the message of Islam, the MSA saw the IAW as an "identity supporter and unifier." It was intended as a week during which the MSA could present and stress its idea of a Muslim identity while simultaneously strengthening the community of its members.

Not all campuses formed or presented the IAW in the same way. Although the MSA National had designated one specific week each year for the event, local chapters sometimes chose a different week, often to accommodate campus scheduling.[50] Further, some MSA chapters extended the IAW. The MSA/UC, for example, chose to hold an Islamic Awareness Month (IAM), and the MSA/UIC held an IAW every semester. In spite of these differences, the Chicago chapters tried to coordinate—or, at least, support—the planning of all local IAWs. During an MSA Chicago meeting in October 1996, the various chapters shared experiences and information: What speakers should they invite? What kind of material did other chapters intend to distribute? How did they advertise? Members were encouraged to participate in events on other campuses, especially when prominent speakers were involved. This encouragement usually worked, as when Professor John L. Esposito of Georgetown University spoke at MSA/NW in November 1995. Much of the audience consisted of MSA members from other Chicago campuses.

Generally, IAWs included three categories of events. One was the ground-level information campaign, located in areas where the general student population was likely to see it. The second category was speeches or movies. These events demanded more planning, with a higher level of interest and action from the audience. The last category addressed the even smaller number of people who answered the MSA's invitation to participate in Friday prayers.

IAW information booths were usually located in areas such as student centers, where many people frequently passed by. All booths handed out free information on IAW events, as well as pamphlets from the local Institute of Islamic Information and Education. In some cases, Islamic literature was displayed and sold from the booths. During the IAW in the spring of 1997, the MSA/UC prepared a "special edition" of its *Khabir* newsletter, with articles on the basic tenets of Islam and Islam in America, and offered the newsletter in the *da'wa* booth.[51]

That same year, the UMMA at DePaul University distributed free Qur'ans, although this action raised concern within the chapter. At meetings preceding the IAW, some members had argued that one could not predict how the Scripture would be used and whether its recipients would treat it with its deserved respect. UMMA solved the problem by distributing Qur'ans written in English only. In that way, some students argued, the sacredness of the text (seen as intimately connected to Arabic) would remain undisturbed while the message was still conveyed. Other chapters got around the problem by asking for small donations (often a dollar) from those who wanted a copy. Their hope was that only "buyers" with a sincere interest in the message would make the investment. Such cases illustrate the resolution of potential conflicts between a group's wish to proselytize and its veneration of a religious text.

In addition to displaying literature and magazines, Muslim students used audiovisual media to attract their intended audience. TV screens showed videos about Muslim countries, conversion stories, or broadcasts from the *hajj* (great pilgrimage). A tape recorder sometimes filled the air with Qur'anic recitations. In 1997, the Muslim students at DePaul University decorated the whole inner court of their student center with colorful posters describing the tenets of their faith. In addition, MSA members were often encouraged to use particular clothing to "embody" Islam, as happened at DePaul, where a planning meeting debated whether IAW participants should dress "ethnically" to show the diversity of the Muslim community.

Constant reference to a broad variety of Muslim countries portrayed Islam as a global faith. In 1997, for example, the MSA/UC prepared a "Cultural Fair," displaying commodities from India, Iran, Palestine, Saudi Arabia, and Turkey. After displaying and selling items, dialogue was the next most prominent way of attracting attention in the booths. Curious students were encouraged to raise questions and doubts, and the Muslim students did their best to answer and encourage people to participate in upcoming lectures with Muslim specialists and activists. In all, the IAW *da'wa* booths were the most effective means presenting Islam as rooted in Chicago campuses, the city of Chicago, and, by extension, the United States.

The second category of events required much more planning. Getting copies of popular videos (such as the film *The Message*[52]) was easy—the students or their families often owned them—but rooms had to be booked and audiovisual equipment installed. Getting speakers was even more time-consuming. Candidates known as exciting and articulate were selected and invited weeks, and even months, before the event and in some cases were flown in from other parts of the country. The MSA often had to find cosponsors to help with expenses such as airplane tickets and hotel rooms.[53] As was the case at 'Id dinners, speakers' topics mostly reflected the perceived needs of the audience—what the planners saw as non-Muslims' misunderstandings in need of correction. Lectures might focus on Islamic interpretations of womanhood, the concept of *jihad* (religious struggle or holy war), the Muslim understanding of Jesus, or the media's presentations of Islam. Other lectures were more missionary, focusing on Islam as a solution for American and global society, Islam as a solution for the African-American population, and Islam as a necessity for the individual salvation.

On one occasion, a microphone was put in the center court of DePaul's student center. Facing it were parallel rows of chairs that were gradually occupied by many of the UMMA members active in the IAW. Hamza, a young African-American convert from Chicago, took the stage. During my fieldwork I had watched his reputation grow because of his status as *khatib* at the University of Illinois at Chicago and DePaul; his charisma and rhetorical talent; and his steadfast, non-negotiable presentations of Islam. He was known as being as tough on Muslims as on non-Muslims, especially in his work as editor of, and contributor to, the local Hizb al-Tahrir (Liberation Party) publication, *Islamic Forum.*[54] Hamza presented Islam that day according to his radical interpretations of Islam as a religion and social system.

Because the school is a place of intellect, he said, stressing his statements with rhythmical repetition, any subject should be judged according to its context, based on information. It is important to keep this in mind within the current American society. The mass media within the country has become the primary provider of information about Islam and does so from a biased and false point of view, such as when it reports that Islam is an Arab or "black" thing, although Islam actually is for everybody, or when it says that Muslim women are suppressed, beaten, and circumcised. Those who read history, he said, will see that 1,300 years ago Muslim women were allowed to inherit and that they owned businesses and fought battles, whereas Christian women during the Middle Ages were burned at the stake.

And, he continued, some might say that Islam is spread by the sword, that Islam is a religion that promotes violence. But it was not Muslims who started the Holocaust. When the Christians took Spain, all the Jews ran to Muslim lands because they knew that the Christians would slaughter them.[55] Wars in Islam are fought only to remove physical barriers to spreading of the message. Muslim Spain was the intellectual center of its time; unfortunately, he noted, a center fostering such intellectual inquiry is missing within today's Muslim world. If we had the proper Islamic system, Muslims would engage in any science for the proper benefit of man. Islam is not against the West, he said. Islam is the alternative.

"That was why I converted," Hamza said. "Because within the present system of this country, oppression is going on, and if we keep on accepting it, we cannot be a part of the solution. It is, like, if you have eaten dirt all your life, you therefore believe it to be good, since it is the only kind of food you believe to exist. But if you were exposed to a different kind of food—a different kind of system—and you had considered it intellectually, you'd be able to make a choice. Islamic Awareness Week is about that choice. It is an invitation to think, not necessarily to convert, because there is no compulsion in religion.[56] Even if we consider the possibility of conversion, this can only take place if the correct information is available, if we have researched it and scrutinized it—that we keep away from the crap that the media feeds us with."

Hamza's speech made clear that the MSAs—and the speakers they chose—did not hesitate to present Islam as politically and socially superior to what the audience could see in the society around them. Islam was presented as the solution to the social and racial ills of American society, as Islam was "for everybody." Hamza's identity as an African-American convert made him focus on and formulate Islam in the light of personal experience: In the late 1990s, African Americans still remained at the bottom of the socioeconomic scale. Again, he portrayed the media as the tool of a nameless oppressor. He mentioned no party, faith, or ethnic group, although his frequent reference to Christianity as the ideology behind the Inquisition and the Holocaust indicated a particular bias. The media did not merely affect the voices of the American public; to a large extent, it *was* this voice, and the images that it produced were therefore more than stories and descriptions. Because this was the "voice" that Muslims often saw themselves pitted against, the media became the central metaphor for misconception, falsity, and "crap."[57] To think as an individual was to free oneself from media representations.

Hamza apparently was aware of both his non-Muslim audience and the Muslims who filled the chairs in front of him. Although his speech emphasized the downfall of powerful Islamic states such as Muslim Spain and his call for a "proper Islamic system," making his non-Muslim audience see Islam in a new light and "think for themselves," his remarks were also aimed at Muslims. If Muslims reconstituted Islam as it was supposed to be— intellectually strong, unified, and socially just—American society would see its message as compatible with, and superior to, the dominant secular values. Hamza saw the IAW as more than an event intended to change the thinking of non-Muslims. It was also designed to "support Muslim identity and unity."

Although lectures such as these were fashioned according to their audiences—shaped according to the language, issues, and scientific skepticism common on Chicago campuses—I found it hard to gauge their persuasive effects. In most of the lectures I attended during various IAW/IAMs, more than half the audience was Muslim, and non-Muslims seldom asked questions or made comments. Dialogue between Muslims and non-Muslims seemed confined to the *da'wa* booths.

The last category of IAW events that most of MSAs organized was to invite the campus community to attend Friday prayers. In the spring of 1997, the MSA/UC decided to pray on the campus lawn to make the ritual more visible. But in the end, the plan was abandoned because prayer was meant to please God, not to draw attention. However, only one or two non-Muslims ever came to Friday prayers. The others stayed away, possibly for lack of interest, but also possibly because of cultural unease about participating in the rituals of a religion not their own. To enter Muslim ritual space indeed seemed like entering a space of total absorption. For most non-Muslims, limiting the encounter to discussions at the *da'wa* booth was apparently more comfortable.

THE STUDY CIRCLE

Reactions to or against the dominant culture notwithstanding, Muslim Americans framed their identity with—and eventually against—other Muslims, locally, nationally, and globally. Young Muslims educated themselves to detect a wrongful, weakening, or fragmenting enemy in their own midst as much as outside it. To attune themselves to such critical distinctions, they studied the Qur'an, the *ahadith* (the narrated traditions of the Prophet Muhammad), and the works of renowned theologians in the hope of discovering the "true" Islam beneath the veil of cultural "innovations."

The Halaqa

The use of the word *halaqa* on American campuses and beyond shows the Americanization of an Islamic term. The Arabic word *halqa/halaqa* (circle) has been used for centuries in the Muslim world to describe the circle that students at religious seminars and universities formed at their teachers' feet during instruction.

Sitting in a *halaqa* marked periods of accumulating of Islamic knowledge, raising the student to the status of religious authority or scholar. On American campuses, the *halaqa* had a similar yet quite different meaning. Although *halaqas* were indeed periods of religious instruction, the participants did not expect to receive any religiously defined authority as a result of their participation. Teachers were usually fellow students, not Islamic scholars, although some teachers came from outside the college environment. The structure of the *halaqa* was mostly democratic, and students took turns preparing and presenting subjects.

This section covers two kinds of *halaqas* for women in which leadership was decided beforehand. These examples clearly describe what the intention of a *halaqa* can be, what may hold it together, and what may make it fall apart. After all, *halaqas* are loosely structured in the sense that they exist only as long as their members find the topics discussed interesting and feel that they gain useful knowledge about aspects of their faith. In the first example, the teacher followed a strict, ideological line, but because this line was not accepted or known by the students in advance, the *halaqa* soon fell apart. The second example introduces a successful *halaqa* based on the so-called Peacenet curriculum. This *halaqa* succeeded because it adhered to a strict form, and the participating students knew exactly where the curriculum was leading them.

Although *halaqas* could consist of men and women, they were often separated by gender. The women I met at various *halaqas* saw this segregation as promoting security and intimacy. In women-only *halaqas*, the participants were more likely to speak up and discuss personal issues. They could relax, discuss, and internalize subjects that were of interest to them not only as Muslims but also as Muslim women.

A Women's Halaqa

For Muslim women at DePaul University in the fall of 1996 and spring 1997, the *halaqas* were significant because they were led by Aminah, an African-American convert, who was not directly affiliated with the campus. She was accepted at the recommendation of Hamza, the powerful IAW speaker quoted earlier. It was not surprising, given Aminah's background, that her *halaqas* came to center on Islam as a social and political system. Hamza and Aminah shared more than their identities as African Americans and converts: Both were affiliated with the Hizb al-Tahrir, a group that gained some ground during my time in Chicago. In Chicago, the ideas of the Hizb al-Tahrir were particularly expressed by the journal *Islamic Forum.*

To both Hamza and Aminah, Islam promoted a divinely decreed social order that stood in absolute contrast to the system of *taghut* (idolatry)[58] that they claimed prevailed within the United States and the current world order. The establishment of an Islamic system was presented as implementing the reconstitution of the *khilafa* (institutionalized government of the *umma*; the caliphate). Although neither Hamza nor Aminah expressed membership in the movement explicitly, Hamza had told me about his engagement in the movement during an interview in the spring of 1996.[59] Aminah, however, did not refer to the Hizb al-Tahrir until late in her teaching. That some people within the DePaul UMMA were affiliated with the movement (or, at least, felt positively about the idea of Islam as a political system and about the re-establishment of the *khilafa*) until then had been visible only in certain items in the UMMA room: copies of *Islamic Forum* lying on the desk and a poster promoting the establishment of the *khilafa* on one of the walls. But nothing indicated who was responsible for these postings.

During the initial *halaqas*, which took place in the UMMA room on Tuesday afternoons, Aminah did not touch on the Hizb al-Tahrir or on Islam as a political ideology. Her focus was methodical and analytical, initially restricted to defensive arguments useful as rhetorical validations of the Muslim tenets of faith: How could the gathered women argue for the existence of a God in a way that non-Muslims could not refute? In mid-November 1996, however, during a discussion of the human actions that please Allah, Aminah moved the discussion toward whether and how Islam could be approached as an all-encompassing social system.

She had started the *halaqa* that afternoon by reflecting on the perfection of the *wahy* (revelation) and the indisputable decrees for humankind that it had fostered. During the ensuing discussion of the implications of *wahy* for the world of today, one of the women stated that no system created by humans had ever provided absolute equality or absolute abolition of evil. Aminah agreed, going on to say that, although some people believed that the Roman Empire and the present system in the United States were good, they did not realize that these systems were transitory and that they were not good for everybody. Such people had not realized that they needed a Creator and those decrees that He has made for them. A country such as the United States promoted a system that was false at its basis. The only system ever built on valid concepts, she said, was the *khilafa*.

Because the meeting fell shortly before the U.S. national elections and because the issue of whether participating in those elections was valid according to Islam had been raised in the larger Muslim community, I asked the group what it had to say on the subject.[60] Aminah responded immediately. Participating in a system that by its constitution was *kufr* (unbelief) could never be validated, and because voting was a fundamental part of that system, it had to be abandoned. The women around me suddenly held their collective breath, viewing the teacher with an air of distrust.

Noticing their mood change, Aminah explained: Whatever present political system we are dealing with, be it the United States or the United Nations, it is a product of *taghut*. A ruling system such as the one we know in America, based on the separation of church and state, was absolutely unacceptable according to Islam. In Islam, ruling was embedded in the commands of Allah. Since democracy was based on the principle that power belonged to the people, how could Muslims, who believed that all power belongs to God, who is above any man-made system, engage in such *kufr*? It was true that a worldwide confusion existed within the *umma* about the concept of democracy, and only one "small group of which I myself am a member" understood what this was all about. Centuries of misinterpretation had blurred the fact that no human beings could make laws against the statement of *la illaha illa Allah* (there is no God but God), and they would be held responsible if they did. She was certain, she concluded, that if she voted, God would hold her accountable on the Day of Judgment, and not for the good. The participating students were far from convinced. During the next meeting, Aminah distributed two photocopied pages titled, "The Ruling of Islam on Elections." The publisher's name, "Hizb ut Tahreer, Wilayah of Jordan," was clearly printed on the second page. Although Aminah still refrained from referring directly to her affiliation, her source of inspiration was exposed in the text:

> The regimes ruling in Muslim lands nowadays are all un-Islamic. That is, they are regimes of Kufr because their systems are not derived from the Book of Allah and the Sunnah of his Messenger (SAWS) (except from some proportion of it). It is forbidden for a Muslim who believes in Allah and his Messenger (SAWS) to help, participate in or be a part of these regimes. Rather must he work with utmost diligence and speed to dismantle it and establish the system of Islam in its place.[61]

Although the text described its targets of critique as "regimes ruling in Muslim lands," the use of English showed that its intended readership was indeed Western—and Aminah did not hesitate to apply the statements to the present state of Muslims in the United States.

From then on, Islam as a political system was the most discussed subject in the halaqas at DePaul. People reacted differently to Aminah's message, most of them with hesitation. The number of people who attended the halaqa slowly decreased, probably because of participants' doubts, although the decrease was generally attributed to the end-of-term increase in homework.

By spring 1997, only two people took their places on the Persian carpet in front of Aminah—the female president of UMMA and me. The president apologized for the small attendance, saying that people had actually promised to come. But Aminah smiled and now seemed confident about discussing her involvement in the Hizb al-Tahrir. She told us that she did not care that we were so few; Allah would reward her for her efforts. As a member of the Hizb al-Tahrir, a party whose goal was to establish the Islamic way of life—to establish the shari'a, the implementation of the akhira (judgment in the hereafter), and the wahy—it was her duty to convey this message to other Muslims.

During the hour that followed, Aminah told us about the party's viewpoint on present Muslim states and on nationalism: They were all incompatible with the Muslim idea of the *umma*. She emphasized her arguments against American society with examples from Chicago and the United States, using them to highlight the Hizb al-Tahrir's ideas about Islamic rule, community, and authority. She argued that, in the United States, there was confusion about almost every subject of Islamic knowledge. Although one of the most important Muslim organizations in the country, the Islamic Society of North America (ISNA),[62] had established a *fiqh* (Islamic jurisprudence) council,[63] people did not know about the society and its *fatwas* (legislative opinions according to Islamic law). People spent a lot of time quarreling about basic issues, she said, because there was no one to tell them about the *hukm shar'i* (legal judgment of the *shari'a*). The Hizb al-Tahrir, however, was not marked by such inner confusion. It could be characterized as a political movement based on the principle of *siyasa* (politics)—"that which is good for the people." It was the people—the community—who gave the assigned person the right to implement the *shari'a*, and they gave that right to one ruler at a time. The *khalifa* was not the absolute possessor of authority, because in the end absolute supremacy belonged only to God.

Aminah's presentations included more than an interpretation of Islam as a social and political system, rooted in divine revelation and pitted against human idolatry and ignorance. Her interpretation positioned itself against other groups of Muslims, who believed that Islam was compatible with democracy, with United Nations resolutions, and with voting in elections. She attacked a national Muslim organization, ISNA, for its alleged lack of efforts in telling people what Islam was about, thus neglecting to create a basis for a coherent community. Islam, according to Aminah, could only be truly implemented if Muslims shunned such organizations, along with the Western societal processes that she found polluted by human conditions.

Still, that so many of the UMMA women stopped attending her *halaqas* implied that hers was not the Islam with which they wanted to affiliate. To renounce political and social activism, both nationally and internationally, was too contradictory to their practice of Islam and their views on raising awareness of Muslim concerns in America. Therefore, the *halaqa* fell apart. People came only as long as they felt that they gained something from the knowledge that the teacher conveyed. If the message was unacceptable, inconsistent, or uninspiring, they simply stopped coming.

Halaqas *according to the Peacenet Curriculum*

Halaqas were created so that Muslim students could learn about and discuss Islam, as well as get to know one another. Because attendance was not always consistent, some MSA chapters adopted the Peacenet Curriculum, which included a defined and disciplined teaching strategy. Peacenet began in 1995, possibly at the University of Michigan (I never was able to verify its origins). Its first training curriculum was developed that year, with eighteen subjects, including *sira, tajwid* (intoned recitation of the Qur'an), *hadith, fiqh,* comparative religion, Arabic language, character building, current affairs, and sports.[64] Peacenet in no way presented itself as an alternative to existing Muslim youth organizations. Instead, it was a program for small *halaqas* (with four to five members) within larger groups such as the MSA. One "sister" from the Chicago area, Noor, was on the Peacenet steering committee. She was also the *amira* (female leader) of a Peacenet group at the University of Illinois at Chicago, where she was studying for her master's in education. During an interview with two young women at the MWA/UIC, I was introduced to the activities and aspirations of Peacenet within that small group of women.[65]

The group had met for a year. Meetings were held every Saturday morning from 6:00 to 8:00 A.M. in the home of one of the students. The group had chosen to meet this early to be able to pray *fajr* prayer (the ritual prayer prescribed for the period from dawn until just before sunrise) together. Rules for attendance were strict. Ordinary members had to pay ten cents for every minute they were late, and the *amira* had to pay twenty-five cents. The only valid excuses were illness or parents' need for their daughter's help. The women appreciated the "class environment" in which the teaching and learning were taken seriously. Members were expected to study, and their knowledge was tested by an exam at year's end. They also stressed the friendship that the group fostered. The women usually stayed after the lesson to continue their discussion of the day's texts or to discuss personal experiences in relation to their religion. The education had proved so successful that one of the informants considered dropping her plans to become a pharmacist and going overseas to study *shari'a*. Another said that her parents were considering enrolling their younger daughter in another Peacenet circle.

Although both women agreed that the structure of the curriculum heightened students' motivation, they were also certain that the group's success depended on the person who was in charge. Had the leader been more "laid back," the group probably would have accomplished less. Peacenet groups depended more on the authority and knowledge of the leader than any other *halaqa*. The success of this particular *halaqa* owed much to the leadership of a woman who was not only one of the brains behind Peacenet's curriculum but also one of the most active young Muslim women in the Chicago area. Other Peacenet groups that I attended had a more relaxed relationship to the curriculum and standards, so that little difference showed between those Peacenet groups and ordinary *halaqas*.

"YOUNG" ISLAMIC INTERPRETATIONS OF SCIENCE, ETHNICITY, AND GENDER

Three predominating concepts in the MSA's understanding of Islam were science, ethnicity, and gender. Looking at these three concepts provides a clear glimpse of the central ideological challenges that Islam faces in American society and the responses of young Muslims to those challenges. Their responses are important because they reveal how young Muslim adults bridge very complex elements in their lives—or, at least, attempt to "interpret away" apparent contradictions.

Science: Showing the Validity of Islam

Science came to play a role within young Muslims' definition of their identity, their community, the world, and the universe through the combination of their academic studies and the role that the natural sciences played in the surrounding society. To simultaneously believe in the absolute power of Allah and in the methods, theories, and results of science, these students had to understand the two as absolutely complementary. Charismatic speakers such as Hamza often used scientific paradigms to argue that Islam encompasses all truths. For example, his continuous appeal to the audience to "ponder" and "scrutinize," and his description of the school as "a place of intellect," stressed the common view among Muslim college students that their faith is verified by rational and scientific ways of thinking.

Another example of the use of science as an argument for Islam came at a *halaqa* held at the University of Chicago in the fall of 1995. The chapter's vice-president was discussing a short, illustrated booklet, *The Amazing Qur'an*, which included a comparison between the Scripture and prominent scientific investigations. He began by arguing that the Qur'an was the proof of God. Although science had been used as an argument against Islam for centuries, he said, it was evident that science had, point by point, proved the Qur'an to be right. Whether we talked about the creation of the world, the "big bang," the theory of atoms, the theory of evolution, or the stages that a fetus undergoes during a nine-month pregnancy, they were all described in the Qur'an. It was just not until now, he said, that we understood the signs in the text.

The relationship between science and Islam was shown as complementary in Hamza's and the MSA/UC's presentations. Speakers used science to interpret and argue for the value of Islam, while Islam was claimed to have predicted the results of science. By using this kind of argument, proponents of Islam claimed an authority for Islam that showed it as consistent with reason and modernity.[66]

Ethnicity: Showing the Universal Message of Islam

Ethnicity—or, rather, the transcendence of ethnicity—was another important element in the way that Muslim college students interpreted and understood Islam. MSA members had roots in many different countries, and the students worked hard to create common ground among them. From time to time, MSA chapters arranged bake sales and rallies in support of Palestinians, the children of Iraq, or the Bosnian population in the Yugoslavian civil war. This public support of Muslims in other parts of the world underscored the MSA's transethnic and activist interpretation of Islam, based on the idea of the suffering global *umma*. Focusing on the living conditions of Muslims in the war zones of the world was seen as a religious obligation, ideally creating fertile ground for change.

By claiming to be Muslims before anything else (such as Pakistani or Tunisian), some MSA members diverged from—if they did not outright break with—the self-definitions of their parents and their ethnic heritage. In so doing, they set the boundaries of what they saw as a *Muslim* community. The break appeared most clearly to me when I visited a Palestinian family on the Southwest Side during Ramadan in January 1997. The family's oldest daughter was a member of the MSA/UIC, and because I had asked her to grant me an interview, she had invited me for *iftar* that evening.

I was introduced to her family and served mint tea while seated on a white, plastic-covered sofa. The girl told me that hospitality was an essential part of Islam. She continued her explanation as we were called to the table. Her mother had prepared a huge dish of Maghluba ("upside-down chicken"), a salad, and a large bowl of fresh dates. As I expressed my gratitude, the daughter once again said that generosity was a fundamental part of Islam. Her mother interrupted, obviously hurt by all the references to Islam alone, and said, "Now we are talking about *my* country and *my* customs. This is *Arab* culture!"

Although both mother and daughter were expressing pride in a communal identity, each saw her "community" differently. The daughter defined it by religion only, while her mother defined it by her ethnic background, of which religion was only one part.

Others more directly expressed an estrangement from—and even a disappointment with—their ethnic heritage. A twenty-year-old student at the University of Illinois at Chicago said:

> Me and my sister, we don't go that often [back to India]. We go probably every nine or ten years, maybe. . . . I was born in India. Until I was six years old, I was in India. Everything just seemed too different [when

we went back]. My cousins—I became very attached to them in the month that I spent there. But then when you get back here—I don't know—you forget about them. When I went back this summer, I was so attached to them. I would write letters to them. The weird thing is that in India, even though there are so many mosques, there are so many people who consider themselves to be educated in Islam, the majority of the people aren't very Islamic. Among my cousins, there is only one family that has the same Islamic knowledge that I do, and I consider myself to have a very low level of Islamic knowledge.... That really hurt me, because I expected them to know so much more, because they know the language, they know Urdu, and there are so many books on Islamic knowledge. But they are so materialistic, and the only thing that they want to do is to come to America, because America is the window to the world, or whatever it is—America or Saudi Arabia. They just want to get out of there.... The only way that I think that I can help them is by praying to *Allah subhanahu wa ta'ala* (Allah, praised and glorified is He) for them.[67]

Certainly, reactions against ethnic pasts are one means of dealing with the demands of a hybrid identity. Whereas parents are often closely attached to memories of places in the Middle East or South Asia, young people who have encountered those places only during vacations do not always feel a sense of belonging.

I found that young Muslim Americans who chose an Islamic definition of identity came from families in which the Islamic tradition was either as strong as the family's ethnic identity or a strong component of it. Both of these last informants came from families in which mosque attendance, weekend schools, and an Islamically defined moral code were the norm. Being Muslim ultimately came to form the younger person's primary self-definition probably because of two factors: her minimal experience with the country or region from which her family came and the ease with which Islam allowed her to carve out her identity. As second-generation immigrants, young Muslim Americans faced the choice of forcefully declaring their heritage or giving it up altogether and assimilating into the American mainstream. Islam offered an ideology and a community (the *umma*) that claimed to transcend national borders and come from divine decree. Such an identification, therefore, undoubtedly looked and felt stronger to these young Muslims than an ethnic definition based on a national state or zone that might disappear tomorrow.[68]

Gender Roles: Showing Islam as Enhancing Female Dignity

MSA strategies for erasing "cultural innovations" also focused on the issue of gender, particularly the formulation of womanhood. Students not only criticized certain practices within their countries of origin; they also condemned ideologues that their parents held in high esteem. Female MSA members, for instance, criticized Abul A'la Mawdudi, the founder of the Jama'at Islami, for his acceptance of physical punishment and seclusion for women. These female students saw it as their God-given right and duty to be intellectually assertive and physically mobile.[69] Being a Muslim woman was associated with a strong sense of pride, marked by one's actions and, ideally, by wearing the *hijab*. The only authority these young women felt obliged to submit to, they claimed, was that of God and His commands.

As they attempted to break the boundaries of submission, silence, and isolation, these active Muslim women resembled non-Muslim feminists. But none of the Muslim women I met ever called themselves feminists, and they encouraged one another not to do so. They saw feminism as an ideology that disgraced women and the family structure. To them, feminism preached an excessive exposure of women's sexuality that Muslim women saw as destructive to their dignity, making them an even more vulnerable target for male exploitation. Their idea of liberation was the toning down of female sexuality.

By moving voluntarily into a "Victorian Age,"[70] these women believed themselves able to fully accomplish what the past decades of Western feminism had accomplished only in part. This is not to say that covering up—even completely—always had the desired effect. As a twenty-year-old college student at the University of Illinois at Chicago observed:

> People have a certain natural beauty. No matter how much you try to cover yourself up, there is always going to be certain things that men find attractive about you. For example, one of my friends, *subhana Allah*, she covers herself very well. She wears the *jilbab*, she wears the *hijab*, and she completely covers herself. Yet there are still some men who find her attractive. When we were in high school, one of my teachers—it was kind of strange—noticed that she had very beautiful

eyes. . . . He called her up to ask her a question about her report. She said, "What is wrong with it?" And all of a sudden, he just looked into her eyes. And she kind of looked away, because she was embarrassed or whatever. And he said, "Ah, you have so beautiful eyes." So you can cover yourself up, but people will have natural beauty. And you can't hide that, because that was something that *Allah subhanahu wa ta'ala* gave you.[71]

A central but unspoken aspect of this quote is that the representative of non-Muslim America was a teacher and a man. The risk and attendant dangers of yielding to the sexual temptations of the dominant society and to those who are powerful in it (for instance, men, teachers) became an implicit argument for wearing the *hijab*.[72] That many young Muslim women chose the *hijab* when they left home represented in part a stand against such temptations, giving them more individual mobility, as well as the necessary trust from parents and family that allowed them to go to college.

The second argument against secular feminism was that it caused the deterioration of the family structure. To many of the MSA women I met, marriage and the fulfillment of wife- and motherhood were inherent in their definition of womanhood. A number of female Muslim students I met on Chicago campuses were already married, whereas others got married or engaged or looked for possible mates while in college.[73] The road to marriage varied. Some got to know their future husbands through the MSA. Others chose arranged marriages, in which family members and friends suggested candidates and then allowed the woman to converse with them. Whether the couple knew each other beforehand or not, contact was initiated and supervised by parents and older relatives. Premarital "dating" did not take place. All my informants stressed that they had been autonomous in their choice of a mate and that, very often, they had considered more than one candidate. As Noor said when she chose to marry:

We [Noor and the man who had asked for her hand] went to Dunkin' Donuts. It was so funny—it was the coolest little thing. We were walking in, and I remember that I was walking toward the table. I noticed his shoes, right? He was wearing these kind of leather sandals with straps up front with white socks. I was like, "Oh, cool! This is a different one," 'cause every time someone would come, they were always dressed up in their black suits. Nice tie. Very formal. It was hard to tell the personality. . . . I had also heard before from my aunt that he was quiet, that he was not going to say anything unless it was necessary. If it will benefit me or anyone else, he will talk. Otherwise, why say anything? So I though, "Oh, great, I have a quiet one," because in my past I have had experiences with proposals where [the man would] introduce himself and in five minutes, I would try to ask him a question, pull something out of him, I would look at my mom who would sit with us, and I was like, "That's it; let's go." So I was expecting something like that.

So my Mom, my aunt, and a cousin, they sat at a group table and let us sit at a two-people table. I noticed that he was tall. When I came to sit down, I was so afraid to bounce into his knees. I was very careful. When I first sat down, I did not push my knees underneath. But I was like, "Sit well; sit well under the table." So I sat down. For some reason, I did not look straight at him yet. And I was like, "*Salam 'alaykum.*" And he was like, "*'Alaykum al-salam,*" and then he started. He started! And he was, like, "How are you?" and he just went on, and it was more like a question-answer session. He asked, and I said something. And I asked. It was back and forth. And I saw his face, and it was so cute. . . . It was, like, when we talked, I started to see little features of him, and it was an interesting conversation. We went on and on. We could have gone on for hours, but we had a guest at our home, and my mother literally had to pull us apart. . . . It was like, "Come on you guys. We gotta go." And I was like, "One more question, please." And she was like, "Okay, Noor, one question." So I was like, "Tell me about your life from the earliest that you can think of until now." But he was brief because of the time we had. But it was a very nice conversation.

And so we got home, and he did not come in. He stood outside. He stayed with my cousin. I stayed with my aunt and my mom. My aunt went to him and asked, "So what do you think? Do you want to go on with this? Talk to her more?" And he . . . said, "Yeah, why not?" And she came back and asked me. She said, "I'll give you time. I'll give you a week to think about it and talk to your parents." And I was like, "O.K., that's fine." So after two days, I called her up: "O.K., let him call me. I'm ready." And then he called after a week. . . . So we talked an hour and a half, . . . and we started e-mailing and then talking on the phone. It was hard to see each other. Finally, we decided that this was it. It came to a point where we had to decide yes or no. We couldn't go any further, otherwise we would have gotten into a major disposition for an unmarried couple. . . . We set a date for him to come, and he came. . . .

The following day, we went to the courthouse [and] got our marriage license. Then we went to Devon [Avenue] to look for jewelry or whatever. We could not find any that day. Afterward, we went . . . to the mosque, [and the shaykh] did our Islamic contract. Afterward, . . . my mother gave him a big hug. It was like, "Oh, my God! You are my son-in-law. You are a part of the family now." Finally I was able to shake his hand, because beforehand he would ask me, "When I come to the airport, we are not going to do anything like hug or shake hands. Definitely no, right?" We got to a point where we were close friends. So the whole process was really nice, considering that I saw him only once.[74]

The man Noor chose to marry was not the first possible husband-to-be to whom she was introduced. As was the case with many of the young women I spoke with, making the choice was the result of a long process. The young women saw it as their Islamic right to say yes or no, to make the choice autonomously. The fact that many of them were well educated made it easier for them to make such claims and to turn down proposals. Both the young women and their parents were aware of this advantage. One mother on the South Side proudly told me that her daughter had refused the many offers she had received from men because she wanted her degree first. Unlike some of their sisters of faith who married in high school, Muslim college women were not expected to marry the first person their parents found for them. From what I observed, their professional and class status, along with their ability to understand and participate in the scientific and intellectual issues of the day, assured them a social and communal value that expanded their relative autonomy. This autonomy extended to when and with whom they wanted to participate in the religious institution of marriage.

Discussion

This chapter calls attention to the ways in which American secular society deeply affects Muslim educational institutions and Muslim college students in its midst. Although Islamic colleges are established as visible alternatives to the dominant non-Muslim-American society, these institutions still adopt the form and terminology of mainstream American institutions. Both the EWU and the AIC were "colleges," their teachers were "professors," and they offered "bachelor's degrees." Their survival depended on offering the full complement of academic programs recognized by society at large as much as on their dedication to a religious worldview. The result mirrored what happened in Muslim full-time schools: Muslim colleges experienced an inner conflict between philosophy and survival. But whereas Muslim full-time schools were saved by a state-recognized curriculum that allowed their wealthier students to attend prestigious non-Muslim universities, a Muslim college such as the AMC was handicapped by a curriculum that left no door open to further specialization.

As for the MSA, although chapters are supervised by campus administrations, the associations are relatively free in their expression of Muslim-ness within the student society at large. Although MSA members are Muslims by heritage and choice, their religious behavior is also affected by the country in which they have lived the majority of their lives. They know America as well as they know Islam. When they discuss their religion, their focus on gender roles and science shows how the larger secular environment affects their focus, their preferences, and their religious interpretations. They see Islam as complementary to reason, not its antithesis, because they value logic and reason.

Dedicated young Muslims see themselves as put in America to correct its ignorance and the innovations that, they argue, corrupt Islam and tear apart the Muslim *umma*. They often see themselves as pitted against the religious interpretations and ethnic nostalgia of their parents. Their rejection of ethnicity reveals their desire for an ideal transethnic identity of mythic dimensions, as well as their hope of forming a unified Muslim-American community.

To many dedicated Muslim college students, Islam was their primary source of identity, even though no final decision about Islam as a belief and a practice evolved within the MSAs. Disputes over Sufism (and the ideas and representatives of the Hizb al-Tahrir as partly included but partly excluded from the community) exemplify some of the internal theological rifts. Whereas the efforts of young Muslims born, raised, and educated in the United States may eventually minimize the effects of ethnic diversity within the Muslim community, new diversities and conflicts are likely to arise along other lines (for example, religious interpretation).

Involvement in the MSAs caused many young Muslim-American students to realize that they are next in line, spiritually and physically, to promote and represent the American community of Muslims—not only on campus but also beyond it. MSA activities therefore involve a redistribution of authority and an incentive for new expressions of institutional forms. In that sense, the MSA and all that it represents pose a personal and ideological challenge to the adult Sunni Muslims who still remain the leaders of the community.

5 The House of God and Beyond

Understanding Islam, Islamic Identities, and Islamic Authority among Adults

A DESCRIPTION of the religious efforts of first-generation Muslim immigrants to the United States can too easily become a description of a transitory period: Muslim immigrants come with certain Islamic practices and interpretations of their faith that change, are rejected, and ultimately disappear in the new environment. Younger generations, influenced by daily living in the United States and by knowing the new system and language, take over, and they forcefully promote their ideas of Islam to fellow believers and to fellow Americans who do not share their faith.

But such a depiction is utterly wrong. As this chapter will show, first-generation Muslims (in Chicago, primarily those who arrived during and after the mid-1960s) have had a profound impact on the outlook of the Muslim-American community as a whole. They have done so mostly through the high offices they have held and continue to hold in the numerous Muslim institutions and organizations that they founded. In addition, whereas the institutional strategies of second- and third-generation Muslims are largely synchronized within organizations such as the MSA, the paths that first-generation immigrants have taken in their implementation of Islam differ greatly. In the 1990s, these differences both accentuated and reinforced the already dynamic character of the Muslim-American community.

In presenting the different kinds of institutions that these Muslim immigrants have created, this chapter introduces some that are particular to the American environment. These institutions can be considered "paramosques," because they are grassroots alternatives or supplements to the mosque.

To exemplify the dynamics that exist among first-generation Muslims in their institutions, the chapter describes a conflict between the Institute for Islamic Information and Education (III&E) and the most prominent Sufi *tariqa* (order) in Chicago, the Naqshbandiyya-Haqqaniyya. While Sufism and Sufi organizations are not paramosques, they have a long history in Islam and are a part of Muslim-American life. However, some members of the community see Sufism as corrupting Islam's genuine message and therefore oppose it on religious grounds. The difference in viewpoints between Sufism and its opponents is covered through a focus on two prominent figures representing these beliefs within the Chicago context.

Because paramosques are not the sole institutions outside the mosque through which Islam is interpreted, a section of this chapter is devoted to describing "professional Muslims." These people, most of them academics, visit churches, mosques, and schools around the city and lecture to both Muslims and non-Muslims about Islam. This section reveals the influence of an American academic career and status on the presentation of a religious message.

The chapter also describes the history and activities of four major mosques in Chicago, looking at the impact of ethnicity within these institutions: In what way does ethnic affiliation affect membership, practices, and leadership? How does ethnicity affect relations among mosques? And how does ethnicity affect the Muslim-American community's ability to act cohesively?

Finally, the chapter investigates the interpretation of Islam and Islamic authority within the mosque. Included are the role of the *khatib* (the person who delivers the sermon during Friday prayers) and a study group for women who gather each weekend in one of Chicago's major mosques to study and discuss their faith. The description of the women's group in particular illuminates the interpretation and role of gender among first-generation immigrants.

In all, this chapter sets the scene for a final discussion of *Islam in Urban America*'s two major questions: Is the Muslim community in America truly unified, and can Islam be seen as an American religion? More specifically, how were differences in Islamic interpretation, ethnicity, gender, and social class affecting Chicago's Muslim community by the late 1990s?

PARAMOSQUES IN CHICAGO

Two categories of institutions uniquely represent American Islam. One is the mosque, a well-known structure throughout Islamic history. The other, the paramosque, is a grassroots organization established by the community as a critical supplement to mosques and other traditional Muslim organizations and structures in the American context.

Larry Poston, the professor of religion who coined the term "paramosque" in the early 1990s, has described how this institution gained ground in America as a result of the new, extended, and exhausting role that mosques were forced to take in this environment: American mosques "combin[e] prayer room, educational center, political forum, social hall, informal law court, and counseling clinic all under one roof."[1] According to Poston, the mosque's transformation into an "Islamic center" weakened the institution's traditional religious character, which in turn was further weakened by internal "excessive competition" along ethnic and national lines.[2] Whereas mosques in America (despite stressing an all-inclusive Islamic ideal) often took on the parental role of helping immigrants deal with homesickness, the paramosques, with their emphasis on Islamic spirituality and activism, emerged as important spiritual alternatives.

In Chicago, the institutional split between mosque and paramosque is much less prominent than in Poston's presentation. Chicago-area paramosques are indeed caretakers of activist, grassroots functions that the mosque, as a community center, is not equipped to handle. But although paramosques by their very existence implicitly criticize the mosque, they need the symbolic value of the mosque to validate their activities. Paramosques often depend on the authority that mosques, as religious institutions, grant them.

National Islamic "paramosque" organizations in the Chicago area include the Islamic Society of North America (ISNA),[3] the Islamic Circle of North America (ICNA), the American Muslim Council (AMC), and the Council on American Islamic Relations (CAIR). A number of ISNA's annual national conventions were held in Chicago in the 1990s. Yet ISNA has no apparent effect on the daily lives and activities of Chicago Muslims. Although the people I interviewed described their experiences at ISNA conventions, they seemed to view ISNA as a distant, uninspiring giant.[4] ISNA pamphlets, flyers, and posters were absent from the major Islamic centers, except at annual-convention time.

By contrast, the activities and aspirations of the ICNA closely affected Chicago-area Muslims. The local ICNA chapter distributed its own magazine, *Assalamu 'Alaikum Chicago Muslims*, which carried short articles (mostly about religious celebrations such as *hajj*, *'Id*, and Ramadan), announcements of local and national meetings, and a comprehensive list of local mosques. The ICNA's strong position in Chicago included productions by the foundation Soundvision. Located near downtown, Soundvision has since the early 1990s produced a wide range of high-quality multimedia products "dedicated to education and *da'wa*" for children as well as for adults.[5] The video series *Adam's World*, which includes the titles *Take Me to the Kaba* and *Happy to Be Muslim*, introduces Islam to the very young, using devices from mainstream children's programs, such as catchy songs and cute puppets.[6] Software such as "*salat* bases" and "*tafsir* bases" targets more mature and computer-literate audiences, and videos such as *Choosing Islam* and *The Book of Signs* present Islam to non-Muslims.

The Book of Signs, with its claim to show equivalence between major scientific breakthroughs and the words of the Qur'an, was also aimed at non-practicing Muslims by asserting a compatibility between Islam and the ideological basis of modern Western society. During my visits to Chicago mosques, libraries at Muslim full-time schools, and Muslim homes, Soundvision's products were almost everywhere, and I often heard Adam (from *Adam's World*) singing about the oneness of Allah from the TV set in the children's bedrooms. Soundvision's commercial success derives from the company's fluency in, and linkage of, two spheres of knowledge—the electronic–digital and the religious. American life, integrated and formulated according to Islamic norms, was fixed on CD-ROMs and videotapes, promoting a hybrid definition of Muslim selfhood in which nation, science, and religion are symbiotic allies, not competitors.

The AMC and CAIR also had a voice in the Chicago area. AMC's telephone hotline announced monthly meetings,[7] and CAIR distributed "Action Alerts" and arranged talks and film screenings in the major Muslim centers. Although both the AMC and CAIR claimed to work on a "grassroots basis,"[8] and their activities were noticeable in the area, their focus on national politics and events put them in the distant and detached position of ISNA, dwelling in the halls of power in Washington, D.C. While community members might discuss the activities of the AMC and CAIR, neither organization inspired or directed local activism.

Though some paramosques in the Chicago area claimed the entire country as their audience, their activities were mainly local. One such organization was the Islamic Information Center of America (IICA), in the suburb of Des Plaines.[9] Founded in 1983 and steered by Dr. Musa Qutub, a professor of geography at Northeastern University, the IICA's primary concern was to provide information about Islam to non-Muslims. Dr. Qutub stressed that the IICA was not proselytizing.[10] Rather, it sought to answer questions that the media and the public and doubts raised about Islam, mostly by arranging seminars and lectures, participating in radio programs, and publishing a newsletter, *The Invitation*. Despite the IICA's seemingly defensive strategy, Dr. Qutub took pride in the number of people who had converted to Islam as a result of the organization's outreach. That "many now accept Islam over the phone," he said, proved to him that Islam was "a religion of proof" appealing to the human intellect.[11]

The Institute for Islamic Information and Education

Another important paramosque, the Institute for Islamic Information and Education (III&E), is housed in the northern corner of the Muslim Community Center (MCC) on Chicago's North Side. The III&E is not an official part of the MCC, but it has a noticeable impact on its host. Whereas the MCC's only public indication of Muslim-ness during my fieldwork was a green sign hanging over the entrance, announcing the name and function of the center in English and Arabic, the III&E proclaimed Islam in every possible way. A faded poster of the *Ka'ba*, surrounded by the names of the prophets of Islam and Christianity, filled the large window facing the street. At the door, a sign welcomed visitors to the "Islamic Reading Room," as the III&E offices were generally known.

Although the sign indicated that the III&E was open at only certain times of the day, the door was usually open, and the rooms behind it teemed with activity. People on their way to or from the mosque dropped by to read magazines, books, and pamphlets available in the book stacks or simply to discuss their faith. To the left of the door lay stacks of the III&E's latest pamphlets and of the *Da'wah Newsletter.* A second room, toward the back, emphasized the organization's focus on publishing, with stacks of small, colorful pamphlets and packed brown cardboard boxes destined for all corners of the nation.

The managing director of III&E, Dr. Amir Ali, was born in the Indian state of Hyderabad and migrated to Pakistan in 1952. He arrived in the United States in 1962, where he completed his Ph.D. in biochemistry. Despite the often provoking and uncompromising viewpoints in his publications, he was a kind, cheerful person who always seemed to have time for a heated discussion. Coffee, pizza, or some of the spicy food of his homeland was generously served in the back office as he presented his formulations of Islam with unshakable certainty. His wife, Mary Ali, was the editor of the organization's newsletter and an often requested speaker on the role of women in Islam. A convert from Roman Catholicism, she shared her husband's deep convictions and persistent dedication to Islamic works.

The couple established the III&E in 1985 when they returned from working in Saudi Arabia.[12] The Islamic Reading Room officially opened on November 25, 1988.[13] Although the III&E stressed independence from any foreign government,[14] a foreign influence was evident in the board of trustees, as three of the eight members were from Saudi Arabia.[15] In its first year, the III&E coordinated its *da'wa* work with the ICNA (an organization that Amir Ali did not speak highly of during our interviews).[16] In 1987, the III&E founders launched a twenty-five-year project designed to reach the entire population of North America by the year 2012. The organization's goals, presented both in the organization's numerous publications and on a large poster in the back of the III&E office, included:

1: The removal of mis-information, mis-perception and mis-appre-
hension of Islam and the Muslims from the minds of the American
people.
2: The education of North American people about the true teachings
of Islam to open the door of their entry.
3: The education and training for Islam for those who revert (or convert) and their integration into the Muslim community at large.
4: The recruitment of Muslims of all ages, genders, and races and train
them to become *da'wah* workers.
5: The development of resources, particularly the material resources,
to carry out the mission mentioned above.[17]

Among the III&E's goals was to reactivate Muslims, educate
converts, and inform non-Muslims about Islam. To Amir Ali, *da'wa*
was equivalent to spreading "correct knowledge." He was convinced that powerful public conveyers of issues within and outside the United States—notably, the press and the government—
hid the truth of Islam from the masses.[18] People's ignorance of
Islam, he argued, was "exploited by atheists, secularists, agnos-
tics, Zionists, Fundamentalist Christians and all those who have
an agenda against the Muslims, world over."[19] Amir Ali's attention was particularly directed toward an alleged "Fundamentalist Christian and Zionist Conspiracy" against Islam.[20] Zionists
were presented as puppeteers steering the U.S. government and
media; fundamentalist Christians were presented as the corrupters of Islam's message.

In the aftermath of the Oklahoma City bombing, when various broadcasts and certain politicians accused Muslims and Middle Easterners of being the aggressors,[21] Amir Ali pondered: "In
America, it appears that the value of life of all Americans is not
equal. By all observations the value of life of Jewish and white
Americans is the highest, the blacks and the Spanish speaking
take the next far lower rung, whereas American Muslims, irre-
spective of their national or racial origin, have no value at all."[22]

Amir Ali offered what he believed to be a sensible explanation
for the perception and treatment of Muslims in the United States:
"We know that the American government had been pressured by
the Israeli government to stop or restrict the immigration of Muslims into the U.S. and find a way to stop the growth of Islam."
He similarly saw fundamentalist Christians, most of all as writ-

ers and publishers of books on Islam, as harmful to the understanding of Islam and the treatment of Muslims within the United States and as deliberately contributing to an intellectual decay within the Muslim world.[23] In that sense, they promoted the downfall of the *umma*:

> The goal of [the Christian] mission [in Muslim countries] has been to cool the flames of establishing Islam as a way of life. Missions took children of aristocrats, bureaucrats, businessmen, teachers and professors, charged them high tuition fees and gave them enough anti-Islamic education in a subtle way and turned the entire leadership into anti-Islam, yet remaining cultural Muslims. Now the entire Muslim land is in the hands of secular minded "Muslims" who hate Islam and practicing Muslims.[24]

It was this alleged status quo of conspiracy and ignorance, formulated as "cultural Islam," that the III&E wanted to counterbalance. It did so by spreading information about Islam to American non-Muslims, "who are, in general, decent and truth loving and would support the right thing,"[25] particularly those who were most capable of causing change. III&E pamphlets were an ever-present part of the literature available at the Islamic Awareness Week's *da'wa* booths, at *'Id* dinners where non-Muslims were among the guests, and when representatives of larger interfaith organizations—such as the Council for a Parliament of the World's Religions—visited Muslim centers in the Chicago area. In 1994, the III&E claimed to have distributed more than 3.5 million copies of its literature, covering sixty titles of tracts, flyers, pamphlets, and booklets, in English and Spanish. By 1995, according to the III&E's founders, twenty-five book titles had been distributed to more than 200 libraries, mainly in prisons.[26]

Publishing pamphlets was not the III&E's only method for reaching and teaching the American public. In 1990, the organization opened the service Islam on the Phone, where curious people could ask questions about Islam. In 1993, the organization aired the program *Welcome to Islam* for three months on a TV channel in the Chicago area. Of higher priority, though, were the meetings and seminars that Amir Ali and his wife gave to non-Muslim groups in the III&E office and elsewhere in the Chicago area. Curiously, such seminars were regularly given to future

Christian missionaries to Muslim countries.[27] Although Amir
Ali argued strongly against what he saw as a "fundamentalist,
Christian conspiracy," he nevertheless advocated interfaith work:
"We should impart the message of Islam, through interaction and
right communication. Interfaith dialogue will be helpful in creating the proper environment in the Land of Liberty."[28] Although
Christians were "adversaries," they might—as might any other
stratum of American society—prove useful as "helpers" if they
received the correct information, the correct teaching.

Amir Ali criticized not only elements of American and other
Western societies for misleading the public about the essence of
Islam. To an even larger extent, he also criticized the community
of Muslims—the people whom he expected to know and act according to the message of their religion—for their lack of engagement. In particular, he believed that Muslims living in America
and Europe, who had access to powerful non-Muslim governments, should understand their obligations: "Muslims living in
the Western countries have a duty to educate the populations so
that meddling in Muslim countries' affairs becomes unpopular
and helping them in a way Muslim countries desire becomes popular."[29] Following this idea, the III&E did its best to engage and
teach the local Muslim community. The organization offered a
number of classes on Islamic and Qur'anic studies, Arabic, and
tajwid (intoned recitation of the Qur'an), as well as instruction
of new "Islamic workers."

*The III&E's Critique of the Current State of
the Muslim Umma*

In the 1990s, the III&E organized several *da'wa* conferences that
were attended by prominent national and international Muslim
activists. The goal was to equip all attentive Muslims with the
understanding and skills necessary for generating the "correct
knowledge," a knowledge that had gone into decay and been
replaced by the ignorance of "cultural Islam." Amir Ali said:

> The immigrant community is so ignorant about their duties and what
> Islam is that they don't know what to do. They think that their own
> culture is Islam. . . . Allah has promised that if you follow the Qur'an
> and do good deeds and not commit *shirk* [belief in more than one God,

which in Islam is understood as a major blasphemy] you will be a superpower in the world. That is a promise of the Qur'an [verse] 24:25.[30] It is a promise, and God keeps the promise. So I ask people if they believe and do good work. And they say yes. And I ask them if they commit *shirk*, and they say no. And I say that Allah has said that if you are a believer, then he will make you a superpower, then how come Muslims are such a disgraced power in the world? Did Allah lie to us? Either Allah lied to us or we are lying to ourselves. And people accept that they must be lying to themselves. But how come they do not correct themselves? Because they don't know how.[31]

That it is duty of all Muslims to reform themselves and thereby—presumably—reconstitute the community of Muslims as the *khair-umma* (the best of nations) is a time-honored motivator among Muslims of the world today.[32] Ideas of "reformulation" and "re-education" are prominent among revivalist Muslim thinkers and movements.[33] Although Amir Ali agreed with the goals of such movements, he claimed no direct affiliation with any of them. In an attack on two *shaykhs* of the Naqshbandiyya-Haqaniyya Sufi order, he stated in a pamphlet that they were "working with Western powers, kings, presidents, and dictators of the Muslim countries to defeat the Islamic movements of *Jamaat-e-Islami, Ikhwan al-Muslimoon, Tanzeem-e-Islami, Khilafah* and similar movements [that seek] to establish Islam in totality in Muslim countries."[34] The pamphlet expressed acceptance of these movements *only* to the extent that their motives resembled those of the III&E. According to Amir Ali, because these movements interpreted God's message in the right way, they also struggled to establish Islam as a political system. Because of this ambition, and because of their truthfulness to Islam, these movements were persecuted by the powers of evil, the "CIA, FBI, all of the other Western powers, Russia, India, Israel and all other Islam and Muslim haters."[35]

Amir Ali saw the apparent apathy of twentieth-century Muslims, in both the East and the West, as resulting from their alienation from the true message of Islam. Muslims, in his eyes, had become the puppets of *imams* and *shaykhs* sponsored by Western governments and agencies. The issues corrupting the faith of today's Muslims were more ideological than cultural. The only way to regain what had been lost was to revert to the primary sources—the Qur'an and *sunna*—to find the unmediated intentions of God. As he told me:

> Don't accept opinions. Accept what is Qur'an and *sunna*. Islam is not a religion of conjecture or doubt or hearsay. Islam is a religion of knowledge. Of revealed knowledge. And all the revealed knowledge is recorded. Unfortunately, today's Muslims have become Muslims of hearsay and [inaudible]. They do not have the attachment to the sources. . . . Today's Muslims have become followers of cultist leaders, and they make people their own followers: "Follow me." . . . People either follow this *shaykh* or this *imam* or this *mullah* or that '*ulama*'. And a lot of people are not teaching strictly from the Qur'an and *sunna*. They are teaching from their own understanding of Islam. Some people are outright dishonest. I have come across some outright dishonest *shaykhs*. They take material out of context.[36]

This statement, along with the III&E's overall ideological profile, left little doubt about the influence of revivalist Muslim movements—notably, the Ikhwan al-Muslimun, the Jama'at-i Islami (see Chapter 1), and the Salafi.

The Salafi is a neo-orthodox Islamic-reform movement that sees secularism and Westernism as the source of all corruption in contemporary Islamic communities. Current Salafis are active in Muslim and non-Muslim societies, although the structure of the "movement" is so loose (with no real leadership) that some Salafis refer to it using the term "*manhaj*" (thought, approach, idea). In the United States, there are notable attempts to create organizations that represent Salafi thought—for example, the Qur'an and Sunnah Society. Some of my informants, mainly those critical of Salafi interpretations, claimed that the Salafis were supported by the Saudi regime, a support that is real in parts of the Muslim world.[37] However, I have no documentation that similar support is generated in the United States. The argument can be seen mainly as an attempt to discredit the Salafis as a group that, in the eyes of many active Muslim Americans, has been bred by a corrupt regime in the Arab world.[38]

However, Amir Ali always stressed that his ideas were his own. His intention was to present Islam in a "new" and "rational" way.[39] It would be fair to assume that he sought to be all-inclusive, to engage as many Muslims as possible (according, of course, to those limits of authority that he set for his interpretation). Still, his self-admitted ideological non-affiliation was put to the test through a conflict in which the III&E was involved during my stay in Chicago. The conflict was played out against the most influential Sufi order in Chicago, the Naqshbandiyya-Haqqaniyya.

The conflict is interesting for several reasons. First, it highlights the diversity of interpretations and practices that exist among Muslim Americans. Second, it expands on a theme raised in the previous chapter—namely, how some immigrant Muslims consider Sufism and Sufi practices controversial and attempt to erase this "fallacy" that has taken firm root in American soil. Third, it exemplifies the potential conflict between "new" paramosque institutions (in this case, the III&E) and older institutions within Islam (in this case, Sufism) while showing the centrality of the mosque to conflict resolution.

REASON AND PASSION: THE III&E VERSUS THE NAQSHBANDIYYA *TARIQA*

The Naqshbandiyya-Haqqaniyya

Sufi orders (sing. *tariqa*, pl. *turuq*) are not paramosques. They were not created in the American context but have a centuries-long history within all parts of the Muslim world. Sufis themselves consider Sufism (*tasawwuf*) as constituted by the Prophet himself. The history of these orders is diverse, as are some of their practices. But some practices are common to them all, such as the ritual of *dhikr*, the status of the *shaykh* as a guide into the spiritual world, the initiation to the order (*bayʻa*), the *silsila* (chain of transmission of knowledge), and the belief that God can be approached on a deep spiritual level.

Branches of three Sufi orders exist in the Chicago area: the Tijaniyya, the Nimatullah, and the Naqshbandiyya-Haqqaniyya. The strategies of the three orders vary. The first two are highly exclusive, allowing only those who have pledged their adherence (*bayʻa*) to the order and its *shaykh* to participate in meetings and *dhikr*. I was therefore unable to make any observations within either of these orders.

The third order, the Naqshbandiyya-Haqqaniyya, displayed a very high level of openness. One of the primary spokespeople of

the *tariqa* in Chicago, Dr. Laleh Bakhtiar, was known in interfaith circles, both on television and in Christian organizations
such as the Lutheran School of Theology in Chicago. *Dhikrs* held
in the Naqshbandiyya-Haqqaniyya were open to whoever wanted
to join in—initiated as well as uninitiated, Muslim as well as
non-Muslim. Some Naqshbandiyya-Haqqaniyya initiates even
claimed that the *shaykh* allowed non-Muslims to join the order.[40]
Because of this openness and outreach, the Naqshbandiyya-
Haqqaniyya received a high level of visibility and attention that
could be perceived as a provocative challenge to those strata in
the Muslim community that judged Sufism to be heresy and
innovation.

Most of the Naqshbandiyya-Haqqaniyya *dhikrs* that I attended
took place in the bookstore of Kazi Publications, a Muslim publishing company on the North Side of Chicago. Kazi Publications,
founded in 1975, claimed to be the largest Muslim publishing
company in the United States. No fewer than 2,000 titles were
in stock, many on Sufism.[41] Its founder, Mr. Liaquat Ali, and
Laleh Bakhtiar directed the affairs of the company. Both were
practicing *murids* (initiates) of the Naqshbandiyya-Haqqaniyya
order.

Every Thursday evening, Kazi hosted the Naqshbandiyya-
Haqqaniyya *dhikr*.[42] The building showed no indications of the
activities inside—and for good reason. In the late 1980s, unknown
arsonists had set fire to the store, which was then located at
another address on the same street.[43] In the late 1990s, between
twenty and thirty people—primarily South Asians, African Americans, and Caucasian Americans—would gather in the main room
of the bookstore, as soft music sounded from a stereo placed
among the piles of books. The women would sit at the back of
the room, near a huge brown couch, and the men would gather
in a half-circle, facing a small platform formed by Persian blan-
kets and pillows. That is where the leader of the *dhikr* would sit.
Although the person taking this position varied, he was usually
the *imam* from the Islamic Cultural Center of Greater Chicago
or a graduate student from the University of Chicago. Whereas
the women's style of clothing was highly diverse, most of the men
dressed stereotypically in red or green turbans, loose pants, and

vests. People would greet one another warmly, the women kissing each other, and the men hugging and pressing their right hands to their own chests.

After the evening prayer, the director would read and comment on a short sermon written by either the Naqshbandiyya-Haqqaniyya *shaykh* of the United States, Hisham Kabbani, or the grand-*shaykh* of the order, Muhammad Nazim al-Haqqani. Then *dhikr* would start, concentrating mostly on the recitation of short *suras* and *ayas* such as *al-Fatiha* and *Ayat al-Kursi*[44] and beautiful names of God (*al-asma' al-husna*), such as *al-Latif* (the Gentle) or *al-Rahman* (the Merciful). *Dhikr* would continue for about an hour, after which coffee, tea, and snacks were served. Several times a year, Shaykh Kabbani visited the congregation, often in connection with large events such as the *Mawlid al-Nabi* (birthday of the Prophet) or the International Milad an-Nabi Conference that the Naqshbandiyya-Haqqaniyya order had held since 1994 at the University of Illinois at Chicago's student center.[45]

A Chicago Murid: Laleh Bakhtiar

One of the most prominent members of the Naqshbandiyya-Haqqaniyya in Chicago is Dr. Laleh Bakhtiar, a tiny woman who always wears her *hijab* so that it leaves a fringe of her black hair visible. Her journey into Islam and Sufism is a story in itself:[46] The youngest daughter of an Irish immigrant mother and an Iranian immigrant father, she was raised a Presbyterian, although she decided to become a Roman Catholic at age eight. Her parents divorced shortly after her birth, so she got to know her father and his religion only when she was twenty-four. She later married an Iranian architect, with whom she published a book on Iranian Sufi architecture.[47]

The couple later left for Iran. While there, Laleh Bakhtiar was introduced to one of the primary American intellectuals on Sufism, Seyyed Hossein Nasr (now a professor of Islamic studies at George Washington University), who became her teacher and whom she considers "one of the most important friends I have ever known."[48] Their friendship initiated her encounter with Sufism and led to her conversion to Islam in 1964. In 1979, she was divorced but stayed with her two children in Iran. Her memory of the revolution was positive—"a positive earthquake, a positive flood"[49]—although she had to struggle financially to keep her life and family together.

In 1979, Laleh Bakhtiar founded the publishing bureau Hamdani Foundation in Tehran. Nine years later, she returned to the United States, where she earned master's degrees in philosophy and counseling psychology and a Ph.D. in educational psychology from the University of New Mexico. When I met her in the summer of 1995, she had worked in Kazi Publications for four years. The depth of her engagement was obvious in the more than fifteen books she had already written or translated.[50]

To Laleh Bakhtiar, Sufism primarily included "traditional psychology": a balancing of reason and passion (the two elements of revelation) representing absolute perfection in word and deed, according to the Qur'an and *sunna*. To her, revelation did not speak merely to human reason but also to human passion and intuition. Through revelation, God made the human soul know and understand its origin, purpose, and true religion: Islam. When I asked Laleh Bakhtiar whether a person could equate Islam with reason, she answered:

> Reason? Very much so. The whole, all the *hadith* and the Qur'an. There are some elements that are based on faith, and you just have to take them or leave them. That God is one, you can never reason that. And we believe that there are angels. We believe in the revelation of the Book. These are things that you can't prove by reason. But everything else—the Islamic sciences and how they developed—is built on reason. Otherwise you cannot be scientific at all. And all the wise words of the Prophet, they are all based on reasoning and controlling the passions. The whole *shari'a* is on controlling your passions. What happens is that reason leads you to understand that you need spirituality. Then, once you get into spirituality, you basically throw reason out and use your intuition. That is where you need a guide [that is, the *shaykh*]. So there is the ability to reason, your parents, your teachers, your environment, those things you can teach yourself or learn by reading books. Intuition you have to learn through a guide. And that is why in Sufism we have this ever-present guide who helps you to train the intuitions. The prayers, the *dhikrs*, the fasting—those things actually increase your intuitive abilities.[51]

For Laleh Bakhtiar, reason was more than an individual capacity. It was tied to revelation and to the teachings and guidance of the *shaykh*. It was exactly here, in the Sufi focus on the *shaykh*, that the seed for a conflict with the III&E lay. As the following section will show, people such as Amir Ali strongly opposed Sufi views and in the end took action against them. Not only did Amir Ali and his allies view the role of the *shaykh* as corruptive; they also saw Sufism as an element planted by malevolent forces to destroy Islam from within.

The Divergent Perspectives of Laleh Bakhtiar and Amir Ali

The role and authority of the Sufi *shaykh* has been a source of conflict within the Muslim community for centuries. For Sufi *murids*, the *shaykh* is the indispensable guide on their mystical path, whereas some non-Sufis find the *shaykh's* role and authority unacceptable. They believe that no one person can stand between the believer and God—as neither a guide nor an intercessor.[52] Among late-twentieth-century Muslims in Chicago, this dispute was still ongoing. When I discussed the subject with my informants, most hesitated before answering. Some called Sufism "an addition to the form of the Muslim constitution,"[53] while others found it religiously radical. As one informant said: "I think they come so deep into it that they do not see the light."[54] A much stronger reaction came from Amir Ali:

Sufi group members, they are not on the main Islam, they are—I consider them on the fringe of Islam. They don't like the whole Islam but only part of Islam. . . . What Sufis have done, in my language, is that they have Christianized Islam . . . [b]y saying that Islam is personal life. You go to the *masjid* and do your prayers, stay home, be a good person, and do the *dhikr*, the remembrance of Allah—whatever they have invented—and that is the whole Islam. From my understanding of Islam, Islam is much more than that. That is the Christian concept of religion: first, be a good person, be a good father, a good mother, and a good family; go to the church once a week and remember Jesus, God, the Lord, whatever; and be a good person, and that's it. Don't try to bring religion into public life or your business life. . . . [The Sufis] have started what they call *bay'a* system, *bay'a* for guidance. But we do not find anything like that in Islam. That is an innovation, because that *bay'a* is to the Prophet Muhammad and his followers, following a total way of life, meaning that we will support the elected or appointed ruler of the country in all . . . political and religious matters. In Islam

> there is no such thing as separation of religion and politics; they are
> one. . . . So what Sufis have done is that they have said, "Let the rulers
> rule the way that they want to," and they have compromised with the
> ruler—respect the ruler, whatever kind of ruler he might be.[55]

Amir Ali's assertions that Sufis have "compromised with the ruler" and respected him no matter who he was (or what he did) introduced another area of historical controversy—namely, how Muslims are expected to behave under a ruler whose government is inconsistent with the message of Islam.[56] This question is particularly crucial for emergent Muslim communities in the non-Muslim West. Immigrant Muslims in these parts of the world face more than the secular division of church and state. Their lives are also directly affected by non-Muslim rulers and governments that base their decisions on societal norms and constitutions that claim respect for humans but not necessarily for the will of God.[57]

On various occasions, the Naqshbandiyya-Haqqaniyya order in the United States has shown a high level of support for the U.S. presidency and government.[58] Given that Amir Ali saw the Western system as highly influenced by anti-Muslim tendencies and conspirators, he could only consider the Sufi orders to be corrupters of Islam, theologically as well as communally. That Amir Ali chose to call the outcome of this alleged corruption "Christian" fit his conspiracy theory. The "corruption" argument supported his claim that Sufis were backed by nations and powers that sought to infiltrate and destroy Islam. Christianity was an obvious metaphor for the dominant "opponent" in American society.

Interestingly, Laleh Bakhtiar did not object when I presented her with the statement that Sufism could be compared to Christianity: "I can see that some might think that, because of the emphasis on love," she said. "Judaism emphasizes fear of God; Christianity emphasizes love of God; but you needed a faith that could bring the two together, and that was Islam—fear of God through *shari'a* and love of God through Sufism. The reason why it is not just Christian is that we follow the *shari'a*."[59] To Laleh Bakhtiar, the only difference between Christianity and Islam was Islam's inclusion of absolute reason (the *shari'a*) controlling the element of passion (love)—an addition that, used with caution, was essential to any development of God-consciousness. By this reasoning, Islam did not erase Christianity. It merely brought it to completion. Islamic tradition, for Laleh Bakhtiar, included much more than the revelation of a message, of a divinely inspired system of knowledge. It also included the gradual development of the human spiritual capacity, in which not only the message but human beings moved toward greater consciousness of themselves and God. Rather than putting an end to Christianity, then, Islam incorporated it as a step toward perfection. Even after the divine message was revealed in its total form to Muhammad, humanity's last prophet, human beings had not reached their potential final stage. Teaching now depended on *shaykhs* who understood the message and knew how to guide their initiates toward that which they, as human beings, were supposed to become.

In contrast to Laleh Bakhtiar, Amir Ali saw the Islamic message as speaking directly and equally to every individual. His Islam also offered guidance for development and God-consciousness but without the need for intermediaries. What most likely made Amir Ali raise his voice against the Naqshbandiyya-Haqqaniyya in particular was its success in North America and Chicago—a success that challenged his interpretations of Islam. Through this challenge, this alleged "twisting of truth," the Naqshbandiyya-Haqqaniyya could be nothing but another trick in the Western conspiracy against Islam, another of the "pseudo-Islamic sects" that Amir Ali believed he had exposed:

And certainly one of their leaders has recently come up with a speech, his name is Nazim Qubrasi, whose home is in Cyprus, but he also operates from England. And his son-in-law, who is the head of the Sufi group in the United States, his name is Hisham Kabbani, he is going way out of the way. He is promoting a new religion, practically. He said in one of his speeches that came out on the Internet that there was an ancient Sufi, called Muhyi al-Din Ibn al-'Arabi, who lived about 1,000 years ago.[60] He said that Muhyi al-Din Ibn al-'Arabi inherited the Seal of the Prophets.[61] It is a blasphemy. Where did he get it from? And then he says that the Seal of the Prophets means [that] the Prophet had the knowledge of the future, and about the last day, and also about after the last day.

This contradicts the Qur'an, [which] says: "No Prophet has been given complete knowledge about the future, of life unseen, except what

Allah wants to give."⁶² When Muhammad was asked when the last day
was coming, he said, "I don't know." The Qur'an confirms that many
times. Only God knows when the last day is coming and what is going
to happen. . . . From then on, he says there is a *Mahdi* [a messiah who
will come before the end of time] who is going to come before the year
2000. Prince Charles of England is to become a Muslim. And all the
kings who have been thrown out of the power, they will conquer their
kingdom and get the kingdom back, and they will become the minis-
ters of this *Mahdi*.⁶³

The idea of the *Mahdi* is relevant to this discussion, because a
number of Muslim sects in America present their founders and
leaders as fulfilling the eschatological, or "end-of-all-times,"
expectation of the *Mahdi*.⁶⁴ The concept of the *Mahdi* is far from
static historically: According to Islamic scholars Yvonne Y. Haddad and Jane I. Smith, it "went from that of a deliverer from present chaotic conditions, to someone who would come at a future
time, and finally (and gradually) to a figure who is to appear at the
end of the world heralding the day of resurrection."⁶⁵ Not surprisingly, Amir Ali, who was raised in India, has written about and
argued against the Ahmadiyya, whose founder claimed to be the
Mahdi. Regardless of whether the Naqshbandiyya-Haqqaniyya
shaykh ever used the title *Mahdi*, Amir Ali's allegation that he
did was a rhetorical device for proving the falsity of Sufi interpretation and authority and the sectarianism of the *shaykhs* and their
initiates.⁶⁶

Further, Amir Ali's rejection of the Naqshbandiyya-Haqqaniyya
and Sufism had its basis in the III&E's conspiracy theory: As the
truth of Islam was globally infiltrated both from beyond and within, the same held true in the United States. Because Zionists and
fundamentalist Christians had been unsuccessful in their attempts
to extinguish the Islamic flame that might illuminate the minds
and hearts of the American people, "they" had redirected their
attack to infiltrate Islam's message from within. The presumed
effect of this "attack" was an ideological fragmentation among
Muslims. According to the III&E, financial support was consequently granted to so-called pseudo-Islamic cults in the United
States, among them the Ahmadiyya and the Nation of Islam. As
Amir Ali wrote in one of his publications:

There is a rise in pseudo-Islamic cults in the West, particularly in the U.S., and such groups are also obtaining moral, technological, financial and media support. Pseudo-Islamic cults create confusion and, sometimes, scare the non-Muslim population away from Islam. A hundred-year-old pseudo-Islamic cult, Qadiyanism, or so-called "Ahmadiya Movement in Islam," is getting support from all sides. Among other American pseudo-Islamic cults are Farrakhanism (so-called Nation of Islam), Moorish Science Temple, Ansarullah Community, Five Percenters and others who are receiving help from anti-Islamic forces.[67]

A third group that Amir Ali described as "pseudo-Islamic" and "cultist" was the Sufi orders (turuq). Whereas groups such as the Nation of Islam and the Moorish Science Temple carried out their activities autonomously, Sufis consider themselves to be orthodox Sunni Muslims and therefore frequent Sunni mosques and Islamic centers for salat al-jum'a and other community and ritual activities. Therefore, it was Sufism—and in particular the Naqshbandiyya-Haqqaniyya—that Amir Ali saw as a threat to correct Islamic practice and the unity of the umma.

Taking Action against Sufism

Amir Ali and his followers did not let their critique of Sufism and the Naqshbandiyya-Haqqaniyya languish in silence. In the summer of 1995, members of the organization Qur'an and Sunnah (an organization until then unknown to the Chicago community) distributed a flyer titled "Excerpts from the Preaching of the Naqshbandi-Haqqani Sufi Order Led by Nazim Qubrasi and Hisham Kabbani" in the MCC just after the Friday prayers. Those of my informants who were in the mosque that day told me that they immediately noticed that one of Amir Ali's co-workers had written the flyer. It claimed to include "genuine material" and "exact quotes" from books, pamphlets, and e-mails distributed by the two Naqshbandiyya-Haqqaniyya Sufi shaykhs responsible for disciples and missions in the United States. Using headings such as "Hisham Kabbani Likes to Look at Madonna on MTV" and "The Mahdi is coming by the year 2,000 and Prince Charles will be his wazir" (vizier), the flyer included strong allegations against the shaykhs' formulation of Islam and their personal credibility.

Although reaction was prompt, it was directed not toward the author but against Amir Ali and the III&E. As Amir Ali said in an interview:[68]

> So what we did was, one of my workers, he put that material on a piece of paper and he published it. But because he works with me, they [assume] that it was I who wrote it and who stood behind all that work. And they are coming with flyers, with material, and they are [putting out] propaganda against me. All the Sufis are joining hands together and attacking my work, just because I supported the expositor of this kind of blasphemous belief.[69]

The following Friday, members of the Naqshbandiyya-Haqqaniyya distributed their own flyers in the MCC. Titled "What the Scholars of Islam Said about Tasawwuf [Sufism]"—and including analyses by Shaykh Muhammad Hisham Kabbani himself—the flyer presented Sufism as deeply rooted in Islamic intellectual tradition. After quoting a number of respected Islamic scholars, the flyer concluded:

> In sum Sufism, in the present, as in the past, is the effective means for spreading the reality of Islam, extending the knowledge and understanding of spirituality, and fostering happiness and peace. With it Muslims can improve, transform, and elevate themselves and find salvation from the ignorance of this world and the misguided pursuit of some materialistic fantasy.[70]

In the flyer, the Naqshbandiyya-Haqqaniyya presented Sufism as an essential means of understanding what Islam is about and to communicate that idea of Islam to non-Muslims. Over the next few months, the Naqshbandiyya-Haqqaniyya and the III&E exchanged a few more flyers. After that, the confrontation died down, mainly because the MCC forbade fighting within its walls and banned the distribution of all antagonistic material. Although the hostilities lasted no more than a few months, and although the MCC's censorship finally silenced the disputants, the conflict was not over. The mosque could neither put an end to nor settle the historical struggle over the essence of Islamic tradition and Islamic leadership—how Islam as knowledge is to be communicated throughout the generations. In that sense, the clash between the III&E and the Chicago Sufis was a continuation of a global tradition of dispute over the boundaries of faith and community.

History aside, the conflict illustrated yet again that Islamic knowledge is not a corpus of static, defined interests pitted against what is outside the boundaries of Islam (whether "outside" is defined as people of other faiths or competing ideologies or religions). The opponent might be another person praying in the same mosque, speaking the same language, and sharing the same sense of "home." In this particular clash, the superiority of the mosque actually shone through, because it proved to have the decisive power to silence the debate and counteract exclusion.

Significantly, the dispute pointed to ideas, practices, and institutions that can fragment Muslim Americans. Although such diverging views rarely lead to direct confrontations, they do have an impact on how people understand one another, what ideas they can agree upon, what actions they can take as a community, and what picture of Islam they present to America. Historically, diversity has always been a part of Islam, and will probably remain so in the American context. However, the question remains whether the diversity in some instances is so great that it creates unbridgeable rifts, making it difficult for Muslim Americans truly to state and share a common agenda and stand forth as a unified community.

PROFESSIONAL MUSLIMS

"Professional" Muslims[71] are individuals (mostly academics) who visit churches, mosques, and schools around the city and lecture to Muslims and non-Muslims about Islam. Although their activities usually are not attached to any organized Muslim structure, they have had, and still have, a noticeable effect on the articulation and presentation of Islam and Islamic authority within the community—in particular, on how the community presents itself to its non-Muslim neighbors.

The authority of professional Muslims came as much from the expectations of the society around them as from the educational priorities of their religious community. Most middle- and upper-middle-class Muslims, while claiming Islam to be the correct way of life, still considered religious study a spare-time activity. A good professional career—not just for their children but for themselves—took precedence over religious studies. People encouraged their children to take degrees in secular studies, not Islamic studies, to secure a stable income and social recognition in the society at large.

Still, the community acknowledged a need for people with a profound, scholarly knowledge of Islam. For decades, although most of the professionally educated *imams* and *ulama* had been brought over from the Muslim world,[72] they did not always succeed in their mission. Their unfamiliarity with American life made it difficult for them to relate to the surrounding society and to the needs of their congregations. (For that reason, Muslims established its first school for the training of *imams*, offered at the School of Islamic and Social Sciences, in 1996.[73])

By the mid-1990s, the community still lacked scholars who combined knowledge of Islam with understanding of the community's American context and who could also present Islam reasonably to non-Muslim Americans. It was in this vacuum that professional Muslims found their niche. Although they were not theologians, they understood both Muslim and non-Muslim terminology and norms, and they had acquired the professional status and social standing that allowed them to talk within both spheres. This combination not only strengthened their position among Muslims but also shifted the standards for religious authority within the community.

One such professional Muslim is Dr. Ibrahim, a medical specialist living in one of Chicago's suburbs. An immigrant from the Middle East, he earned his Ph.D. in the United States. Although he spent a considerable amount of his day in his practice, he often dedicated an evening or an afternoon to telling other Chicago citizens, Muslims and non-Muslims alike, about Islam. On Sunday afternoons, he would lead a study group at an Islamic center in one of the northern suburbs, and once a month he would drive to a center in the western part of the city to discuss Islam and Christianity with a Methodist minister in front of an audience comprising both religious communities. Dr. Ibrahim also lectured at Muslim full-time schools and Christian seminaries and spoke to the press about Muslim festivals such as Ramadan. Moreover, he was highly respected for his charitable work.

Like other professional Muslims, Dr. Ibrahim had no formal religious education. His decision to study, at the outset, was quite personal. He told me that when he married his American wife, who was a Roman Catholic, they decided to study the Bible and the Qur'an together. They continued this study for several years until they concluded that Islam was the superior religion. His wife converted to Islam and raised their children in that faith. Both have since been highly involved community members and dedicated speakers on Islam.

During my time in Chicago, I joined Dr. Ibrahim several times to hear him address the Muslim–Christian discussion forum. He was well versed in both Christian and Islamic scriptures and obviously found great pleasure in a good discussion. Although his listeners were dedicated Christians, and he knew he had no chance of converting them, he continued these interfaith meetings for several years. Most interesting was that none of the participants seriously challenged any of his statements. He came out the rhetorical winner every time.

One of these meetings took place in November 1995, just after the evening prayer. Although the prayer hall was next to the room in which we were sitting, only a few Muslims participated. The subject that evening was racism. The two speakers, Dr. Ibrahim and the Methodist minister, Reverend Johnson, had an equal amount of time to present their religiously based comments on the topic. Dr. Ibrahim was the first to speak. Smiling, with the calm voice of a man certain of his convictions, he started by saying that no religion had ever found slavery acceptable as such. Still, when Islam appeared, slavery was widespread, and so Muslims had to confront this social reality.

"I will argue from the Qur'an," the doctor said, pointing to the book in front of him, that God was a merciful God, a God that was the creator of all humanity. The Prophet Muhammad came with the message that all God's creatures were of one family, and the one who loved the most was the one whom God put highest. "Oh Mankind, we have created you as a single male and a single female. The one who is most honored of you in the sight of Allah is the one who is most righteous," the doctor recited from the Qur'an.[74]

He then pointed to events in Muslim historiography. "Fourteen hundred years ago," he said, "the Prophet Muhammad, peace be upon him, said that there is no preference of an Arab over a non-Arab or the opposite. The only condition determining the value of a human being is his faith and his obedience."[75] Fourteen hundred years ago, Islam took action to stop slavery, step by step.[76] This not only had an effect on how slaves were treated; it also meant that people of other faiths could live peacefully in the Muslim society. "When I got to the United States twenty-five years ago," Dr. Ibrahim concluded, "I got completely shocked when I saw that one could discriminate against another person because of his color. That would never happen in a Muslim society."

Reverend Johnson, an African American, now presented his understanding of Christian views on slavery. Although he had the confidence of most of his audience, he seemed much more defensive than Dr. Ibrahim. He briefly cited a statement in Leviticus that slaves should not be treated cruelly, that they should be treated as a part of the family. Then he put an apparent trump on the table: These statements were written 4,000 years ago; therefore, the Bible had spoken against slavery long before the Qur'an.

Dr. Ibrahim seemed far from impressed by these arguments. "Why is it," he asked, "that you do not give any references to the New Testament?" he asked. "Why is it that Jesus did not speak about slavery, an institution that was so widespread in those days? We want to see teachings that reform human beings and human society, especially in a society like this, which is so racist. In the churches, they used to preach that Africans were worth nothing. It is scientifically proven that we are all products of our culture, our environment, and if you grow up in a racist society like this, you will be a racist yourself. But since Muslims learn from day one that all humans are equal, we do not have the problem of racism. Racism is not a part of Islam."

The majority of Dr. Ibrahim's activities were aimed at non-Muslim participants, because his idea of da'wa included using rhetoric that would both shock and silence. He might not win hearts, but he would win the debate.

Not all professional Muslims that I met in Chicago, including those from other parts of the United States, shared this rhetorical strategy. Whereas some used doomsday warnings or rhetorical provocation, others chose calm, tolerant dialogue. What they all had in common was their audience, their status as professionals, and their social standing. Their audience was mainly non-Muslim, often interested in Islam as a faith and therefore susceptible to religious persuasion. But perhaps the main factor that allowed professional Muslims to reach their audience was their social and secular academic status, which their listeners accepted as authoritative.

Professional Muslims who appeared in lecture halls and at conventions and seminars, and who spoke about Islam in the media, were doctors, lawyers, social scientists, and engineers. By taking prestigious degrees in various scientific fields, they had accumulated a level of knowledge that brought them not only wealth but credibility and admiration. What made professional Muslims trustworthy communicators of religion was, first, that they were Muslims, and second, that they were "specialists." Perhaps most important, belonging to the educated middle- or upper-middle class granted professional Muslims mobility, social confidence, and self-esteem and assertiveness. Because they had done so well in America, the community viewed them as hardworking, reliable citizens who had earned the right to be heard—and whose word on all subjects, including Islam, carried considerable weight.

MOSQUES IN CHICAGO

The number of mosques that actually exist in the Chicago area is uncertain because mosque locations seem to constantly change. A study published in 1988 estimated the number of mosques at twenty-seven.[77] By 1997, nearly ten years later, an unpublished survey listed sixty-two in the six-county metropolitan Chicago area.[78] As the community itself had not thoroughly looked into the numbers, estimates still varied. Some of my informants claimed that at least 110 mosques existed in Chicago, while ICNA's local *Assalamu 'Alaikum Chicago Muslims* newsletter listed only thirty-one.[79] Whatever the truth, the number of mosques increased considerably in the 1990s, a trend that seemed to continue into the new millennium. The importance that the community gave to the mosques showed clearly in the frequent fund-raisers for the building of new mosques.

But what exactly is a mosque? Certainly, no institution is as central to Muslim communities as the mosque. Although prayer itself is almost independent of locality—Muslims may pray alone or together, in their homes, at work, or in airports—the mosque as place and form is a key symbol of faith. The mosque is shaped not only according to function but also according to the conditions of a community. It visibly manifests Islam to both believers and non-believers, either by taking on a particular architecture or by just "being there." As part of a long historical tradition, the mosque is therefore a strong Muslim community symbol. Although mosques are built differently from Texas to China, across this diversity the mosque symbolizes a common ideal, something that is beyond history: It is a space in which Muslims face their God across time and context. As the scholar of Islam Patrick D. Gaffney puts it:

> By its very existence, the local mosque in any Islamic community embodies a paradox. On the one hand it represents a universal and permanent ideal. To believers it recalls events regarded as unique, absolute, enduring, and of normative consequence.... On the other hand, every actual mosque is contingent, incidental, and contained by concrete facts. The empirical qualities of every real mosque ... all belong to the flux of human affairs that are forever partial and subject to change.[80]

Although molded on a "universal ideal," the form of the mosque seems "incidental," even in Chicago. In the run-down neighborhoods on the South Side, where dust piles up in front of doors hidden behind metal grating, the "ideal" is nothing but a storefront with darkened windows. A small sign or painting on the front wall may indicate the purpose of the building, but it seems as desolate as the area around it. In the downtown area (the Loop), the fifth floor of an office building contains another mosque. On the far North Side, where trees and gardens surround expensive villas, a mosque built of red stone, with a stereotypical high minaret, stands proudly. In Chicago, as elsewhere in the United States, the shape of a mosque depends on the economic and social conditions of those who worship there.[81]

As individual mosques reflect the social class and architecture of their surroundings, so do they emphasize communal knowledge. They do so based on an ideal, pointing to a specific period in history (the life of the Prophet and his community in Medina), gaining absolute authority as a model through the divine, through revelation. As the *imam* of the Islamic Cultural Center of Greater Chicago, one of the city's major Islamic centers, stated in a publication:

> Islam is the religion of learning. Its miracle is a Book and spiritual strength. The first revelation was about learning, reading, and writing. At that time, there existed no school or college to enroll in. The place where those seeking guidance could easily find it was the mosque of the Prophet. His house was right next to the mosque. It was their school.[82]

Four Mosques in the Chicago Area

Ground was broken for the most impressive Chicago-area mosque on June 18, 1995, in the suburb of Villa Park. A budget of $3.6 million[83] covered the construction of prayer rooms with space for 1,000 to 2,250 people, *wudu'* (ablution) areas, a bookstore, a library, banquet and lecture halls, and a cafeteria. The mosque—one of the first in Chicago to do so—also houses a funeral home.[84]

The increase in mosque establishment involves three overlapping trends. First, it points to demographic changes since the 1950s. Second, it points to the greater role that Islam has come to play among certain groups of immigrants who have moved to Chicago from countries with Muslim majorities. And third, it points to the community's wish to make this city "home"—not merely a temporary place of residence but a place of cultural "known-ness,"[85] manifested in the buildings that the community has established.

While I was in Chicago, I became well acquainted with four mosques in the area: the Islamic Cultural Center of Greater Chicago in Northbrook, the Mosque Foundation in Bridgeview, the Downtown Islamic Center in the Loop area, and the Muslim Community Center on the North Side. All four are among Chicago's major Muslim centers. In the late 1990s, three of them drew between 500 and 1,500 people to Friday prayers.

Of the four mosques, the Islamic Cultural Center of Greater Chicago (ICCC) is the oldest.[86] Its history dates back to a mosque founded by the Bosnian American Cultural Association on North Halsted Street in 1954. The location functioned as both a Sunday school and a mosque. In the 1960s, the area around the mosque deteriorated economically, and the community decided to look for a location elsewhere. Groundbreaking for the new center took place in the suburb of Northbrook on September 8, 1974. The project was funded mainly by donations from members in Chicago and elsewhere—notably, the government and king of Saudi Arabia ($200,000) and the government (and embassy) of Kuwait ($33,000).[87] The center opened its doors in 1976.

The ICCC is one of the most meticulously designed mosques in the Chicago area, with a dome and minaret rising above the quiet suburban neighborhood. It is usually referred to as the "Bosnian mosque," and with good reason: Although many Middle Easterners and South Asians attend the mosque, the atmosphere and many of the activities in the center point to Balkan cultural roots. The current *imam*, hired in 1989, came—as did his two predecessors—from Bosnia. Although *khutbas* are held in English, announcements after *jum'a* are often given in Bosnian. During community celebrations such as the *Mawlid al-Nabi* (the birthday of the Prophet), a number of *qasidas* (poems) are also read in Bosnian.

The mosque differs in two respects from the other mosques in this study. First, the banquet and lecture hall in the basement is used for folk dancing, a practice that seems to have disappeared from the other Chicago mosques.[88] Second, there is a strong Sufi influence, among both regular attendees and the mosque's appointed personnel. In the 1990s, *dhikr* was held weekly in the mosque, and common Sufi rituals and celebrations such as *Mawlid al-Nabi* and the *tarawih* prayer of Ramadan were celebrated. Naqshbandiyya-Haqqaniyya *shaykhs* often visit the ICCC, as Muhammad Hisham Kabbani did during the *Mawlid al-Nabi* in the fall of 1995.

Although established in 1954, the Mosque Foundation (MF) mosque did not actually open its doors until the early 1980s.[89] The mosque was funded by donations. Much of the work was done by the Arab-American Ladies' Society. Arab influence is prevalent in the MF, and most members are Jordanian Palestinians. The mosque experienced a split in its early years. Some people had hoped for a cultural center where Muslim and Arab cultural activities and celebrations could take place. Others found such activities incompatible with the teachings of Islam. The case evidently went to court, and an agreement—that the building was for religious activity only—was signed.

Louise Cainkar writes in her study of Muslim Palestinians in Chicago that "a fundamentalist Moslem leadership from outside this community has taken charge of Mosque affairs to the dissatisfaction of the people who paid to build it."[90] Some of my informants in southwestern Chicago stated that a conflict over leadership existed in the MF, but that it was caused by ethnic affiliations rather than by religious or "fundamentalist" differences. I was told that the Bridgeview community had hired the present *imam* not on the basis of his education (he was trained in Saudi Arabia and initially sent to Chicago to work with the African-American community[91]) but, rather, because his mother was a Palestinian and his father a Jordanian. An Egyptian Islamic scholar who lives in the Bridgeview area was not hired, even though he had graduated from the prestigious al-Azhar University in Cairo and was a former president of the ISNA. Despite the MF's membership-based structure, these informants said, ethnic affiliation alone gave the *imam* his unlimited authority.[92]

The affairs of the MF were also troubled on several occasions by outside pressure, especially when a number of members—including the *imam* and members of the board—were suspected of supporting the Palestinian-Islamist movement Hamas. On March 19, 1996, journalist Steven Emerson testified before the U.S. Senate's Foreign Relations Committee, Subcommittee on Near East and South Asia, that "American law enforcement confirms Palestinian Hamas testimony that a principal leader of Hamas in the United States [name] is the Imam of the Mosque Foundation in Bridgeview, Illinois."[93] Whether Emerson (whom most Muslim Americans see as an anti-Muslim hate-monger[94]) was correct in making such allegations was not something I could verify during my stay.

The Downtown Islamic Center (DTIC) was founded in 1976.[95] In those days, a handful of people simply got together to pray at a small place on East Adams Street, in the center of the Loop's financial district.[96] In the early 1990s, the congregation had to move, because about 300 people were coming to Friday prayers and because the building in which the mosque was located was demolished. The center moved to a spacious fifth-floor location on South Wabash Street. By the late 1990s, 400–500 people were turning up for Friday prayers, packing the prayer hall. In the fall of 1996, the DTIC announced that its board had entered into negotiations to purchase a building on North Michigan Avenue. Although the center's leaders often pledged to donate generously, and although the North American Islamic Trust (NAIT) offered a considerable interest-free loan, the purchase of the building had not been settled by the time I left Chicago in the summer of 1997.[97]

Like the two other mosques, the DTIC was membership-based. Although the people who came to the mosque were of various ethnic backgrounds, they had in common that they were either working or running errands in the downtown area. The DTIC's major function was Friday prayers, but other functions included a Wednesday gathering for Qur'anic studies. The DTIC also maintained a *zakat* (alms) fund to help the needy and recent immigrants. The Council for Islamic Organizations of Greater Chicago, which I will discuss later, had its office in the DTIC.

The MCC, mentioned several times in previous chapters, was a giant within the Chicago Muslim community. Its influence was particularly evident at its twenty-fifth anniversary in 1995, when Illinois Governor Jim Edgar and Chicago Mayor Richard M. Daley announced the week of May 15–21, 1995, as American Islamic Community Week.

The MCC was established as a nonprofit organization on September 18, 1969. In 1972, the MCC bought its first building on North Kedzie Avenue[98] and soon established a Sunday school. In 1981, the MCC moved to a former ballroom on North Elston Avenue, receiving financial support from the Muslim World League and NAIT. The reasons for the move were lack of space and the small number of Muslims living in the neighborhood around the Kedzie Avenue building.[99] At the time of the purchase, the community consisted largely of people from the South Asian subcontinent. But the mosque also absorbed members of the Arabic Masjid Aliman, then located at West Montrose

Avenue. Since then, these two communities have worked side by side in the MCC.

The MCC is membership-based and led by a board of twenty-four members.[100] No fewer than thirty-four subcommittees take care of various functions, such as publicity and media,[101] medical services, interfaith relations, and neighborhood study circles.[102] As discussed in Chapter 2, the MCC building houses a Sunday school (and is also in charge of the Muslim Education Center in Morton Grove) and a *Dar ul-Uloom* (a school focusing on the teaching of the Qur'an). Adults receive Islamic education in the Elston building. Arabic classes, Qur'anic classes, and women's study groups meet several times a week. On Sundays, the busiest day of the week, a *Dars al-Qur'an* (lesson presenting the teaching of the Qur'an) in Urdu is given between 12:00 and 12:45 P.M., and an English lecture is given between 12:45 and 1:30 P.M. For those who want to study on their own, the center offers a bookstore and a library with a considerable collection of books, magazines, and videos. A number of social services are carried out, ranging from support of the needy to funerals. During Ramadan in 1995, the center collected money and distributed food to 1,000 needy Muslim and non-Muslim families in the Chicago area.[103] In 1989, the MCC bought 1,500 graves at the Rosehill cemetery, where the community's dead are now buried.

The MCC has organized a great variety of conferences. In July 1975, it held a three-day *hadith* seminar in commemoration of Imam Bukhari, attended by more than 1,000 delegates.[104] In 1978, a national conference on Muslim community development was held in cooperation with the Institute of Muslim Minorities at Abdulaziz University in Jeddah. A week-long youth camp is held annually outside the Chicago area.

In contrast to the other three mosques, the MCC had no appointed *imam* during my stay, although hiring was in process by the summer of 1997. That it had taken almost three decades to reach such a decision was the result of two major considerations. First, the MCC wanted an *imam* on whom all members, no matter what their ethnic background, could agree. Second, they wanted an *imam* who knew American society as well as he knew Islam.[105]

The Impact of Ethnic Affiliation on Chicago's Mosques

Ethnicity always plays a significant role in the issue of who seeks out these mosques and in what language Islam is presented to those who attend. At the MF, *khutbas* were given in Arabic by a Palestinian *imam*; at the MCC, an Urdu lecture was given every Sunday; at the ICCC, announcements were given in Bosnian, reporting on the often grave situation "back home."

The role of ethnicity was visible in the clothes people wore when they came to the mosque and the food that was served in the cafeteria after lectures and noon prayers. Some people tried to counter this divisiveness ideologically, by following the ideal of the transethnic and all-encompassing aspects of Islam as articulated by the MCC and by heeding Amir Ali's thundering against the ignorance of "cultural Islam." On a practical level, organizations such as the MCC fostered peaceful cooperation between South Asians and Arabs.

A direct initiative for resolving this ethnic fragmentation was the Council of Islamic Organizations of Greater Chicago. After initial discussions in 1989–90, the Council was founded in 1992.[106] It now coordinates major Muslim institutions in Chicago, including mosques, organizations, and schools. In 1995, thirty-three institutions were registered members, seventeen of them mosques.[107] The Council sought to coordinate its members' activities and projects, particularly during Ramadan.[108] Nevertheless, the Council proved most effective as an informative body, addressing and responding to the non-Muslim media, particularly Chicago's newspapers and TV stations. In 1995–96, the Council tried to broadcast its own TV program, a project that eventually failed for economic and organizational reasons.[109] The Council also arranged religious festivals and functioned as an umbrella organization for community boards such as the Chicago Fiqh Council and the *'Id* Committee.

The celebration of *'Id* inevitably emphasized the significant ethnic divisions in the community. In 1997, *'Id al-Adha*, the commemoration of Abraham's sacrifice, was celebrated on not one but two different dates; the community in Bridgeview celebrated one day before the rest of Chicago Muslims, for reasons both theological and ethnic. The city's leading *'alim* later said that he had contacted the *imam* in Bridgeview to solve the problem, but the *imam* had defended his position according to a *hadith* saying that if the new moon was sighted in Saudi Arabia, the sighting was valid for the rest of the world. The '*alim* had explained that this particular *hadith* applied only to Ramadan, not to the months before and after.[110] Although the *imam* agreed, he added that his community might want to continue celebrating the holiday as they were accustomed to—now and in the future.[111] In this case, old ethnic traditions proved more powerful than the theological judgments of the community's religious leaders.

Identifying themselves through religion that was interpreted ethnically—and through ethnicity that was interpreted religiously—also enhanced feelings of safety, as a member of the MF observed:

> Most of the people who come into the Mosque Foundation are from Arabic backgrounds. It is like our mosque back home. So always the *jum'a* speech is in Arabic and prayer is in our Arabic language, and the classes are in Arabic. And the habits. The generosity of the people. It is exactly like back home. In the Mosque Foundation you feel as if you visit any mosque in Egypt, Palestine, or Jordan. It is the same thing. I am happy with the Mosque Foundation.[112]

This feeling of safety, of having a space "exactly" like home, was critical for a generation of immigrants now living in a context in which familiar elements of identification—language, culture, and place—were overshadowed by powerful new ideas and habits.

But the mosque became a safe haven for others, as well. It "protected" those who wanted separation from others who were "almost equal" in religious observance. Converts felt this demarcating line most directly and described the isolation they experienced when they came to a mosque.[113] One woman furiously told me that she had taken her children out of the local mosque's weekend school because the principal treated them differently because they were "Americans." In such situations, some converts looked for other mosques, while most adopted the ethnic habits of their local mosque. In South Asian mosques, women converts wore the *shalwar kamiz*; in Middle Eastern mosques, they wore the *jilbab*. Male converts tended to create their own distinctive styles, combining clothing from the Middle East,

South Asia, and the Balkans. Such patterns of ethnic imitation were not restricted to dress, however, but also extended to language and cuisine. In that sense, converts adapted to Islamic practices that were more than generic; they adapted to the practices of the particular ethnic group with which they had chosen to live and worship.

Ethnicity created spaces of safety and isolation, but it also created expectations among groups. Most significantly, certain ethnic groups within the community received religious authority simply on the basis of their national origin. Muslims from the Middle East, willingly and unwillingly, played such a role. For example, during a conversation about the dynamics of ethnicity and religion, a Pakistani informant told me that Arab Muslims were perceived as "more" Muslim than others. The reasons were that Arabs were the first to embrace Islam and they spoke Arabic, the language of the Qur'an, presumably giving them a deeper intimacy with the message of the scriptures and ritual.[114]

Although non-Arab Muslims sometimes expressed such ethnic expectations directly, I never heard Arab Muslims claim this authority for themselves. Nevertheless, when I observed the teaching of converts within mixed groups from various ethnic backgrounds, the Arabs were generally the first to speak, often basing their arguments on their knowledge of the Arabic language. Arabs also may have been regarded as more "culturally" inclined than South Asians (who were seen as "ritualistic"), because the community identified Arab culture as linguistically and geographically integral to the origins and practice of Islam.

The centrality of ethnicity in the Chicago Muslim community determined the creation of certain groups (for example, Bosnians, South Asians, Arabs), the lack of consensus among certain groups (for example, South Asians and Arabs), and the exclusion of certain groups and people (for example, African-American and Caucasian converts). However "universal and permanent" an Islamic ideal the mosque might be, in its American reality it was neither.

Mosques were also segregated by gender. Women had their areas and men had theirs. The level of segregation, most apparent in the prayer hall, varied. I once saw a man and his wife praying side by side, but that was an exception. In that particular mosque, women—except in this instance—always prayed behind the men, although no curtain or screen separated the sections. Still, physical separation existed in most of the mosques, with screens made of colored cloth or bamboo sticks or bulletin boards. In some instances, the women prayed in a separate room, usually the basement, and in two Tablighi Jama'at mosques, I saw no facilities for women at all.

Regardless of the level of segregation in the different mosques, gender separation became more important as an issue during my time in Chicago.[115] Not only was the prayer area split in two, but the remaining areas became increasingly divided according to similar patterns. Entrance doors that had been used by men and women now sported signs saying, "Women's Entrance" and "Men's Entrance." The banquet hall in the basement of the huge mosque in Villa Park had a removable wall so religious and family celebrations could be segregated by gender. Mosques had apparently evolved into more than safe havens for the totally different and ethnically "almost different." They had also become safe havens for men and women against one another, against the "sexually different."

THE MAN AND THE WORD: THE *KHATIB*

The mosques in Chicago were collectives, and collectives within collectives, defined by ethnicity, age, or gender. Such distinctions appear vital for the life of the mosques: who comes for Friday prayers, who engages in decision-making on boards and subcommittees, and who donates the money for the rent or mortgage. But one person in particular represents both members and leadership: the Islamic preacher, or, as he is mostly known in Chicago, the *khatib* or *imam*. He is the one who speaks on behalf of the Scripture and the congregation at the same time, and does so during the most important hour of the week: the Friday prayers.

The role of the *khatib* and his *khutba* (sermon) in the Middle East has been delineated in several studies, among them Richard T. Antoun's *Muslim Preacher in the Modern World: A Jordanian Case Study in Comparative Perspective* (1989) and Patrick D.

Gaffney's *The Prophet's Pulpit: Islamic Preaching in Contemporary Egypt* (1994).[116] These studies focus on countries in which Islam plays a prominent role in public and political life. A decisive dynamic between government institutions and Islamic institutions and academies clearly exists in countries such as Jordan and Egypt,[117] for example, where the government must always take into account the power that Islam has on the lives of its citizens. However, because of their minority status, Muslims in Chicago and elsewhere in the United States face a very different situation. Before the events of September 11, 2001, Islam was seen as having only minor relevance to the U.S. administration and public life. This status quo was reinforced by the American separation of church and state, because the state had no role in appointing or regulating religious functionaries. At the turn of the millennium, then, the question arises: On what grounds did the *khatib* or *imam* in America base his authority within the community?

An answer to this question can be found in the *khutbas* I began taping at the DTIC during Ramadan in 1997, a project I later extended to include the MCC, with the agreement of both mosques. Dr. Yakub Ahmed Patel of the DTIC was particularly helpful, assisting me during my first recordings and bringing me tapes of his earlier sermons. Later that spring, we sat down in the meeting room to discuss his role as a *khatib*, as well as the activities of the center as a whole. The interview began as follows:

GS: Could you briefly introduce yourself?

YAP: We say in the beginning, "*Bismillah al-Rahman al-Rahim.*" It means, "In the name of Allah, the most Merciful." Actually, this is one very unique thing in Islam: that in the Qur'an every *sura* except one begins with this sentence. There is a specific reason why. All the other chapters, they begin with this statement. It is like a Muslim way of beginning anything. You know, if you write a letter to somebody, you begin with *Bismillah al-Rahman.* [Whenever] we do anything—driving, going out, writing, beginning any work—it means that we begin in the name of God, the Most Merciful, the Mercy-Giving. This is really [based] on two attributes of God: *Rahman* and *Rahim* [the Merciful, Compassionate]. The *Rahman* is, according to the Qur'an, the being of God. That means that God is *Rahman.* He is *Rahman*, it is His essence. He is the One full of mercy Himself, which means that

He *is* mercy. And *Rahim* is the actualizing of this mercy into the creation. There is a flowing of that into everything. *Rahman* is like the soul, and *Rahim* is like the utilizing of the soul into the creation.

According to the Qur'an, Allah's—God's—mercy covers everything. It does not mean believer, nonbeliever, atheist, someone criminal, non-criminal. It does not matter. He [Allah] is mercy generally. In other words, *Rahman* is like a general mercy. *Rahim* is like a specialized kind of mercy that He gives to the believers that are very close to Him. So the Qur'an says *wa rahmati wasi'at kulla sha'in*, meaning, "my mercy covers everything."[118] Therefore, the Qur'an, from page to page, sees the world and repeats this. In every few *ayas*, you will find this to emphasize that the human being, that the only thing that he can expect, is repentance or coming to God with constrained heart. Those kind of things. Not our actions. Actions are very trivial in the sense that it can never save a human being. Even the Prophet, peace be upon him, was asked, "Will you be saved by your actions?" And he said, "No." He said, "Only if the mercy of God covers me, then I will be saved."[119]

Instead of answering my question directly, Dr. Patel presented the Qur'an and Islamic terminology. His reason for making this jump most likely reflected his intentions for the interview. Given time with an interested non-Muslim, he undoubtedly saw himself as religiously obligated to play the role of missionary. The quote highlighted a particular element of Dr. Patel's narrative style: He often used the semantics of the Arabic language to introduce and support his arguments, both in his *khutbas* and in the books he had written on Islam. Although Arabic was not his native tongue, the roots and patterns of the language gave him the option of continuous interpretation. Further, the use of Arabic as the "truth language"[120] gave his interpretations complete credibility among his congregants.

Dr. Patel was born near Bombay, India, and emigrated to the United States in 1965. He studied engineering at the Massachusetts Institute of Technology and later earned a Ph.D. from the Illinois Institute of Technology in Chicago. While pursuing a professional career, he became engaged in what he called a "volunteer study of Islam." As a child in India, he had studied the Qur'an and Arabic at a *madrasa* (religious academy). Although he never gave me an in-depth description of these studies, the community at the DTIC must have seen his knowledge and continuing religious studies as considerable. At one point, Dr. Patel had also been a member of the Fiqh Committee of the MSA of the United States and Canada. He had written numerous short booklets on Islam, mainly to communicate Islam to non-Muslim audiences.[121]

Dr. Patel was the most frequently called on *khatib* at the DTIC. During my time at the center, he gave the *khutba* about twice a month. When I asked him about the procedure for choosing *khatibs*, he told me that the mosque's steering committee elected one person to make the arrangements. This person set up a monthly schedule, appointing "different people who are actively involved in Islamic work." They might be university professors with degrees in Islamic studies, presidents of other Islamic centers in the area, or visitors from Mecca, Medina, or Indonesia. Then he added:

> But there is no priesthood in Islam. What it means is that any person sincerely interested to convey a message to benefit the community and please God he can recommend that "I would like to take care," and then generally we allow them, dependent on the schedule. But most of the time, we give to the people who have worked in Islamic work for years and years. Those are the people we generally allow. Generally, they are people very fluent in the Qur'an, in the *hadith*. They have good knowledge. And they are people who can address—communicate better.[122]

In this statement Dr. Patel illustrated what has been called the "essential looseness of the vocation."[123] Apparently, this "looseness" brought about a democratization of the role of the *khatib* and the subjects he conveyed: There was "no priesthood" in Islam, and any sincerely interested person could convey the message. But the last lines of Dr. Patel's statement show that this "looseness" contained certain implicit requirements. The *khatib*'s message had to benefit the community and please God, thereby giving both God and the congregation the final authority. Of these two, the congregation (or community at large) appeared stronger, with its power to accept or reject how the message was brought alive in the here and now. What the congregation saw as important— and what it saw as pleasing God—was stated in a particular time, in a particular space, relative to a fixed set of holy scriptures.

In Chicago, the factors that determined claims of religious authority were based less on the candidate's religious education than on his level of religious commitment—and his secular education. Because they wanted their children to become lawyers, engineers, and doctors, community members tended to choose people in these professions to lead the prayers and interpret their religion. This preference has greater strength in America than elsewhere, because only a few 'ulama' (Islamic scholars) live and work in the United States. The ability to interpret holy scripture becomes something that any Muslim can undertake, as long as that person has the secular social position, credibility, and personal time and dedication to do so.

As the section on professional Muslims showed, a secular education and middle-class status heightens not only a Muslim speaker's respectability but also his or her credibility in matters of religion. Moreover, because Islam is not the dominant religion in a country that separates church and state, all claims to Islamic authority (and access to powerful positions in community institutions such as mosques) tend not to be based on institutionalized religious schooling. Instead, the Muslim-American community values personal commitment and the ability to successfully address a particular Muslim or non-Muslim audience.

The consequences of this difference are numerous, both within and outside the mosque. The establishment of paramosques, the independent interpretations of professional Muslims, and the activism of young MSA members all demonstrate the power of different Muslim-American "communities" to create their own distinct identities and Islamic viewpoints. The diversity of interpretations among Muslim Americans—and the sometimes confrontational dynamics within the community—result from a confrontation between Islamic tradition, history, and ethnic affiliations and a very American understanding of who is entitled to participate in the debate.

When Dr. Patel spoke about the "looseness" of the vocation, he was pointing to more than the position of the khatib. He was also speaking about a broad group of people whom the community considered capable of interpreting, speaking for, and presenting Islam. Although those with social standing and personal dedication were deemed more trustworthy than others, this "looseness" still reflected great diversity and change within and outside the mosque. Although this diversity may have hampered any community claims to unity, it nevertheless demonstrated the community's profound adaptation to the surrounding society.

THE OPENING OF THE HEART: A WOMEN'S STUDY GROUP

In Chicago, as elsewhere, Muslim women have established study groups in which they can discuss their faith, share experiences, and learn more about Islam from knowledgeable women within the community. These groups meet in private homes or in mosques. During my fieldwork, I participated in one women's study group on several occasions to learn how the discussions were structured and how authority was distributed among the members. This eyewitness view of the group provides a "gendered" perspective on Islamic interpretations and practices within the American context. It also helps explain the question of why many Muslim women feel they need to participate in such groups and interpret their religion among themselves.

Stories of Faith and Sisterhood

"I want to tell you a story," the woman said.[124]

"During this past Ramadan something remarkable happened. It was in New York. They are still talking about it all over, and the *imams* there are mentioning it in their *khutbas*. I tell you, this story always makes me cry. There was this Spanish guy who saw the Prophet in one of his dreams, and in that dream the Prophet told him: 'I am the Prophet Muhammad. Embrace Islam.' The man was then given the directions to a mosque. When he woke up, he went there—he had never been to a mosque before— and he told the people there about his dream. He asked them— because he did not know—'How do you embrace Islam?' And the people told him that you must take *shahada* [the proclamation of the Islamic attestation of faith, the first pillar of Islam, marking conversion to become a Muslim].

"So he went home, took a shower, and returned to the mosque to take *shahada*. They told him how to pray, and he went with them to pray in congregation. But when he went down in prostration—*Subhana Allah*—he did not get up again. At first, people did not notice that much—after all, he might just be sincere in his prayer. But then some of them thought that it was strange that he stayed in the position, so they went to him to see if there was something wrong. They pushed him gently on the shoulder, and he fell to the side. He was dead. And I tell you, this story truly tells us about our ignorance. Perhaps this man had done something really special in his life, since Allah showed him that mercy. But we don't know. I mean, it doesn't even matter to me whether this story is true or not. It just opened my eyes to what God may grant human beings."

Umm Ahmad, an energetic Arab woman in her late thirties, told this story in a study room at one of Chicago's large Islamic centers.[125] While she was speaking, other women were filling the chairs around the long table in the middle of the room. This was a women's study group, and it was common practice for the women to talk about events of the previous week as they waited for their teacher, Umm Khadija. The stories usually had communal or religious value: Who had gotten married or engaged in the past few days? Had anything happened that showed the greatness of Allah?

The tale of the sudden convert and his dramatic death typified the mystique and drama often included in these stories: God intervened in someone's life, changed it, and destined the person to eternal reward or punishment according to his or her deeds. The relevance of the story was even greater because the event had occurred close to home—a mosque somewhere in America, a convert saved at the eleventh hour. Because many of the women in the group were converts, the story reaffirmed the validity of their decision to choose Islam. As Umm Ahmad said, it did not matter whether the story was true. What was important was the message it transmitted and its effect on the listeners. The willingness to transform—to "open one's heart" and live Islam to the fullest— was a primary aspiration for the women in the group. It signified their submission to the will of God.

The group, which had been meeting for several years, was ethnically mixed, with Middle Eastern, South Asian, Hispanic, and Caucasian converts. The "regulars" described their friendships as so deep that they "could feel when one of the others was in pain."[126] Much hugging and sharing of personal stories, both glad and sad, showed bonds of affection. They called one another not only friends but "sisters," claiming to share a bond of divinely determined kinship that transcended those defined by humans.

The meeting time for the group changed from time to time— sometimes it met at 11:00 A.M., sometimes at noon, sometimes later. No matter what the hour, however, Umm Khadija was always late. Her usual excuse was that she had been delayed by something at home or at the small business she and her husband managed in the downtown area. Often she was joined by one or more of her five daughters, who, in contrast to the rest of the group, remained silent during their mother's instruction.

Umm Khadija had become the teacher for two reasons. First, although she never spoke about her accomplishments, she was known for being a *hafiza* (a woman who had memorized the entire Qur'an) and for having earned degrees in Islamic studies from a college in the Middle East and from the American Islamic College. Second, Umm Khadija created her authority through her behavior, in the ways in which she sacrificed parts of her earthly life for the pleasure of God and the hereafter. All members of the group were aware that Umm Khadija had not had an easy life, a condition to which she often referred when giving examples of her broader theological points.

Preparing for the Day of Judgment

On this particular occasion, Umm Khadija arrived as Umm Ahmad was finishing her story. As always, she sat at the far end of the table and opened a large notebook. The pages were neatly organized, with all the words written carefully in black ink and the important sentences underlined in red. Umm Khadija once told me that she got her information from various sources. Not only did she read a lot; she also listened to the growing number of audiotaped *khatib*s (by well-known American *imams*) that had become available on the U.S. market.[127] Rather than commenting on Umm Ahmad's story, Umm Khadija calmly asked whether everyone had benefited from Ramadan, which had just ended. The women answered that Ramadan had been full of peace and blessings. "Oh yes," Umm Khadija concluded, "I wonder where we all would have been without Ramadan? Probably somewhere in a dance club. *Astaghfir Allah* [may God forgive]!"

She closed her eyes and began reciting a long segment of the beginning of *sura Ya Sin* (*sura* 36): "*Wa al-Qur'an al-hakim. Innaka lamin al-mursalin*" (By the Qur'an, full of wisdom, you are indeed one of the messengers). As *amin* (amen) left her lips, she opened her eyes and looked around, saying:

Today I want to talk to you about the meaning of being a Muslim. Allah has chosen Muslims to come from many nations, so being a Muslim has nothing to do with where you are born. *Fiqh*—knowledge in depth—is given to you if God likes you. When Allah likes somebody, He wants them to learn. He likes people who worship Him, but He likes people who worship Him with knowledge better. It is not so that you have to be a scientist. What matters more than anything is the light in your heart. You can gain much knowledge about all matters in the world, but there is nothing like knowledge of Allah. Like the first Prophet on this earth—Idris [Enoch]—he was a tailor. Nuh [Noah] was a carpenter. Many of the Prophets were shepherds—including Musa [Moses]. Everything that is not connected to Allah's knowledge, Allah calls ignorance, because the Qur'an has knowledge about everything. The Prophet knew about space, he knew about the universe. He knew about what is under the earth and that it was round. He knew all these things that science proved only centuries later.

The first word that was given to Muhammad was *iqra* [read]. Whenever you feel tired, go and read Qur'an. You will find yourself refreshed, even if you don't understand the words, because there is a healthiness to be gained through them; they are the words of God. And that is why we say *ihdina sirat al-mustaqim*[128] when we pray: Lead us to the straight path. Allah responds to every prayer that you present to him. Allah works in mysterious ways. Sometimes when you see a car accident, you may say to yourself, 'Oh, this is terrible.' But you have no idea if these people are good. Maybe it is a test for them. Maybe the driver is a runaway. Maybe Allah has waited for a couple of months, six months, and then He pays the driver back for what he has done.

God created everything and measured everything. Sometimes we are so blind that we don't see the work of the Creator. Like the girls who expose themselves in front of a camera—where is their respect for what the Creator has given them? I tell you, we are all under watch. But when people forget this, they begin to do bad deeds. They may say that, 'I am so small that God won't care.' But such people are going to become the people of *nar* [hellfire]. It is stated in the Qur'an that every human being is going to testify against himself. Allah looks through our vision, He hears what you hear. He observes if you let your eyes look on *haram* [forbidden] things or look away. On the Day of Judgment you will be tested on your knowledge and how you used it—if you taught or offered it to someone else, because every Muslim in this world is a messenger of Allah. You will be asked how you spent your time. What did you listen to—music on the radio or a recitation of the Qur'an? My life is my inhaling and my exhaling. That, too, will be measured.

Umm Khadija did not end by describing the questions that each individual would be asked on the Day of Judgment. Instead, she told the listeners a story about what might happen to the person who was not aware of the importance of her deeds:

There was a woman who died, and she had been in her grave for a long time. But her daughter, she wanted to see her [mother] very, very badly; she wanted to assure herself that her mother was doing well in the hereafter. Then, one night, her mother appeared to her in a dream. First the daughter got very happy, and she asked her mother, 'Mother, how are you doing?' But the mother did not look happy at all—she looked as if she was in severe pain, and she told her daughter why. She told her that she had once borrowed a needle from her neighbor, and she had forgotten to return it. For that reason, she had been punished until that very day when she showed herself to her daughter.

Umm Khadija covered several subjects in a very short time, from how to "define a Muslim" to a perspective on knowledge, from a perspective on human deeds and their consequence, to a perspective on the hereafter. This loosely structured teaching was typical of Umm Khadija's lessons. Despite her neatly ordered notebook, she always seemed to digress from her initial intentions. Part of the distraction came from the group's questions and comments. From time to time, another woman might walk in, bringing news and stories, and that person had to be taken into account, too.

Umm Khadija's explanations were bound together by clear-cut definitions of how knowledge was distributed, what it included, and how it should be used. Knowledge came from the absolute possessor of knowledge, God. Knowledge was not the result of scientific investigations, because all science could do was verify what was already stated in the revelation, and no scientist had ever gained (or, rather, been granted) the same level of knowledge as the prophets. The requirements for knowledge were piety, commitment, and faith—staying on the "right path." God watched every human action, judged whether it was affiliated with His order or "the knowledge of the world." And as God watched His creation, so every creation, intentionally and unintentionally, watched itself to give testimony on the Day of Judgment. Salvation would not be given to someone just because she called herself a Muslim; salvation required complete commitment in even the smallest actions. To Umm Khadija, human access to knowledge was therefore inherently connected to self-control—through awareness of the potential for eternal punishment—and to divine selection.

Umm Khadija used stories to make points clearly and convincingly. Leaving no areas for doubt, the stories showed either the corruption of, and terrible punishment for, the sinful or the blissful reward of the person who lived according to God's will. The women cheered at the positive stories, exclaiming *al-hamdu li-llahs* (thanks be to God), or they sighed with shock or worry, mumbling *astaghfir Allahs* (may God forgive) at the terrible accounts of the lost souls that they did not want to become. "It is not enough to be a Muslim," Umm Khadija told them. "It is only the *muminun* [true believers] who get into heaven."

Umm Khadija often moved away from the original theme of the lesson because she was driven toward convincing experiences in her own life. Of these, the strongest themes dealt with getting older and, most frequently, with her relationship to her husband. At the end of this particular lesson, she stated: "Allah is your exit for everything. Your husband might like you when you are young and strong. And your children, they leave you when they get their own family. They might even move to another part of the world. But I tell you, when all these people turn their backs to you, Allah will still be there for you. When they have put you under the dirt and left you there, there is no one but Allah for you. And Allah will call you: *'Abd* [servant/slave of God], it is you and me now.' For that moment we have to prepare."

Umm Khadija's conviction that Allah was indeed the only trustworthy constant in her life also showed in her stories about her marriage. Umm Khadija often mentioned that she had left her husband for a period of time when their marriage was not happy. Although she felt deceived by him, she considered this break in their relationship to be a result of her determination to follow God's commands. In another lesson, she mentioned that "there will come a time when distractions make people confused, like when I look and I see people and I must ask myself: 'Am I wrong? Am I too extreme?' Like when I had problems in my marriage. People might think that I spent too much time on religious duties, that I did not take care of my husband. But I did. I did everything. This could happen to everybody."

Umm Khadija was not the only woman in the group who told stories to stress and exemplify what was seen as religiously defined and thereby true. But although the other women sought recognition through their stories, the credibility of their stories depended on the amount of personal authority that the group was willing to give them.

Because Umm Khadija was the acknowledged teacher, elected on the basis of her knowledge of the Scripture and Islamic traditions and her willingness to engage in self-sacrificing behavior, her statements were close to unquestionable. Even when she moved into areas in which her grip of rhetoric slipped, her listeners did not object. For example, at one meeting, a woman asked whether it was acceptable to keep things that you had borrowed and that the borrower later told you that you might keep. In that situation, Umm Khadija said, you should return the thing for the sake of Allah. It might be acceptable to keep things given within your own family, but accepting things from others might be risky. People might take advantage of you. Although also at issue was the lender's kind gesture—the accepting of which was religiously recommendable—no one questioned Umm Khadija's statement.

Several of the women in the group were converts. Their journeys into Islam differed (although many had converted through marriage to Muslim men), but their role in the group, their reason for being there, seemed clear. Becoming a Muslim involved a long, steep learning process that was highly dependent on knowing Muslims who could teach them how to live a Muslim life—and teach them well. Such teaching called for a safe social network where the converts felt accepted and appreciated for the steps they were taking to live Islam to the fullest. These women asked the most questions, wanted the deepest and most comprehensive explanations, and took the most notes. Their stories reflected the ideals they pursued and the behaviors they rejected, such as when they despaired over stories of converts-to-be who had been scared away from Islam by family or "so-called friends" and when they proved their engagement in the social fabric of the community by bringing news about engagements, weddings, deaths, and divorces. Because none of these converts could claim authority as teachers, community gossip became their best avenue for social acceptance. In addition, beyond their stories, they could be counted on to wear the *hijab, shalwar kamiz,* or *jilbab.*

One woman in the group, however, was in a class by herself: Umm Ahmad, who told the story about the man who had died in prayer. Umm Ahmad was present at all of the meetings I attended and often was the first to show up. She was the only one who openly criticized Umm Khadija for being late and for the disorganization of the group. As an Arab raised in Islam from early childhood, she knew Islam's tenets and the language of the Qur'an in a way that the others did not. While Umm Khadija gained her authority by being calm, reflective, and somewhat emotionally distant, Umm Ahmad made herself known as a vibrant, loud, and motherly person. "I know that I am extrovert," she exclaimed on a day when we were sitting alone together, "but that is just the way I am. I tell people how I am feeling."

Umm Ahmad gained stature not only through what she said but also by serving others with ceaseless energy. Just after Ramadan, she decorated an entire table with colorful candles, flowers, and pearls for the group's 'Id celebration. And, at least when I joined the meetings, she brought some of her home-made crafts (decorated with feathers, pearls, and silk flowers inscribed with "Allah" or "Muhammad" in Arabic), either to sell or to fill an order from the group. Umm Ahmad seemed to be everywhere, appealing with her kindness to every member's heart. Ironically, she was therefore something of a threat to Umm Khadija's position.

Friendly Competition: Umm Khadija and Umm Ahmad

Both Umm Khadija and Umm Ahmad were significant authorities in the group. Because each had her own way of doing things, along with somewhat different ways of looking at Islam, their relationship was often competitive. This competition showed in the stories they told. Neither needed to use gossip to solidify her position— Umm Khadija had spoken strongly against this practice in her lessons—because both had been born and raised as Arab Muslims and both wore the Islamic uniform. The major difference between them was that Umm Khadija's authority came from her formal education in Islamic studies, while Umm Ahmad's was manifested in her unselfish deeds and her ethnic background. Like Umm Khadija, Umm Ahmad told exemplary stories and allegories, although hers were more joyful and miraculous than frightening and judgmental. Like Umm Khadija, Umm Ahmad dared to interpret the Qur'an and the life of the Prophet. She even dared to correct or argue with Umm Khadija's statements, as on the day that Umm Khadija once again used a well-known segment of Muslim history to prove that Allah was the only one to be trusted.

"Muhammad," Umm Khadija remarked, "was raised an orphan. He never said, 'my mother . . .' or 'my father told me to.' He always said, 'Allah told me to.' He never referred to what other people said, only to what Allah said. The fact is that people may claim that they look after you, that they care for you. But in reality they don't." A young woman jumped in and supported Umm Khadija's statement. When she gave birth too early to her infant son—whom she had on her lap—it almost seemed as if people were happy. It seemed as if they were only satisfied when something went wrong.

"But," Umm Ahmad interrupted, "it is not always like that. A lot of people behave decently."

"I know," Umm Khadija said, smiling with confidence. "I did not say this to scare you. I am telling you this to make you see that the *umma* needs to be one. The *umma* needs to be in a state where—how should I put this?—if one part hurts, the whole body aches. I can tell you this story. It is just like when the Prophet left Mecca. Abu Bakr al-Siddiq[129] went with him on that journey. At night they came to a cave where they decided to rest. Now, they knew that the Meccans were looking for them, so Abu Bakr filled all the holes in the cave with strips of his clothes, until nothing but his *awra* (those parts of the human body that must be covered according to Islamic tradition) was covered. Then they went to sleep. At the same time, the Meccans had begun to look for the Prophet, and sure enough they came to the cave. But in the meantime, a spider had made a web in front of it, and a bird had made a nest in it. So they walked away again, because they did not believe that the Prophet was there."

"Ah, how dumb they were," Umm Ahmad exclaimed.

"No," Umm Khadija argued calmly. "Allah made a block in their hearts."

"But I was talking about the *Jahiliyya* (time of ignorance)," Umm Ahmad said, defending herself.

"But we are talking about the sickness of the heart."

"That is exactly what I mean."

Umm Khadija continued her story. The woman with the infant asked how one should deal with people who "looked like Abu Bakr on the outside but were Abu Jahl (father of ignorance) on the inside?"[130] Umm Khadija told her to be cautious:

"Just say *al-hamdu li-llah* when they ask," Umm Ahmad argued. "These people are tests."

Umm Khadija continued her calm instructions, without taking much notice of the interruption. "After twenty years," she said, "I do not trust my husband. Things really do change, I can tell you, when you are no longer young, no longer strong."

"It is the opposite with me," Umm Ahmad said.

"What I have experienced," Umm Khadija said, "is that the only one who stays next to you, the only one that never leaves you, is Allah."

In this case, Umm Ahmad created and held authority for herself through exclamations, the use of specifically religious terminology, and a perspective that was lighter than Umm Khadija's. Yet I never felt that the two women disliked each other, or that Umm Ahmad was trying to take over. The interplay of their perspectives created a fascinating, dynamic coherence. Neither could speak with total authority; neither claimed the mantle of a religious scholar. Instead, they relied on life experiences—marriage, friendships, womanhood, motherhood—comprehended, communicated, and integrated in a shared religious framework.

The activities of women's study groups must be seen in the light of the conditions under which Muslim women live in the United States. That Muslim women create these spaces of learning for themselves can be attributed to four factors. First, non-Muslim surroundings directly and indirectly question and criticize the religious knowledge by which these women live (especially through their dress). Because those conditions are stressful, joining a group of like-minded people for support is both attractive and necessary. Second, American converts to Islam want to learn more about the religion they have chosen, and the education of converts was indeed primary to these groups. Third, both American-born converts and immigrant women lack the supportive network of an extended family that is common in the Muslim world. Women's study groups allow them to create social mobility and a sense of community that is important for personal self-assurance. Fourth, the group positioned itself against pressures from men as much as it positioned itself against pressures from the secular or Christian society. As much as America was perceived as trying to drag the women away from their religious duties, so, in the teacher's words, were their husbands. Although it would be misleading to claim that a Muslim feminist consciousness sprang from Umm Khadija's group, the interpretation of womanhood and Islam among the members ran counter to patriarchal domination and reinforced the women's sense of empowerment within Islam.

DISCUSSION

In this and the previous chapters, the influence of American society on Muslim community institutions has been evident. Paramosques carried names such as "center" and "institute." The III&E had a "reading room" that is comparable to those at many American Christian churches. In this way, the community adopted institutional structures and titles familiar to the outside society, thereby giving Muslim institutions an aura of intellectual and theological respectability that could ideally attract the non-Muslim majority. The influence of American society is also noticeable in the tools that the organizations have used to carry out their mission: speeches, seminars, booklets, and computer programs.

This chapter, perhaps more than the others, illustrates the impact of ethnic fragmentation within the Muslim-American community. People chose a particular mosque because it reminded them of their life "back home." On an individual level, the result for some was a feeling of safety; for others, a feeling of isolation and discrimination. On a communal level, ethnic fragmentation caused disagreement on such points as when to celebrate important holidays. These rifts reveal the impossibility of speaking about Muslim Americans as one community. Although efforts made by the Council of Muslim Organization of Greater Chicago, the III&E, and others demonstrated a communal desire for change, the Islamic house of God remains divided.

Religious authority within the community is deeply influenced by social class. The prevalence of professional Muslims shows that the right to interpret Islam within the United States is determined by an individual's success and status according to prevailing American secular norms. Furthermore, within mosques and paramosques, authority depends on two factors: The first is the proof of having done well in America, of succeeding in fields that within that society are connected to prestige, power, and money but not necessarily religion. The second is the dedication of time to the practice, study, and teaching of Islam—a dedication usually made possible only by economic and social status and comfort (that is, from money earned professionally in the non-Muslim world).

While people who are granted the power to speak to, and on behalf of, a congregation or community must be "good Muslims," this moral requirement is in very few instances authoritative in itself. Although the Muslim-American community embraces people of all social classes, those who are able to interpret and witness their religion on behalf of their community are members of the middle and upper-middle class—the ones whose voices, not surprisingly, are primarily heard in this book.

This chapter also covered the roads that some women take to religious authority and interpretation. Because the system in many ways is based on the viewpoints of men, Muslim-American women therefore feel the need to define the Islamic interpretations and authority for themselves, according to their experiences and aspirations. As a number of earlier studies have concluded, women within a patriarchal minority or immigrant community often become the essential bearers of culture for present and future generations.[131] That Muslim women in Chicago were proudly taking on this role showed, for example, in their distinctive style of clothing and their dedication to live Islam to the fullest. The frameworks within which women moved in the community also emphasized their distinctiveness. Women's visibility enhanced their stature, to be sure, but it also heightened their vulnerability, ironically "validating" paternal observance and control.

As the focus on women's roles increases, so does the need for self-definition. The definitions of Muslim womanhood that emerged in the women's study group included stands against non-Muslim norms and certain male behavior and privileges, both of which were seen as corrupting the religious dedication of women. Non-Muslim values were also perceived as threatening because of the power of the surrounding society to restrict Muslim practices or tempt Muslim women away from their religious beliefs. Interestingly, Muslim men (not all, of course, but many) were perceived as threatening because of their lack of religious dedication; they were seen as having the potential to undermine the authority and activism of their female partners.

Overall, complex religious divisions and interpretations make the road to religious authority among first-generation Muslim Americans complicated and sometimes conflicted. Age, gender, ideology, class, and ethnicity are highly influential elements in the presentation and practice of Islam in America. Although the results at times are conflicts and disputes, the diversity nevertheless demonstrates the vibrancy of the Muslim community, not only in Chicago but across the continent.

6 Muslims in America
E Pluribus Unum

GIVEN THE NATURE of Muslim religious life in the American context, seen through the microcosm of the Chicago community, it is time to revisit the two questions with which this book began: Is Islam, after its century-long encounter with America, an "American religion" or simply a temporary transplant that will never take root? And do Muslim Americans constitute one community? Both questions, although important in the late 1990s, are equally central to the present and future of Muslims in America. If Islam becomes deeply woven into the religious fabric of the United States, then Muslim Americans have a big stake in the country's future and the right to claim acceptance on a larger scale. And if Muslims ever establish themselves as a unified voice in American society, they may—considering the community's potential size and economic and educational assets—eventually influence the wider society on many levels.

The preceding chapters have shown how Islam has adapted to the United States and developed within the American social context. Although this process of contextualization changes neither the sacred texts nor the basic dogmas, it affects the ways in which the community reads, understands, and practices them—and brings them to life. Islam has become an American religion because its interpretations, institutions, and practices are constantly reacting to, or being influenced by, the American environment. This adaptation of Islam to American society showed itself in numerous ways, from IMAN's social and educational efforts to counter the malaise of a deprived neighborhood to the contention of young Muslims that Islam and its scriptures predict scientific discoveries and support equal status for women.

Islam is an American religion because America is the environment in which new generations of Muslims are socialized and

189

in which they carry out their Islamic activities. *Khutbas* are held in English, Islam is propagated on American campuses, and Muslim-American institutions and organizations engage locally and nationally with the larger non-Muslim society. Even when Muslims take a strong stand against certain values or behavior in American society, that very society remains an important reference point in their practice and presentation of Islam. For example, although the Hizb al-Tahrir views any participation in American society as *kufr* (unbelief), it still uses American institutions (such as universities) to spread its message. Whether Muslim Americans like it or not, non-Muslim America is the daily reality to which they have to relate, even when attempting to create alternative or even secluded ways of living.

Just as American society values individual choice, the central components of the formation of Islam and Islamic identities in America are personal choice, conviction, and dedication. Parents choose to send their children to weekend schools and Muslim full-time schools. Muslim students choose to enroll in the MSA. Young women choose the *hijab.* Muslim professionals choose to dedicate their spare time to publicizing and explaining Islam, with some even establishing paramosque institutions. Community members who lecture about Islam to non-Muslims or hold the office of *khatib* within the mosque do not have to hold a degree in Islamic theology; instead, their status is a direct consequence of their personal desire to participate in these fields.

Critical voices among both Muslims and non-Muslims would probably argue that Islam is not, and can never be, an American religion. Among Muslims, one likely argument is that Islam as a divine message cannot be changed and cannot bow to human context, and, further, that it should not do so because *fitna* (disagreement, chaos) within the global *umma* must be prevented. Among non-Muslims, critics are likely to point to the occasions on which Muslims worldwide have used their religion as an excuse to inveigh against or wage terrorist attacks on the United States. Despite their many differences, however, what both camps have in common is a view of Islam and Muslims as homogeneous and unchangeable. Both fail to see that religion is nothing without practice and that practice is always affected by time and place. Islam as practiced in America has become, and continues to become, American.

The most fundamental argument against adjusting Islam to the American context lies in the ties that Muslim immigrants have to the countries they left behind. Ethnic nostalgia and deeply felt responsibilities toward family and the culture of origin can make it difficult, and even frightening, to accept the norms of a new country. Ethnic preferences make people choose to pray and participate in the activities of certain mosques, while avoiding others. But even when immigrant life centers on keeping familiar traditions, practices, and ties "unpolluted," change inevitably occurs.

One of the most common reactions to life in a new environment is the strengthening of behaviors that seemed less important in the "old country." In some instances, for example, the importance and meaning of religion will grow in reaction to a person's or family's suddenly becoming part of a minority, so that the community becomes more religiously observant than it was, or might have been, in its original homeland. That it became important for Muslim parents to send their children to Muslim full-time schools "free of Western social ills" is an example of this intensified religious commitment. Life in the United States, with its assimilationist values, actually fosters this intense redefinition of religion among minority newcomers.

The main challenge that ethnic nostalgia and ethnic preference present to Muslims in America is their fragmentary effect. Whereas a unifying religion could ideally bring diverse ethnic groups together and give them a coherent voice with a political impact, such coherence is more the exception than the rule. That is also why the influence of ethnic affiliation is the strongest argument against the existence of a unified Muslim-American community. Although Muslim institutions, organizations, and individuals speak out against ethnic fragmentation, almost all of the organizations and groups that this book describes expressed ethnic preferences and beliefs. IMAN, for example, struggled with the problem of children's teasing other children for not being Arabs. And ethnicity was visible among MSA members not only at cultural fairs but also in the clothes that students wore at 'Id dinners.

It would be misleading to claim that the Muslim community in America will grow out of ethnic fragmentation when the next generation takes the reins of leadership. Muslim immigrants continue to bring with them their own form of Islam, contextualized in their country of origin. Although ethnicity may eventually diminish in importance, its indicators and traces do not readily disappear from people's faces, family histories, rituals, or kitchens. Even if ethnic fragmentation among Muslim Americans is actually overcome, the historical rifts between Sunnism and Shi'ism—or between those who consider Sufism in perfect accordance with Islam and those who consider it an innovation—are likely to come to the fore. Newer rifts (for example, between those who consider active involvement in American society to be absolutely Islamic and those who do not) will also arise to divide the community. Although Muslims in America see themselves as members of an inclusive *umma*, rooted in the same religious scripture and tradition, their understanding of what this community stands for will continue to change and evolve.

However, diversity—whether ideological or ethnic—is not necessarily negative, depending upon how diversity is handled and what it produces. Closely tied to the ethnic diversity of the Muslim-American community is the vibrancy of its ideas, institutions, and cultural differences. Because diversity has always been a part of Islam, it does not change the Muslim self-image of honoring the same divine message and belonging to the same *umma*. Muslims in America handle diversity as both a condition and a challenge, sometimes praising it, sometimes fighting it. Either way, diversity is a given, fostered by both the many cultures and levels of religious observance that Muslim Americans represent and the individualist values of American society.

So what is the future of Muslims, as one or perhaps several communities, in the United States? There is no doubt that Muslims in America have a long way to go to attain social inclusion and acceptance—especially since the events of September 11, 2001—and to overcome ethnic fragmentation. However, their establishment in the 1990s of schools, mosques, community centers, and grassroots and lobbying organizations showed that Muslims want influence and acceptance as contributing citizens—not in spite of but because of their religious heritage. Even if this ambition proves infertile in the wake of September 11, Muslims already have a felt effect on American society as doctors, academics, neighbors, and classmates. They have social influence—especially those with professional, educational, and social status—in their daily lives, both within and outside of their own community.

In particular, the community efforts of the 1990s underlined a strong, conscious effort to establish organizations that speak with weight for all Muslims in America. The community wanted a voice directed toward and speaking within a country in which a great variety of Muslims now live. Although not necessarily accepted by all Muslims as "delivering the right message," these organizations demonstrated the community's desire to create one voice out of many, *e pluribus unum*. This challenge faces not only Muslim Americans, of course, for it is the challenge and strength of the country itself.

The familiarity of Muslim Americans with the academic system, superpower technology, and American system may have effects that reach far beyond their community. In today's global environment, Muslim Americans may eventually influence the practice and understanding of Islam in the very countries from which their parents, grandparents, or great-grandparents came. By the same token, these Muslims may have a growing influence on America itself, especially through the institutions that they establish. As they continue to mold both American Islam and the Muslim-American community, these institutions may one day have a great effect on American social, political, and religious life, as well as on Muslims throughout the world.

No religious or ethnic community immigrates to America and remains unchanged. English words creep into the language of home; children do not always follow the "old ways"; and young adults rebel by becoming more religious or less. Like all of the communities that preceded it, the Muslim-American community practices and interprets its religion in the social context called the United States of America.

But by the sheer weight of its numbers alone, it is a community to be reckoned with in the coming century. Regardless of whether the American *medina* remains fragmented or not, Islam is in America to stay.

Notes

CHAPTER ONE

1. Faree Nu'man, *The Muslim Population in the United States: A Brief Statement* (Washington, D.C.: American Muslim Council, 1992); Richard B. Turner, *Islam in the African-American Experience* (Indianapolis: Indiana University Press, 1997), 12 ff.

2. Yvonne Yazbeck Haddad, "American Foreign Policy in the Middle East and Its Impact on the Identity of Arab Muslims in the United States," in *The Muslims of America*, ed. Yvonne Yazbeck Haddad (New York: Oxford University Press, 1991), 217.

3. John Esposito, "Introduction: Muslims in America or American Muslims?" in *Muslims on the Americanization Path?* ed. Yvonne Yazbeck Haddad and John L. Esposito (New York: Oxford University Press, 2000), 3.

4. Nu'man, *Muslim Population*, 13.

5. Ilyas Ba-Yunus and Moin Siddiqui, *A Report on the Muslim Population in the United States* (New York: Center for American Muslim Research and Information, 1999).

6. Ihsan Bagby et al., *The Mosque in America: A National Portrait. A Report from the Mosque Study Project* (Washington, D.C.: Council on American–Islamic Relations, 2001); Howard Fienberg and Iain Murray, "How Many U.S. Muslims? Our Best Estimate," *Christian Science Monitor*, November 29, 2001; Barry A. Kosmin and Egon Mayer, "Profile of the U.S. Muslim Population," American Religious Identification Survey 2001, *ARIS Report*, October 2001.

7. *CIA World Fact Book*, website (last viewed August 2002); available at http://www.cia.gov/cia/publications/factbook.

8. About 12 percent of the Indian population and 97 percent of the Pakistani population is Muslim, according to the *CIA World Fact Book*.

9. Peter Xenos et al., *Asian Indians in the United States: A 1980 Census Profile*, Papers of the East–West Population Institute (Honolulu: East–West Center, 1989), 15; Karen I. Leonard, *The South Asian Americans* (Westport, Conn.: Greenwood Press, 1997), 173.

10. Karen I. Leonard, "South Asian Leadership of American Islam," in *Muslims in the West: From Sojourners to Citizens*, ed. Yvonne Yazbeck Haddad (New York: Oxford University Press, 2002).

11. Ibid.

12. Leonard, *South Asian Americans*, 90.

13. Michael W. Suleiman, "Introduction: The Arab Immigrant Experience," in *Arabs in America: Building a New Future*, ed. Michael W. Suleiman (Philadelphia: Temple University Press, 1999), 9–11.

14. For descriptions of rejection of "Arab American money" during elec-
toral campaigns, see Nabeel Abraham, "Arab-American Marginality: Mythos
and Praxis," in *Arab Americans: Continuity and Change*, ed. Baha Abu-
Laban and Michael W. Suleiman, AAUG Monograph Series 24 (Belmont,
Mass.: Association of Arab-American University Graduates, 1989), 19; Abeen
M. Jabara, "A Strategy for Political Effectiveness," in Abu-Laban and Su-
leiman, *Arab Americans*, 204; Yvonne Yazbeck Haddad, "The Challenge of
Muslim Minorityness: The American Experience," in *The Integration of
Islam and Hinduism in Western Europe*, ed. P. S. van Koningsveld and
W. A. R. Shadid (Kampen, Netherlands: Kok Pharos Publishing House, 1991),
145.

15. For notices about federal surveillance and possible internment of
Arab Americans in the 1990s, see Laura McCoy, "Questioning of Arab-
Americans Protested," *Sacramento Bee*, January 24, 1991; Haddad, "Amer-
ican Foreign Policy," 220, 223; Louise Cainkar, "Palestinian Women in the
United States: Coping with Tradition, Change and Alienation" (Ph.D. the-
sis, Northwestern University, 1988), 131–32; Kathleen Moore, *Al-Mughtaribun, American Law and the Transformation of Muslim Life in the United
States* (Albany: State University of New York Press, 1995), 104; Louise
Cainkar, "Immigrant Palestinian Women Evaluate Their Lives," in *Family
and Gender among American Muslims: Issues Facing Middle Eastern Immi-
grants and Their Descendants*, ed. Barbara C. Aswad and Barbara Bilgé
(Philadelphia: Temple University Press, 1996), 56; Nadine Naber, "Ambigu-
ous Insiders: An Investigation of Arab American Invisibility," *Ethnic and
Racial Studies* 1 (2000): 49; Hussein Ibish, " 'They Are Absolutely Obsessed
with Us': Anti-Arab Bias in American Discourse and Policy," in *Race in 21st
Century America*, ed. Curtis Stokes et al. (East Lansing: Michigan State
University Press, 2001), 134.

16. Descriptions of the American movie industry's representation of
Arabs and Arab Americans are found in Naber, "Ambiguous Insiders," 44–46;
Ibish, " 'They Are Absolutely Obsessed with Us.' "

17. Asma Gull Hasan, *American Muslims: The New Generation* (New
York: Continuum, 2000), 131. See also pages 56–57, 127–129, and Garbi
Schmidt, "Dialectics of Authenticity," *Muslim World* (Spring 2002).

18. Larry Poston, *Islamic Daʿwah in the West: Muslim Missionary Activity and the Dynamics of Conversion to Islam* (New York: Oxford University Press, 1992), 79.

19. Ronald Robertson, *Social Theory and Global Culture* (London: Sage
Publications, 1992), 6.

20. See also Peter Beyer, *Religion and Globalization* (London: Sage Publications, 1994).

21. Armando Salvatore, *Islam and the Political Discourse of Modernity* (Reading: Ithaca Press, 1997), 18.

22. Most often this interpretation cites Qur'an 49:13 as an argument.

23. *A Rush to Judgment: A Special Report on Anti-Muslim Stereotyping. Harassment and Hate Crimes Following the Bombing of Oklahoma City's Murrah Federal Building, April 19, 1995* (Washington, D.C.: Council on American-Islamic Relations, 1995), 9–20. See also Mary Abowd, "Arab-Americans Suffer Hatred after Bombing," *Chicago Sun-Times*, May 13, 1995; Penny Bender, "Jumping to Conclusions in Oklahoma City?" *American Journalism Review*, June 1995; Richard Roeper, "Media Stumble Badly in Rush to Judgment," *Chicago Sun-Times*, April 24, 1995;

24. See pages 24–25.

25. See Ibish, " 'They Are Absolutely Obsessed with Us,' " 130–31. See also Kathleen Moore, "A Closer Look at Anti-Terrorism Law: *American-Arab Anti-Discrimination Committee v. Reno* and the Construction of Aliens' Rights," in Suleiman, *Arabs in America*.

26. " 'Islam Is Peace,' Says President," remarks by the president at Islamic Center of Washington, D.C., September 2001 White House website (last viewed August 2002); available at: http://www.whitehouse.gov/news/releases/2001/09/20010917-11.html.

27. "Important Safety Info, UCI Campus" (e-mail), MSU-UCI, September 13, 2001.

28. *The Status of Muslim Civil Rights in the United States 2002, Stereotypes and Civil Liberties* (Washington, D.C.: Council on American Islamic Relations, 2002), 9.

29. Ibid., 16.

30. Examples of Muslim-American lobbying organizations are the Council on American Islamic Relations (CAIR) and the American Muslim Council (AMC). For a description of Muslim political organizations in the United States, see also Steve A. Johnson, "Political Activity of Muslims in America," in Haddad, *The Muslims of America*.

31. Paul Findley, *Silent No More: Confronting America's False Image of Islam* (Beltsville, Md.: Amana Publications, 2001). Also Kamiz Ghanea-Bassiri, *Competing Visions of Islam in the United States: A Study of Los Angeles*, Contributions to the Study of Religion 50 (Westport, Conn.: Greenwood Press, 1997), 94–102.

32. The Center for Muslim–Christian Understanding at Georgetown University, founded in 1993, is prominent in this respect. In addition to offering courses on Islam and the history of Muslim–Christian relations, the center seeks to interpret Islam, nationally and internationally, through lectures, symposia, conferences, and media coverage: see Center for Muslim–Christian Understanding: History and International Affairs, *Report on Activities 1995–1996* (Washington, D.C.: Edmund A. Walsh School of Foreign Service, Georgetown University, n.d.).

33. Dialogue between Muslims and other religious groups has, for example, been initiated by the Council for the Parliament of the World's Religions.

34. Examples of media coverage presenting Islam and American Muslims as a growing part of American mainstream are numerous. See Gustav R. Niebuhr, "American Moslems: Islam Is Growing Fast in the U.S.; Fighting Fear and Stereotypes," *Wall Street Journal*, October 5, 1990; Richard Bernstein, "A Growing Islamic Presence: Balancing Sacred and Secular," *New York Times*, May 2, 1993; Robert Marquand and Lamis Andoni, "Islam Takes Root in Land of Levis," *Christian Science Monitor*, January 22, 1996.

35. See Robert Marquand, "Muslims Learn to Pull Political Ropes in U.S.," *Christian Science Monitor*, February 5, 1996.

36. Amatullah Sharif Okakpu, "U.S. Senate Invocation—A Muslim First," *Muslim Journal*, February 14, 1992; Nu'man, *Muslim Population*, 26.

37. Amatullah Sharif, "First Lady Hillary Rodham Clinton Hosts Muslims for *Eid al-Fitr* Celebration," *Muslim Journal*, March 15, 1996.

38. Bob Dole gained some Muslim support because of his pro-Bosnian stance: see "Bosnian Refugees and Genocide Victims Endorse Mr. Bob Dole," MSANEWS, Internet distribution list, October 16, 1996; Marquand, "Muslims Learn." The tendency to address Muslim voters increased during the 2000 national election. Muslim organizations such as CAIR also did their best to gather Muslim voters around one candidate (George W. Bush).

39. See U.S. Congress, House of Representatives, *Supporting Religious Tolerance towards Muslims*, 105th Cong., 2nd sess., August 6, 1998.

40. Muslims in Chicago were described in four earlier academic works of various lengths, three of which focused on one ethnic group. These three dissertations were written in the late 1940s and early 1950s: see Lawrence Oschinsky, "Islam in Chicago: Being a Study of the Acculturation of a Muslim-Palestinian Community in that City" (M.A. thesis, University of Chicago, 1947); Abdul-Jadil al-Tahir, "The Arab Community in the Chicago Area: The Muslim Palestinian Community" (M.A. thesis, University of Chicago, 1950); and idem, "The Arab Community in the Chicago Area: A Comparative Study of the Christian-Syrians and the Muslim-Palestinians" (Ph.D. thesis, University of Chicago, 1952). More than three decades later, in 1988, Louise Cainkar presented her dissertation: Cainkar, "Palestinian Women." Finally, see Asad Husain and Harold Vogelaar, "Activities of the Immigrant Muslim Communities in Chicago" in *Muslim Communities in North America*, ed. Yvonne Yazbeck Haddad and Jane Idleman Smith (Albany: State University of New York Press, 1994).

41. Estimates of size of the Chicago Muslim community vary. In 1993, the National Survey of Religious Identification claimed that 1 percent (28,000 people) in Chicago were Muslims: Barry A. Kosmin and Seymour P. Lachman, *One Nation under God: Religion in Contemporary American Society* (New York: Crown Trade Paperbacks, 1993), 110. However, a few years later the social scientist Ilyas Ba-Yunus estimated the total number of Muslims living in the Chicago area in 1994 at 285,126: Ilyas Ba-Yunus,

"Muslims of Illinois: A Demographic Report," *East–West Review*, special supp. (Summer 1997). Ba-Yunus's study was broken into the following ethnic groups: 46 percent indigenous (mainly African Americans), 20 percent Arabs, 19 percent South Asians, 7 percent Turks, 4 percent Eastern Europeans, and 4 percent other ethnic groups.

42. See also Yvonne Yazbeck Haddad, "The Dynamics of Islamic Identity in North America," in Haddad and Esposito, *Muslims on the Americanization Path?* 37–39; Aminah Beverly McCloud, "Racism in the Ummah," in *Islam: A Contemporary Perspective*, ed. Mohammad Ahmadullah Siddiqi (Chicago: North American Association of Muslim Professionals and Scholars Publications, 1994).

43. Bruce Lawrence, "Islam in America," in *Religion and American Cultures: An Encyclopedia of Traditions, Diversity and Popular Expressions*, ed. Gary Laderman and Luis Leon (Santa Barbara, Calif.: ABC-Clio, 2003), 123–32.

44. Ibid.

45. Bruce Lincoln, *Authority: Construction and Corrosion* (Chicago: University of Chicago Press, 1994), 9.

46. Of the eighty people with whom I taped interviews, thirty were men and fifty were women.

CHAPTER TWO

1. See *Oriental and Occidental Northern and Southern Portrait Types of the Midway Plaisance* (St. Louis, Mo.: N. D. Thompson Publishing, 1894).

2. Nations with Muslim majorities represented at the exposition were Algeria, Egypt, Nubia, Persia, Sudan, Tunisia, and Turkey. India also displayed artifacts representing its Muslim population. For a full description of the Muslim representation at the World's Columbian Exposition, see Moses P. Hardy, ed., *The Official Directory of the World's Columbian Exposition, May 1st to October 30th, 1893* (Chicago: W. B. Conkey Company, 1893); Gertrude M. Scott, "Village Performances: Villages at the Chicago World's Columbian Exposition" (Ph.D. thesis, New York University, 1991); Adele L. Younis, *The Coming of the Arabic-Speaking People of the United States* (New York: Center for Migration Studies, 1995), 150–59.

3. The public was allowed to observe prayer in the mosque on Cairo Street. This was not the case in the Turkish Village, where only Muslims were allowed into the mosque during prayer, except for those who obtained special permits: See Scott, *Village Performances*, 162, 219–20; "Cairo Street Open," *Chicago Tribune*, May 28, 1893.

4. Sufism is often characterized as the mystical path of Islam.

5. Scott, *Village Performances*, 161.

6. Cited in Turner, *Islam in the African-American Experience*, 64.

7. Scott, *Village Performances*, 166.

8. Walter R. Houghton, ed., *Neely's History of the Parliament of the World's Religions Compiled from Original Manuscripts and Stenographic Reports* (Chicago: F. T. Neely, 1893), 460.

9. Ibid., 613–15. A short presentation of papers given on Islam during the 1893 parliament can be found in A. Al-Ahari Bektashi, *The 1983 World Parliament of Religion Papers: Papers on Islam* (Chicago: Magribine Press, 1993).

10. In an immigration statute enacted two years before the exposition, polygamists were added to people guilty of "moral turpitude" and accordingly denied admission to the United States: Moore, *Al-Mughtaribun*, 38.

11. Some evidence can be traced through unpublished sources, such as when a group from the city's social establishment in the late 1930s decided to visit the Syrians. "We usually associate Syrians with house to house vendors of oriental laces and rugs. . . . After the Exposition they settled around 18th Street and State Street": "Syrians in Chicago," *Tour Topics* 36 (January 9–15, 1938).

12. By 1910, the number of immigrants from Turkey fell into two categories: Turkey in Asia and Turkey in Europe. In that year, 1,486 immigrants came from Turkey in Asia, and 758 came from Turkey in Europe: see *The People of Chicago: Who We Are and Who We Have Been: Census Data on Foreign Stock and Race: 1837–1970 (Mother Tongue Addendum 1910–1970)* (Chicago: City of Chicago, Department of Development and Planning, 1976).

13. Adele L. Younis, "The Growth of Arabic-Speaking Settlements in the United States," in *The Arab-Americans: Studies in Assimilation*, ed. Elaine Hagopian and Ann Padden (Wilmette, Ill.: Medina University Press International, 1969), 104; Younis, *Coming of the Arabic-Speaking People*, 111–14.

14. Michael W. Suleiman, "Early Arab-Americans: The Search for Identity," in *Crossing the Waters: Arab-Speaking Immigrants to the United States before 1940*, ed. J. E. Hooglund (Washington, D.C.: Smithsonian Institution Press, 1987), 39; Younis, *Coming of the Arabic-Speaking People*, 180.

15. See Moore, *Al-Mughtaribun*, 29, 42.

16. Edith M. Stein, "Some Near Eastern Immigrant Groups in Chicago" (M.A. thesis, University of Chicago, 1922), 77–78. The Muslim settlement in this neighborhood is briefly described in an article published in *Muslim World* a few years earlier: "How will a worshipper in a 'swell' Lake Shore Drive church in Chicago like if that Mohammmedan boy does go back and tells all he saw in America, as he found conditions on 18th and South State Streets, or the junction of Halsted Street and Milwaukee and Grand Avenues? For all that he saw in America year after year was in that section of the city, where he was doomed to live": M. M. Aijian, "The Mohammedans in the United States," *Muslim World* 10 (1920): 32.

17. Stein, *Near Eastern Immigrant Groups*, 77.

18. Oschinsky, *Islam in Chicago*; al-Tahir, *Arab Community in the Chicago Area*; idem, *Arab Community in the Chicago Area: A Compar-*

ative Study. I have found no studies made between 1922 and 1947 of Muslims or Palestinians in Chicago.

19. Al-Tahir, *Arab Community in the Chicago Area*, 16.

20. Idem, *Arab Community in the Chicago Area: A Comparative Study*, 57.

21. Al-Tahir mentions that, between 1912 and 1932, only 50 percent of the Syrian and Palestinian immigrants to the United States could read and write. Still, some of them pursued academic careers, and fifteen male Palestinians were attending college in the Chicago area at the time of al-Tahir's study: ibid., 182, 210).

22. Ibid., 73, 88. The Syrian enclave that was prominent in Chicago in the 1920s has disappeared today: see Louise Cainkar, *Meeting Community Needs, Building on Community Strength* (Chicago: Arab American Action Network, 1998).

23. Poston, *Islamic Daʿwah in the West*, 28.

24. Hagopian and Paden, *The Arab-Americans*, 9.

25. All of the restaurants were established in the neighborhood of 18th Street and Michigan Avenue: Al-Tahir, *Arab Community in the Chicago Area: A Comparative Study*, 95.

26. Ibid., 104.

27. Ibid., 105. Chicago immigrants contributed $20,000 to the Baituniya School. Other recipients of aid in the early 1950s were Palestinian refugees: ibid., 204.

28. Ibid., 107–108.

29. This was also the case among South Asian immigrants (Leonard, *South Asian Americans*, 107).

30. The first Arabic newspaper, *Kawab America*, was founded in New York in 1892. For a comprehensive description of the Arab press in the United States, see Joseph Ajami, "The Arabic Press in the United States since 1892: A Socio-Historical Study" (Ph.D. thesis, University of Ohio, Athens, 1987).

31. Cited in al-Tahir, *Arab Community in the Chicago Area*, 95.

32. In the mid-1930s, the number of people coming to Chicago from what was then Yugoslavia was estimated at 40,000–60,000. The proportion of this group that was Muslim is uncertain: Joseph S. Roucek, "The Yugoslav Immigrants in America," *American Journal of Sociology* 5 (1935): 604.

33. *People of Chicago*, 15, 33.

34. Sucheta Mazumdar, "Racist Response to Racism: The Aryan Myth and South Asians in the United States," *South Asia Bulletin* 1 (1989): 50.

35. Moore, *Al-Mughtaribun*, 55.

36. Ibid., 49.

37. Cainkar, *Palestinian Women*, 53.

38. Ibid., 87.

39. Cainkar, *Meeting Community Needs*.

40. Richard Taub, "Immigrants from the Indian Subcontinent and the Social Experience of Ethnic Groups in America," in *Immigrants from the Indian Subcontinent in the USA: Problems and Prospects*, ed. Hekmat Elkhanialy and Ralph W. Nicholas (Chicago: Indian League of America, 976), 2; Raymond Brady Williams, *Religions of Immigrants from India and Pakistan: New Threads in the American Tapestry* (New York: Cambridge University Press, 1988), 243.

41. See also Leonard, *South Asian Americans*, 91. It has been estimated that 15,000–150,000 South Asians lived in Chicago by 1988: Williams, *Religions of Immigrants*, 242. Of these immigrants, 50–60 percent came from Hyderabad, 30 percent from Gujarat, and 10–20 percent from other parts of India: ibid., 302 n. 5).

42. Husain and Vogelaar, "Activities," 240.

43. *Islam in North America—Muslim Community Center: Accomplishments and Aspirations, MCC 25th Anniversary Commemoration* (Chicago: Muslim Community Center, 1995).

44. Interview with member of the MCC (taped), June 30, 1997.

45. For an introduction to Tablighi Jama'at in the West, see Felice Dassetto, "The Tabligh Organization in Belgium," in *The New Islamic Presence in Western Europe*, ed. Tomas Gerholm and Yngve Georg Litman (London: Mansell, 1988), 159–73; Barbara D. Metcalf, "New Medinas: The Tablighi Jama'at in America and Europe," in *Making Muslim Space in North America and Europe*, ed. Barbara D. Metcalf (Berkeley: University of California Press, 1996); Dale E. Eickelman and James Piscatori, *Muslim Politics* (Princeton, N.J.: Princeton University Press, 1996), 148–50.

46. Roy Larson, "Feasting . . . Fasting: Two Weeks with Muslims—A Reporter's Diary," *Chicago Sun-Times*, October 13, 1974.

47. Eric Zorn, "Morton Grove Tells School Board to Get Off Muslim Neighbors' Backs," *Chicago Tribune*, November 8, 1990; Rashid Ghazi, *MCC 25th Anniversary Video* (videocassette), Muslim Community Center, Chicago, 1995.

48. See, for example, Janan Hanna, "FBI Questioning Irks Some Arabs in the U.S.," *Chicago Tribune*, January 10, 1991; Charles F. Williams, "FBI Overstepped Consent Decree, ACLU Charges," *Chicago Daily Law Bulletin*, June 14, 1994.

49. "Metro Briefings," *Chicago Sun-Times*, June 15, 1994.

50. See Leila Diab, "A Sea of Injustice: A Palestinian-American Muslim Family's Imposed Crisis," *Muslim Journal*, February 19, 1993; Stephen Franklin, "U.S. Probing Chicago Connection to Hamas," *Chicago Tribune*, November 16, 1994; Tom Hundley, "Two Chicagoans Aided Militants, Israelis Say," *Chicago Tribune*, February 1, 1993; Judith Miller, "Israel Says That a Prisoner's Tale Links Arabs in U.S. to Terrorism," *New York Times*, February 17, 1993; Maureen O'Donnell, "Israel Convicts Hamas Backer," *Chicago Sun-Times*, January 4, 1995, idem, "Israeli Consul to Check Detained Local Muslim," *Chicago Sun-Times*, February 17, 1995; Bonnie Mil-

lar Rubin, "Chicago Ridge Man Being Held in Israel," *Chicago Tribune,* February 18, 1995; Sharman Stein, "Grocer Tied to Terrorists Comes Home," *Chicago Tribune,* July 28, 1993.

51. "FBI Steps Up Inquiries of Muslim Groups in U.S.," *Chicago Tribune,* February 4, 1993.

52. Teresa Puente and Stephen Franklin, "Fight Persecution with Politics, Muslims Told," *Chicago Tribune,* January 2, 1997; "Chicago News: A Summary of the Developments around the Forfeiture of Mohammad Salah," *MSANEWS,* Internet distribution list, June 14, 1998.

53. Matt O'Connor, "Hamas Laundering Charges Denied," *Chicago Tribune,* June 13, 1998; Holly Sullivan, "Arabs Battle Bias," *Daily Southtown,* June 21, 1998; "A New Brand of American Justice?" editorial, *Chicago Tribune,* June 19, 1998; Anne Bowhay, "Salah Seeks Access to Cash; Family Claims to Be Financially 'Destitute,'" *Daily Southtown,* June 16, 1998.

54. *MCC 25th Anniversary Video.*

55. According to "List of Muslim Participants" (photocopy), Parliament for the World's Religions, 1993. Also "Parliament of the World's Religions Meet in Chicago," *Muslim Journal,* November 24, 1989.

56. List of the trustees of the Council for a Parliament of the World's Religions (photocopy), obtained at the 1997 Parliament dinner, June 1, 1997.

57. Shi'ite centers are located in Rogers Park, Dunning, Glenview, Northlake, and Forest Park: Paul Numrich, "African-American Muslim Congregations in Six-County Metropolitan Chicago" (photocopy), November 1996. For a description of the Shi'ite communities in Chicago, see also Williams, *Religions of Immigrants,* 245–46.

58. Interview with member of the MCC (taped), June 30, 1997.

59. Sufis claim that *dhikr* comes from the Qur'an. The Naqshbandiyya-Haqqaniyya order in the United States mentions the following verses, among others: "Those who remember their Lord standing, and sitting, and lying, on their sides" (Qur'an 3:191); "O, Believers, make abundant mention of Allah." (Qur'an 33:41): see "Dikhr—Remembrance of God," website (last viewed April 2001); available at: http://www.sunnah.org/ibadaat/dhikr.htm. For a general introduction to the interpretations of *dhikr,* see *Encyclopedia of Islam,* new ed. (Leiden, Netherlands: Brill, 1967–), s.v. "dhikr."

60. Al-Tahir, *Arab Community in the Chicago Area: A Comparative Study,* 173. According to al-Tahir, in the early 1950s the Ahmadiyya mosque had about 200 members, most of whom were converted African Americans. See also Turner, *Islam in the African-American Experience,* 119.

61. Turner, *Islam in the African-American Experience,* 232.

62. Debra Washington Mubashshir, "Forgotten Fruit of the City: Chicago and the Moorish Science Temple of America," *Cross Currents* (Spring 2001): 15.

63. *Tour Topics,* vol. 46 (April 3, 1938).

64. Turner, *Islam in the African-American Experience,* 106. For a description of the Moorish Science Temple, see also Yvonne Y. Haddad and Jane

Idleman Smith, *Mission to America: Five Islamic Sectarian Communities in North America* (Gainesville: University Press of Florida, 1993), 79–104.

65. Mattias Gardell, *In the Name of Elijah Muhammad: Louis Farrakhan and the Nation of Islam* (Durham, N.C.: Duke University Press, 1996), 46, 209–10.

66. Haddad and Smith, *Mission to America*, 49–8.

67. Specific anti-Ahmadiyya writings written in the Chicago context can be found on the Internet: See "Pseudo-Islamic Cults," website (last viewed March 2002); available at: http://www.iiie.net/main/pseudoislam.html.

68. Studies of the Nation of Islam include Eric C. Lincoln, *The Black Muslims in America* (Boston: Beacon Press, 1961); Lawrence H. Mamiya, "Minister Louis Farrakhan and the Final Call: Schism in the Muslim Movement," in *The Muslim Community in North America*, ed. Earle Waugh et al. (Edmonton: University of Alberta Press, 1983); Steven Barboza, *American Jihad: Islam after Malcolm X* (New York: Doubleday, 1995); Aminah Beverly McCloud, *African American Islam* (New York: Routledge, 1995); Gardell, *In the Name of Elijah Muhammad*; and Turner, *Islam in the African-American Experience*.

69. Gardell, *In the Name of Elijah Muhammad*, 138; "Muslims Seek 500,000 Protesters for October 15 Demonstration in Chicago," *Muslim Journal*, October 4, 1985.

70. Garbi Schmidt, "På middag hos Louis Farrakhan," *Tidskrift för Mellanöst Studier* 1 (1997).

71. See pages 154–155.

72. Conversation with Ali Baghdadi, editor of *Arab Journal*, January 24, 1997.

73. Lawrence, *Islam in America*.

CHAPTER THREE

1. Interview with female college student (taped), November 5, 1995.

2. The Kuwait (or Gulf) war took place between January 16 and March 3, 1991.

3. The bombing took place on April 19, 1995.

4. Interview (taped), October 26, 1995.

5. That Muslim children changed their names to hide their religious and ethnic identity was reported by people involved at various levels in the community—for example, IMAN activists and professional counselors.

6. A verdict in the case was given on February 1, 2001. One Libyan citizen, accused of committing the deed, was convicted, and another was found not guilty: Donald G. McNeil, "The Lockerbie Verdict: The Overview; Libyan Convicted by Scottish Court in '88 Pan Am Blast," *New York Times*, February 1, 2001.

7. Interview (taped), September 3, 1995.

8. Interview (taped), December 15, 1995.

9. Interview (taped), October 4, 1995.

10. Some Muslim-American organizations, such as the California-based Council of Islamic Education, try to change the presentation of Islam in public schools. The council gives seminars to textbook authors and publishers: *Islam in Textbooks: A Dialogue between Textbook Publishers and Muslim Scholars, Sunday October 4, 1992*, Council of Islamic Education, 1992. American-Muslim publishers such as Kazi and IQRA Publications, both in Chicago, also independently publish textbooks on Islamic subjects. IQRA alone published eighty-five books in its Islamic curriculum between 1983 and 1995. According to one of its editors, its goal is a full curriculum of 350 books, covering such subjects as Arabic, *fiqh*, Qur'an, Islamic social studies, and Islamic manners: interview with IQRA editor, July 19, 1995; see also "IQRA International Education Foundation," *Muslim Journal*, January 27, 1989. A number of Muslim children's fiction books, intended to educate children about Islam, have also reached the market: see, for example, Zeba Siddiqui, *Karem and Fatima* (Indianapolis: American Trust Publications, 1990).

11. On the concept of Islamic education in the United States, see Kamal Ali, "Muslim School Planning in the United States: An Analysis of Issues, Problems and Possible Approaches" (Ph.D. thesis, University of Massachusetts, Amherst, 1981); idem, "Islamic Education in the United States," *American Journal for Islamic Sciences* (1984); Nimat Hafez Barazangi, "Perceptions of the Islamic Belief System: The Muslims in North America" (Ph.D. thesis, Cornell University, Ithaca, N.Y., 1988); Nimat Hafez Barazangi, "The Education of North American Parents and Children: Conceptual Change as a Contribution to Islamization of Education," *American Journal of Islamic Social Science* 3 (1990); Zakiyyah Muhammad, "Dilemmas of Islamic Education in America—Possible Alternatives," *Muslim Education Quarterly* 4 (1990); Shukery Bin Mohamad, "Growing Up Muslim in America: The Dynamic of Cross-Cultural Learning in a Small U.S. Community" (Ph.D. thesis, University of Ohio, Athens, 1992); and Karen Lynn Selby, "An Integrated versus a History-Centered Arrangement of Social Studies Content Used by Full-Time Islamic Schools in the United States" (Ph.D. thesis, University of Michigan, Ann Arbor, 1994). A number of handbooks for Muslim parents on teaching strategies also exist: see, for example, *Parents' Manual: A Guide for Muslim Parents Living in North America* (Indianapolis: Muslim Students' Association/American Trust Publication, 1992); and Norma Tarazi, *The Child in Islam: A Muslim Parent's Handbook* (Plainfield, Ind.: American Trust Publications, 1995).

12. According to *Islam in North America*, 249 students attended the first shift, and 109 students attended the second shift in 1995. The first shift was held between 10:00 A.M. and 1:30 P.M. and the second shift from 2:30 P.M. to 5:30 P.M. Tuition costs depend on the number of children each family sends to the school. The center also offers a Saturday school for Arab children. In 1995, the Saturday school had 300 students from kindergarten to

ninth grade. During the week, the MCC houses a Qur'an school, called the Dar ul-Uloom. In 1995, the Dar ul-Uloom had 87 students.

13. For a discussion of the Islamic uniform, see pages 106–110.

14. Muhamed Ismail, *Teaching Tips and Effective Strategies for Weekend Islamic Schools* (Plainfield, Ind.: American Trust Publications, 1994), 81–82, 118–20.

15. Interview (taped), December 3, 1995.

16. For another description of the Arab community in southwestern Chicago, see Louise Cainkar, "The Deteriorating Ethnic Safety Net Among Arab Immigrants in Chicago," in Suleiman, *Arabs in America.*

17. See *Social and Economic Characteristics of Chicago's Population* (Chicago: City of Chicago, 1990), 399. The actual number of Arabs living in Chicago Lawn is probably higher than stated in the report. A sizable proportion of these immigrants have come without papers and may be expected to hide from officials, including those in charge of gathering statistics. Community activists estimate that the number of Palestinians in the neighborhood is as high as 30,000: Cainkar, *Palestinian Women,* 59; idem, *Meeting Community Needs.*

18. *Social and Economic Characteristics,* 399.

19. Cainkar, *Meeting Community Needs.*

20. According to a conversation with a former project leader, March 9, 1996. The local press has covered IMAN on various occasions: see, for example, Meghan Deerin, "Arab-American Center Provides Kids Safe Haven," *Daily Southtown,* February 16, 1997.

21. Jon Anderson, "Video Peers into Lives of Arab-American Girls," *Chicago Tribune,* March 26, 1997.

22. Louise Cainkar mentions that several Palestinian community centers closed after the Gulf War, from which the Palestine Liberation Organization emerged weak: Cainkar, "Deteriorating Ethnic Safety Net," 198. The resulting weakening of ethnic pride may have increased Islamic activism and activist projects such as IMAN.

23. Interview (taped), December 13, 1997.

24. Interview (taped), September 6, 1995.

25. The Southwest Youth Collaborative was founded in 1991 by the Southwest Community Congress, the Southwest Catholic Cluster Project, and the West Communities YMCA: see *Southwest Youth Collaborative,* pamphlet, n.d. The collaborative has initiated a number of projects, such as the West Englewood Youth and Teen Center, and the *Southwest Side Tabulations from the 1994 Metro Survey* (Chicago: Metro City Information Center, 1994), a statistical survey of the city's southwestern side. A cooperative community effort with IMAN, "Taking It to the Streets," took place in the summer of 1997.

26. For a description of this project, see Cainkar, "Deteriorating Ethnic Safety Net."

27. Interview (taped), December 13, 1997.

28. The verses follow the arrangement of one of the most widely used translations of the Qur'an: Abdullah Yusuf Ali, trans., *The Meaning of the Holy Qur'an*, (Brentwood, Md.: Amana Corporation, 1993). So, to a large extent, does the translation. A notable exception is *sura* 29:46, where "the People of the Book" are not described as Christians or Jews: see idib. That a reference to Christians and Jews was included in the translation that IMAN presented at the 'Id dinner probably revealed the intention of reaching a particular audience.

29. Interview (taped), December 13, 1997.

30. Other centers in the Chicago area work among Muslim women and children who have suffered physical or psychological assaults. The Apna Ghar, founded in 1989, works among Hindu and Muslim women from the South Asian subcontinent. The center stated in its 1996 report that 142 women and children had stayed there in 1995–96: *Apna Ghar Inc.* (Chicago: privately printed, 1996). Another social-service center, the Hamdard Center, directed its services toward the South Asian and Middle Eastern community in the suburbs: *Hamdard Center* (Chicago: privately printed, 1996).

31. Interview (taped), December 13, 1997. Immigration to the United States may be a conscious choice made for Middle Eastern women who expect to better their own situations and that of their daughters. Cainkar (*Palestinian Women*, 47) says that families often bring their daughters to the United States to let them benefit from the educational opportunities. Similarly, Maryam said that some of the mothers with whom she worked had almost "forced" their families to migrate, because they wanted their daughters to have "equal opportunities for education and jobs, or choose to wear *hijab* or not to wear one, choosing who they can marry": interview, December 13, 1996.

32. Interview (taped), December 13, 1997.

33. See also Sue Ontiveros, "Rooting Out Domestic Violence," *Chicago Sun-Times*, November 1, 1997.

34. Interview (taped), December 13, 1997.

35. Ibid.

36. "IMAN Meeting" (e-mail), MSA-Chicago Net, March 4, 1997.

37. "Taking It to the Streets" (e-mail), MSA-Chicago Net, March 20, 1997.

38. "Taking It to the Streets" was funded by IMAN and the Muslim Youth Center, the Southwest Youth Collaborative, Youth Place, the Council of American Muslim Professionals, the Arab Community Center, Sanad, MSA Illinois, Benevolence International, the Muslim Youth Council, Masjid Qadir, the Latino Organization of the Southwest, Parents for a Better Community, Chicago Islamic Center, Chicago Park District, and the Crescent Brotherhood. Further, according to a pamphlet titled "Taking It to the Streets" (n.d.), the DePaul UMMA donated the surplus of its 'Id dinner to the project.

39. "Make DUA—No Rain" (e-mail), MSA Chicago Net, June 20, 1997.

40. "Jazakum Allah Khair" (e-mail), MSA-Chicago Net, June 25, 1997.

41. The College Preparatory School of America was established in 1989, and the Islamic Foundation School was established in 1988: see Mazhar Hussaini, "Islamic Foundation of Villa Park: A Dream Comes True with Full-Time Islamic School Opening," *Muslim Journal*, September 2, 1988; *Islam in North America.*

42. The al-Aqsa School differed from the other schools in one additional way: In the higher grades, Islamic studies and Arabic were taught only in Arabic. In all other schools, these subjects were taught in English. For a description of the school, see Mildred El-Amin, "Aqsa School, an All Girls Muslim Environment," *Muslim Journal*, May 24, 1991; Daa'Iyah Abdul-Muhaimin, "Career Day at al-Aqsa Muslim Girls School," *Muslim Journal*, June 12, 1992.

43. Mildred El-Amin, "The Universal School," *Muslim Journal*, November 9, 1990.

44. *Universal School Board News* (Fall 1995).

45. See Jessica Seigel, "Moslem School in Dispute," *Chicago Tribune*, August 12, 1990; Zorn, " Morton Grove"; "Islamic Group's Purchase of $2 Million Property in Morton Grove Creates Residential Stir," *Muslim Journal*, November 24, 1989; *MCC 25th Anniversary Video.*

46. Interview with the principal of a Muslim school in the Chicago area (taped), October 4, 1995. Similar statements were made by other interviewed principals: interviews, taped, October 30, 1995, and December 20, 1996.

47. *Universal School: Teaching Muslim Minds to Lead the Future* (pamphlet, n.d.).

48. *C.P.S.A.: Discover the Balance!* (pamphlet, n.d.).

49. Interview (taped), December 20, 1996.

50. Interview, March 24, 1996.

51. Interview (taped), March 25, 1997.

52. Interview (taped), March 25, 1997.

53. Interview (taped), October 30, 1995.

54. Interview (taped), March 25, 1997.

55. Interview (taped), October 4, 1995.

56. This point was emphasized by staff members at the schools: interviews (taped), March 24, 1996 and December 20, 1996.

57. The low priority that parents and the board of education give to Islamic studies may be influenced by the academic status of the Islamic teacher. Although Islamic studies teachers may have bachelor's and master's degrees in various social subjects, no state certification in religious studies exists. At the time of this study, religion as a subject was not included in the Basic Skill tests preceding teaching certification in the State of Illinois and was mentioned only as part of teachers' general education (that is, background) requirements under the category "humanities": "Minimum Requirements for State Certificates Issued by Illinois State Board of Education," website (last viewed October 1998); available at: http://206.166.105.103/isbesites/

teacher/minreq.htm. Also interview with teacher at full-time Muslim school (taped), December 20, 1996.

58. Abul A'la Mawdudi, *Let Us Be Muslims* (New Delhi: Markazu Maktaba Islami, 1995).

59. Interview with teachers at a Muslim school in the Chicago area (taped), March 24, 1996.

60. Cainkar, *Palestinian Women*, 152.

61. See also Cainkar, "Deteriorating Ethnic Safety Net," 202.

62. Deoband Islamic University was established in 1869. The teaching is described as traditional and is concerned more with building a religious personality than with helping students use their knowledge to fulfill current social requirements: see *Encyclopedia of Islam*, new ed. (Leiden, Netherlands: Brill, 1967–), s.v. "Deoband."

63. More than one *hafiz* school exists in the Chicago area. According to one informant, the first *hafiz* school in Chicago was located in a Tablighi Jama'at *masjid* on the North Side of Chicago. It closed in the mid-1990s, despite its large student body: interview with board member of the MCC (taped), June 30, 1997. During my visit, the Tablighi Jama'at ran a *hafiz* school at a North Side location with twelve to fifteen students. None of the students lived at the school. A *hafiz* program was also taught at a *masjid* in Bensenville.

64. Interview with director of *hafiz* school (taped), May 20, 1997.

CHAPTER FOUR

1. See MSAs in the USA Contact Info, website (last viewed April 2001); available at: http://www.msa.natl.org/resources/msa_usa_addresses.html.

2. According to "First Commencement Convocation," photocopy, American Islamic College (1988).

3. Trustees of the AIC have included the OIC and the Islamic Development Bank. The OIC, established in 1969, comprises fifty-two member states. The organization is committed to the advancement of solidarity among its members and thereby speaks as one voice for the interest and well-being of Muslims globally. A short history of the OIC can be found in Eickelman and Piscatori, *Muslim Politics*, 139–41. The Muslim World League, established in 1962, is a member of the OIC. The league also seeks to safeguard the interest of Muslims worldwide and, at the same time, is involved in transnational *da'wa* efforts. For a description of the league's work in the United States, see Yvonne Yazbeck Haddad, "Arab Muslims and Islamic Institutions in America: Adaptation and Reform," in *Arabs in the New World: Studies on Arab American Communities*, ed. Sameer Y. Abraham and Nabeel Abraham (Detroit: Center for Urban Studies, Wayne State University, 1983), 69–70.

4. Al-Faruqi was one of the most important Muslim-American thinkers of the late twentieth century. In addition to being among the founders of

the AIC, al-Faruqi spearheaded the International Institute of Islamic Thought in Herndon, Virginia. On al-Faruqi's projects and thoughts and their impact on American Islam, see John Esposito, "Ismail R. al-Faruqi: Muslim Scholar–Activist," in Haddad, *The Muslims of America*; Poston, *Islamic Da'wah in the West*; Muhammad Shafiq, *Growth of Islamic Thought in North America: Focus on Isma'il Raji al-Faruqi* (Brentwood, Md.: Amana Publications, 1994); Tamara Sonn, "Arab Americans in Education: Cultural Ambassadors?" in Abu-Laban and Suleiman, *Arab Americans*; Leif Stenberg, *The Islamization of Science: Four Muslim Positions Developing an Islamic Modernity*, Lund Studies in History of Religions 6 (Lund: Religionshistoriska Avdelingen, University of Lund, 1996). Dr. al-Faruqi and his wife, Lois al-Faruqi, were murdered in 1986: see *The al-Faruqi Murders*, ADC Special Report, American-Arab Anti-Discrimination Committee, Washington, D.C., 1986; Imam Nuri Muhammad, "Faruqis' Assassination Remains Unsolved," *Muslim Journal*, January 16, 1987.

5. In the spring of 1997, the school's tuition was $1,444 per semester (for twelve to eighteen credit hours), exclusive of fees. Fifteen classes were offered. Of these, six were in Arabic studies, five in Islamic studies, and four in "general studies" (covering such subjects as introduction to computer programming, English composition, college algebra, and political science: "Spring Class Schedule" (flyer), American Islamic College, 1997.

6. The academic qualifications of the AIC's staff are high. The president of the college, Dr. Asad Husain, who is also a professor of political science at Northeastern Illinois University, holds a Ph.D. in international relations from the University of Minnesota. The assistant professor of Islamic studies, Dr. Ghulaim Haider Aasi, holds a Ph.D. and a master of arts degree in religion from Temple University, where Dr. Aasi studied under Dr. al-Faruqi.

7. Interview (taped), November 5, 1995.

8. The activities of the AIC are often covered by the *Muslim Journal*: see "American Islamic College Offers Intensive Arabic Program," *Muslim Journal*, November 22, 1985; "American Islamic College," *Muslim Journal*, June 30, 1989; "The American Islamic College Fulfills Many Roles," *Muslim Journal*, May 22, 1992; Mildred El-Amin, "Islamic Education in America," *Muslim Journal*, August 12, 1988; Atique Mahmood, "American Islamic College Graduates," *Muslim Journal*, September 4, 1992; Ahmad Nadim, "American Islamic College: An Institution of High Academic Standards," *Muslim Journal*, November 18, 1988.

9. See, for example, Atique Mahmood and Ayesha K. Mustafaa, "Muslim–Christian Dialogue," *Muslim Journal*, October 4, 1991. By the late 1990s, both Dr. Aasi and Dr. Husain were active in the Conference for Improved Muslim–Christian Relations and the Council for a Parliament of the World's Religions. That two prominent staff members participated in these organizations highlighted the college's growing focus on interfaith relations. In 1997, Prof. Husain was listed as a member of the board of the Council for a

Parliament of the World's Religions. The AIC has also on various occasions worked with Chicago's Jewish community. Dr. Aasi spoke about Jewish–Muslim relations in local synagogues, and in the summer of 1996, a joint Muslim–Jewish conference, supported by the AIC, was held at the Jewish Spertus College in downtown Chicago: interview with Dr. Ghulaim Haider Aasi (taped), September 14, 1995.

10. Amatullah Sharif, "First Islamic Chaplain for the U.S. Navy Commissioned," *Muslim Journal*, September 6, 1996; Larry Witham, "2nd Muslim Chaplain Picked for Armed Forces," *Washington Times*, August 10, 1996.

11. *East–West University Catalog 1996–1999* (Chicago: East–West University), 7.

12. According to the university's chancellor, M. Wasiullah Khan, who holds a Ph.D. in education and administration from Indiana State University, 80–90 percent of the EWU's board members in 1996 were Muslim: interview (taped), February 19, 1996. Non-Muslim board members, according to a later interview with the chancellor, included two Christians and one Hindu: interview, June 12, 1997.

13. For a thorough introduction to the works and thought of Sardar, see Stenberg, *Islamization of Science*, 41–96.

14. *East–West University Catalog 1996–1999*, 39–40. See also "East–West University Adds to Muslim Options in Education," *Muslim Journal*, August 21, 1992.

15. "International Academic Scholarships 1995–1996" (flyer), obtained at the EWU. According to Wasiulllah Khan, the reduction by 1996 was no less than 30 percent: interview (taped), February 15, 1996. In the academic year 1996–97, the tuition for undergraduate studies at the school was $2,150 per quarter (ten to sixteen credit hours), exclusive of fees. Dr. Khan said during the interview that in 1995–96, eighty-nine students were enrolled in the Islamic course and that by 1996–97, the number had risen to about 100.

16. Chancellor Dr. Mohammad Wasiullah Khan to "Patron and Friend of East–West University," correspondence, June 14, 1992. A list of the EWU's Council of Patrons mentions Abdullah Naseef as a "distinguished patron" having donated more than $100,000 to the College: "East–West University Council of Patrons" (photocopy), 1994.

17. *Hadith* (Chicago: East–West University/Umran Publications, 1986); the quote is from the cover.

18. "East–West University Summary of Audited Financial Statements from Inception to August 31, 1994" (photocopy).

19. In February 1979, the EWU was incorporated as a nonprofit corporation without stock: *East–West University Catalog 1996–1999*, 7.

20. Interviews with the EWU chancellor, February 15, 1996 (taped), and June 12, 1997. In the summer of 1998, the EWU claimed to have about 600 students, which seems more comparable to the 1995 numbers. The ethnic

distribution of the students was described as 55 percent African American, 15 percent Hispanic, and 28 percent "international" (students from overseas): East–West University, website (last viewed October 1998); available at: http://www.eastwest.edu/service.htm.

21. Interview, June 12, 1997.

22. Kosmin and Lachman, *One Nation under God*, 258.

23. MSAs in the USA Contact Info, website (last viewed October 1998); available at: http://www.msa-natl.org/resources/msa_usa_addresses.html.

24. See Poston, *Islamic Da'wah in the West*, 102; Haddad, "Arab Muslims and Islamic Institutions in America," 70. For a description of the Ikhwan al-Muslimun, see, for example, Jakob Skovgaard-Petersen, *Defining Islam for the Egyptian State: Muftis and Fatwas of the Dar al-Ifta* (Leiden, Netherlands: E. J. Brill, 1997), 155–57.

25. Since then, the MSA/IIT has maintained a position that distinguishes it from other MSAs in the Chicago area. Then, as during the time of my fieldwork, most members were first-generation immigrants who had come to the United States to pursue higher academic degrees than they had earned in their homelands. The membership in the MSA/IIT is therefore older than that in the rest of the MSA population. These older students also often bring their spouses and children; thus, the MSA chapter is a community of families rather than a student association representing single individuals.

26. *Challenges and Promises: A Handbook of the Muslim Students' Association of the United States and Canada, Its Objectives, Functions, and Activities*, Muslim Students' Association of the United States and Canada, 1968, 29.

27. *The Educational Guide: A Handbook for Foreign Muslim Applications to U.S. and Canadian Universities* (Plainfield, Ind.: Association of Muslim Scientists and Engineers, 1979), 100. The two mosques that accommodated the MSAs were the MCC (then located on North Kedzie Avenue) and the as-Salaam Mosque on South Ashland Avenue. The third MSA chapter mentioned was located at the YMCA College at West Wacker Drive.

28. The following description is based on publicly accessible publications and on a number of interviews that I conducted with MSA members.

29. The Naqshbandiyya order is probably the most active and visible Sufi order in the United States. It and its activities in the Chicago context are described at length in Chapter 5.

30. Interview (taped), December 1, 1995. Whether Islam permits music (including singing) is often a hot topic of debate among Muslims. To some, music is an element that drags human beings away from Allah, whereas to others it can be a means of getting closer to Him.

31. Interview, December 14, 1995.

32. Interview (taped), August 30, 1995.

33. Interview with four female UMMA members, DePaul University (taped), October 30, 1996.

34. The conference was held on August 2–4, 1996. See "125 Speakers, 7,000 Guests Attend 1st International Islamic Unity Conference," *al-Ummah Newsletter,* vol. 1 (1996).

35. Funds for MSA chapters are generated by the campus student union, membership fees, and fund-raising: see "MSA Starters Guide," website (last viewed April 2001); available at: http://www.msa-natl.org/publications/starters.html, and "MSA Chapter Affiliation," website (last viewed April 2001); available at: http://www.msa-natl.org/msaaffil.html.

36. Interview (taped), October 30, 1996.

37. Ibid.

38. Interview (taped), November 28, 1995.

39. Although it was conducted in another part of the world, Leila Ahmed's study of Muslim women in Egypt is informative in this respect. As she says, by wearing the *hjiab,* the female student "carves out legitimate public space for herself"; she might be seen talking and studying with men without family and peers suspecting that she is behaving morally incorrectly: Leila Ahmed, *Women and Gender in Islam: Historical Roots of a Modern Debate* (New Haven, Conn.: Yale University Press, 1992), 224.

40. The film version of Betty Mahmoody's bestseller *Not without My Daughter,* directed by Brian Gilbert (Ufland/Pathé Entertainment, 1991), was often given as an example of a stereotypical presentation of the role of Muslim women.

41. Interview, February 9, 1997.

42. Interview, December 15, 1995.

43. Jan Hjärpe, "The Contemporary Debate in the Muslim World on the Definition of 'Human Rights,'" in *Islam State and Society,* ed. Ferdinand and Mehdi Mozaffari (London: Curzon Press 1988), 26.

44. *Sura* 24:31 and *sura* 33:59 are often cited to support this position.

45. Interview (taped), February 29, 1996.

46. "The Muslim Students' Association of the US and Canada: Islamic Awareness Week—A Resource Book," website (last viewed April 2001); available at: http://www.msa-natl.org/national/iaw/iawrb.96.doc.

47. *Media Relations Handbook for Muslim Activists* (Washington, D.C.: Council on American Islamic Relations, n.d.).

48. "Media Panel," First Annual Islam in America Conference, Chicago, Ill., September 30, 1995.

49. The speech was delivered by Prof. John E. Woods on the topic "Islam and the Middle East in American Popular Culture." See also John E. Woods, "Imaging and Stereotyping Islam," in *Muslims in America: Opportunities and Challenges,* ed. Asad Husain et al. (Chicago: International Strategy and Policy Institute, 1996).

50. Although Islamic Awareness Week in the school year 1996–97 was set to take place October 11–16, most of the Chicago MSAs held the event later. Northwestern University and the University of Illinois at Chicago

held their IAWs on November 10–15; the UMMA at DePaul University celebrated IAW on January 20–25, 1997; and the MSA/UC held an Islamic
Awareness Month from April 22 to May 16, 1997.

51. *Khabir*, Islamic Awareness Month special ed., 1997.

52. *The Message* (Filmco International Productions, 1976), which is also
known as *Mohammad, Messenger of God*, a movie directed by Moustapha
Akkad with actors such as Anthony Quinn, is highly popular among Muslim Americans, especially for its positive description of Muhammad and its
integration of the American film industry with the historiography of Islam.

53. External financial support for IAW/IAM lectures and events comes
most often from associations representing ethnic or religious minorities,
such as Arab, Asian, South Asian, African-American, and Jewish student
associations.

54. The Hizb al-Tahrir was established in 1952 in Cairo by Taqi al-Din
al-Nabahani (1905–78). The structure of the Hizb al-Tahrir is transnational/
global, and its message often includes a hard rhetorical stand against the
principles of Western democracy. According to the Hizb al-Tahrir, the only
legitimate social and political system is the *khilafa* (the caliphate); the
establishment of an Islamic state is therefore an ideal. For an introduction
to the movement, see Suha Taji-Farouki, *A Fundamental Quest: Hizb
al-Tahrir and the Search for the Islamic Caliphate* (London: Grey Seal,
1996).

55. Here "Hamza" refers to the historical situation after the Christian
takeover of Spain in the fifteenth century. Before that, the Jewish community was fairly well protected under Muslim rule.

56. This is a reference to *sura* 2:256 of the Qur'an.

57. Muslim Americans do not deny the favorable reports, articles, and
programs (on Islam and Muslims) that have been produced in recent years.
Cheerful postings are often distributed on Muslim Internet lists when a
newspaper or broadcast company has presented Islam positively: see, for
example, "Newsweek Article—'The New Islam'" (e-mail), MSA-Chicago
Net, March 13, 1998.

58. In the Qur'an, *taghut* is referred to as "the idol" or "the Evil": See
sura 39:17.

59. Interview (taped), February 23, 1996.

60. The question of whether it was correct according to Islam to vote in
national elections was highly debated during the 1996 presidential campaign. Organizations such as the AMC vigorously advocated voter registration: see "AMC News Bulletin: Voters Registration," *AMC Report*, June
1995; Akilah Rabb, "AMC News Bulletin: AMC and MLV Sponsor Press
Conference on Voter Registration," *AMC Report*, October 1995; Qasim
Rashad, "AMC News Bulletin: One Million Voter Registration Drive in the
City of Brotherly Love," *AMC Report*, November 1995. However, they were
countered by groups such as the Hizb al-Tahrir. The debate was also highlighted on the Internet: see "MAVA: Voting in America: Is It Halal or Haram

[Licit or Illicit]?" (e-mail), MSANEWS, October 24, 1996. The *Islamic Forum* also debated the issue (from the standpoint of voting as *haram*), but not until after the elections: see "Voting: When Is It Haram? Muslims Being Led to Hellfire!" *Islamic Forum*, vol. 6 (1997). During the 1996 elections, one Muslim from Chicago, Dr. Jalil Ahmad (Democrat), was running for a seat in the U.S. Senate.

61. "Ruling of Islam on Elections" (photocopy, n.d.).

62. ISNA was established by the MSA in 1982 as an umbrella organization for Sunni Muslim groups in North America. The organization provides a wide range of services to the Muslim-American community, including national and zonal conventions, help for the needy, and the issuing of Islamic marriage certificates.

63. The Fiqh Council of North America, established in 1986, is affiliated with ISNA. The Fiqh Council presents itself as "advising and educating its members and officials on matters related to the application of Shari'ah in their individual and collective lives in the North American environment": see "What Is the Fiqh Council of North America," website (last viewed August 2002); available at: http://www.fiqhcouncil.org/aboutus.asp.

64. *Welcome to Peacenet (Work in Progress as of September 1995)* (Winnipeg: privately printed, 1995), 2.

65. Interview (taped), February 29, 1996.

66. Interestingly, a survey conducted among Muslims in Los Angeles in 1993–94 showed that no less than 62 percent of those interviewed agreed with the statement that "recent scientific research has confirmed the validity of Islamic teachings": see GhaneaBassiri, *Competing Visions*, 81.

67. Interview (taped), February 29, 1996.

68. Although it was conducted in another Western setting, Jessica Jacobson's study of British Pakistani youth is enlightening in this respect: see Jessica Jacobson, *Islam in Transition: Religion and Identity among British Pakistani Youths* (London: Routledge, 1998), 147–49.

69. For a short introduction to Mawdudi's ideas on women, see Ann Elisabeth Mayer, *Islam and Human Rights: Tradition and Politics* (Boulder, Colo.: Westview Press, 1991), 100–102.

70. The existence of a "Victorian age" within American Islam was pointed out by Yvonne Yazbeck Haddad at the American Academy of Religion's Annual Meeting, New Orleans, 1996.

71. Interview (taped), February 29, 1996.

72. For an analysis of the *hijab* as marking a "feminism in the reverse," see Helen Watson, "Women and the Veil: Personal Responses to Global Processes," in *Islam, Globalization and Postmodernity*, ed. Akbar S. Ahmed and Hastings Donnan (London: Routledge, 1994), 152.

73. A description of Muslim-American college marriages is found in Richard Wormser, *American Islam: Growing Up Muslim in America* (New York: Walker and Company, 1994), 59–68.

74. Interview (taped), January 31, 1996.

CHAPTER FIVE

1. Poston, *Islamic Da'wah in the West*, 95. Poston's definition of the paramosques goes further than mine, as he presents the structure as an "alternative" to the mosque. As I show in this chapter, his definition can be contested. Paramosques and mosques often depend on each other rather than exist in a competitive relationship.

2. Ibid., 94.

3. ISNA is an umbrella organization that includes organizations such as the MSA. Despite its stated purpose, ISNA is generally seen as having its own agenda and scope.

4. This understanding of ISNA was mentioned and discussed at the organization's annual convention on September 1–4, 1995, in Columbus, Ohio. What seems to be a major obstacle for the activities and appeal of ISNA is its geographical location. Located on a 124-acre site in Plainfield, Indiana, ISNA is remote from major Muslim demographic centers such as Chicago, New York, and Los Angeles.

5. "SoundVision," website (last viewed October 1998); available at: http://www.icna.com/soundvision/info.html.

6. For a description of the *Adam's World* series, see Misbahu Rufai, "ICNA's Appeal Night with Yusuf Islam a Success," *Muslim Journal*, August 23, 1991.

7. The AMC's activities in Chicago are described in Larry Witham, "Muslims Stress Unity in Opening First National Assembly in Hill," *Washington Times*, April 26, 1997.

8. See, for example, *Rush to Judgment*.

9. For a short presentation of the IICA, see Poston, *Islamic Da'wah in the West*, 99–101.

10. Interview (taped), September 25, 1995.

11. Ibid.

12. Amir Ali tried to establish a *da'wa* organization, the American Islamic Committee, before his stay in Saudi Arabia. The committee published a couple of pamphlets but fell apart after six months, according to Amir Ali, because the members got jobs outside Chicago: interview (taped), August 1, 1995.

13. Atique Mahmood, "Opening of Islamic Reading Room," *Muslim Journal*, January 20, 1989.

14. Interview (taped), August 1, 1995.

15. In 1996, the members of the Board of Trustees of the III&E were Dr. Maneh Hammad al-Johani (Riyadh), Dr. Abdullah O. Naseef (Jeddah), Mr. Sobhi Betterjee (Jeddah), Dr. Muzammil H. Siddiqi (Orange County, Calif.), Mr. Riaz H. Waraich (Chicago), Dr. Jamal Badawi (Halifax), Dr. Amir Ali (Chicago), and Imam Siraj Wahaj (New York). See *Da'wah Newsletter*, vol. 1 (1996). The III&E, according to material obtained at the organization, is

registered in the State of Illinois and with the Internal Revenue Service (IRS) as a nonprofit religious organization: See "What Is III&E?" (flyer, n.d.).

16. According to III&E publications, fieldwork for the organization started with a *da'wa* seminar in Chicago organized by the ICNA in 1986. Amir Ali presented his project at the seminar (*Da'wah Newsletter* [1996]). During my interviews with Amir Ali, he described the prospects of ICNA and other *da'wa* organizations as "hot air": interview (taped), August 1, 1995.

17. *Da'wah Newsletter* (July 1995). The goals of the III&E, although often quoted in its material, are not always formulated identically (though the message is coherent). For example, the poster in the III&E office formulates the organization's objectives as (1) to eliminate the [negative] image of Islam and Muslims in North America; (2) to invite the indigenous North American population to open their hearts to Islam; and (3) to activate and train Muslims and make efforts at integration and interaction in the Muslim community. See also Ayesha Mustafaa, "Institute of Islamic Information and Education," *Muslim Journal*, January 14, 1994.

18. *Da'wah Newsletter*, vol. 1 (1995), 5.

19. *Da'wah Newsletter* (1996).

20. The idea of a fundamentalist Christian and Zionist conspiracy is presented in a number of flyers published by the III&E, whose titles include "Fundamentalist Christian–Zionist Conspiracy," "Terrorism in America, Cowardice and Evil," and "An Open Letter" (all undated). See also *Da'wah Newsletter* (1996).

21. See, for example, John Hanchette, "New Attack Was Anticipated since Trade Center Bombing," *Chicago Sun-Times*, April 20, 1995.

22. "Terrorism in America" (III&E flyer).

23. In particular, the author Robert Morey and the fundamentalist Christian publishing company Chick Publications have Amir Ali's attention. In books and on the Internet, Morey claims that Allah is a pagan moon god and that Muhammad was either a liar or mentally ill: see Robert Morey, *Islam Unveiled* (Sherman Dale, Pa.: Scholars Press, 1991); idem, *The Islamic Invasion: Confronting the World's Fastest Growing Religion* (Eugene, Ore.: Harvest House, 1992). Morey's presentations of Islam can also be found on "FAQs Concerning Islam," website (last viewed April 2001); available at: http://www.chick.com/information/religions/islam/. Chick Publications is known for distributing a number of pamphlets that denounce Islam (as well as Judaism and Catholicism).

24. "Fundamentalist Christian–Zionist Conspiracy" (III&E flyer).

25. "Terrorism in America" (III&E flyer).

26. *Da'wah Newsletter* (1995), 2.

27. For example, on July 24, 1995, Mary Ali spoke to a group of missionaries-to-be at a camp in Kenosha, Wisconsin. Four days later, the same group visited the offices of the III&E and observed Friday prayers at the MCC.

28. *Da'wah Newsletter* (1995), 1.

29. "Bullies, Dogs, Rats and the Muslim Ummah" (flyer, n.d.).

30. "On the day Allah will pay them back (all) their dues, and they will realize that Allah is the (very) Truth, that makes all things manifest": *Surat al-Nur*, v. 25, trans. Yusuf Ali. The word "*shirk*" is not mentioned in this or the preceding *aya.*

31. Interview (taped), September 20, 1995.

32. *Sura* 3:110.

33. See also Poston, *Islamic Da'wah in the West*, 64–80; John Esposito, *The Islamic Threat: Myth or Reality?* (New York: Oxford University Press, 1992).

34. "Response to Anonymously Written Flyer Distributed in Chicago Area on Friday, June 16, 1995, Defaming Amir Ali, Usama Hussein, and the III&E" (flyer, n.d.).

35. Ibid.

36. Interview (taped), September 20, 1995.

37. See Quitan Wiktorowicz, *The Management of Islamic Activism: Salafis, the Muslim Brotherhood, and State Power in Jordan* (Albany: State University of New York Press, 2001), 125.

38. The Salafi should not be confused with the Salafiyya movement of the late nineteenth century, represented by famous scholars such as Muhammad 'Abduh and Jamal al-Din al-Afghani. Although both movements reject the *madhahib* (schools of Islamic law) in an attempt to "regenerate" Islam as it was lived and understood among the first followers of the faith (*al-Salaf al-Salih*), the Salafiyya was opposed not to secularism but to the rigidity of *taqlidi* (strict obedience to canon) scholars (for example, in Egypt). On the Salafis in the United States, see Johnson, "Political Activity"; Wiktorowicz, *Management of Islamic Activism.*

39. See, for example, Amir Ali, *How to Present Islam: A Rational Approach* (Chicago: Institute of Islamic Information & Education, 1994), i–ii.

40. Interview with Naqshbandiyya Sufi (taped), March 17, 1996.

41. Liaquat Ali, "The Essence, History and Future of Muslim Publishing in North America," speech presented at the First Annual Islam in America Conference, Chicago, September 29, 1995.

42. The Naqshbandiyya-Haqqaniyya order arranged *dhikr* on Thursdays and Saturdays. On Saturdays, the location varied. In 1995, the Saturday *dhikr* was held at the ICCC in Northbrook, in the Rockefeller Chapel at the University of Chicago, in the Haqqani Community Center on the South Side, or in a private residence in the suburb of Oakbrook.

43. Interview with Laleh Bakhtiar (taped), August 3, 1995.

44. *Sura* 1 and *sura* 2:255.

45. The conference gathers the Sufi congregation around its leaders and attracts a number of Muslim-American Sufi intellectuals. The Naqshbandiya Foundation for Islamic Education published a "proceedings" of the first

conference: see Alan A. Godlas, ed., *Remembrance: Proceedings of the First Annual International Milad an-Nabi Conference* (Chicago: Naqshbandiya Foundation for Islamic Education, 1994).

46. The following account of Laleh Bakhtiar's life is compiled on the basis of my interviews and discussions with her (especially on August 3, 1995 [taped]) and on the article "In Profile: Laleh Bakhtiar: A Bridge between Two Cultures," *Publishers Weekly*, March 15, 1996.

47. Laleh Bakhtiar and Nader Ardalan, *The Sense of Unity: The Sufi Tradition in Persian Architecture* (Chicago: University of Chicago Press, 1973).

48. Interview (taped), August 3, 1995.

49. Ibid.

50. See, for example, Laleh Bakhtiar, *Traditional Psychoethics and Personality Paradigm* (Chicago: Institute of Traditional Psychoethics and Guidance, 1993); idem, *Moral Healers Handbook: The Psychology of Spiritual Chivalry* (Chicago: Institute of Traditional Psychoethics and Guidance, 1994); idem, *Moral Healing Through the Most Beautiful Names: The Practice of Spiritual Chivalry* (Chicago: Institute of Traditional Psychoethics and Guidance, 1994); idem, *Sufi Women of America: Angels in the Making* (Chicago: Institute of Traditional Psychoethics and Guidance, 1996).

51. Interview (taped), August 3, 1995.

52. See, for example, Ira Lapidus, *A History of Islamic Societies* (New York: Cambridge University Press, 1988), 184; Haddad and Smith, *Mission to America*, 18.

53. Interview (taped), August 10, 1995.

54. Interview (taped), August 24, 1995.

55. Interview (taped), August 1, 1995.

56. See, for example, Seyyed Mohammad Fazlhashemi, "Förändring och kontinuitet. Al-Ghazalis politiska omsvängning" (Ph.D. thesis, Umeå University, Umeå, Sweden, 1994).

57. Yvonne Yazbeck Haddad, "Towards the Carving of Islamic Space in 'the West,'" *ISIM Newsletter* (October 1998); Garbi Schmidt, "Sufi Charisma on the Internet," in *Living Sufism*, ed. David Westerlund (London: Routledge Curzon, forthcoming).

58. Schmidt, "Sufi Charisma."

59. Interview (taped), August 3, 1995.

60. Ibn al-'Arabi (A.D. 1165–1240) was a Spanish-born Muslim philosopher and mystic.

61. Sunni Muslims argue that Muhammad was the last prophet sent by God—that is, that he was the "Seal of the Prophets." Arguing that other prophets could come after him is therefore considered heresy.

62. This is a possible reference to *sura* 5:109.

63. Interview (taped), August 1, 1995.

64. Haddad and Smith, *Mission to America*, 12.

65. Ibid., 15. For the historical development of the term, see *Encyclopedia of Islam*, s.v. "al-Mahdi."

66. For Naqshbandi expectations of the coming of the *Mahdi* (messiah) by the turn of the millennium, see Jørgen S. Nielsen, "Transnational Islam and the Integration of Islam in Europe," paper presented at the Second Mediterranean Social and Political Research Meeting, European University Institute, Florence, 2001.

67. *Da'wah Newsletter* (1996), 4. For a study of the III&E's understanding of the Nation of Islam and the Ahmadiyya, see "Islam and Farrakhanism Compared" (pamphlet, n.d.) and "Qadiyanism: A Brief Survey" (pamphlet, n.d.). For a more comprehensive study of new Islamic movements in North America, see esp. Haddad and Smith, *Mission to America*; Turner, *Islam in the African-American Experience*.

68. Although the III&E did not declare itself to be the initial debater, it was generally viewed as being so, especially because of the accusations against Sufism Amir Ali had made in his earlier publications.

69. Interview (taped), August 1, 1995. Amir Ali's denial of any direct connection with his associate's attack on Sufism was repeated in the later flyer "Response to the Anonymously Written Flyer Distributed in Chicago Area on Friday, June 16."

70. "What the Scholars of Islam Said about Tasawwuf" (Naqshbandiyya-Haqqaniyya order flyer, n.d.). The conflict between Naqshbandiyya-Haqqaniyya and Salafi-inspired movements and organizations is not limited to Chicago. In 1996, the as-Sunnah Foundation of America, which is affiliated with the Naqshbandiyya-Haqqaniyya, published two books that directly addressed the topic of Sufism versus the Salafi: see Jamal Effendi al-'Iraqi al-Sidqi al-Zahawi, *The Doctrine of Ahl al-Sunna versus the "Salafi" Movement, Translated by Sheykh Hisham Kabbani* (Mountainview, Calif.: As-Sunna Foundation of America, 1996); Shaykh Muhammad Hisham Kabbani, *Islamic Beliefs and Doctrine According to Ahl al-Sunna: A Repudiation of "Salafi" Innovations* (Mountainview, Calif.: As-Sunna Foundation of America, 1996). The subject was also discussed during the Sufi Mawlid an-Nabi Conference in Chicago in 1997. There Shaykh Kabbani denounced the "neo-Salafi Movement" as having "tried its worst to cut the heart out of Islamic belief and practice": "Chicago Speech on Milad Annabi," website (last viewed October 1998); http://www.sunnah.org/events/milad97/chicago_speech.htm. The term "neo-Salafi" must be seen as referring to both Wahhabis and the Salafi movement of current days that seek to denounce their claims to imitation of *al-aslaf* (the first generation of Muslims). The conflict between Salafis and Sufis in the United States is evident on the Internet: see Schmidt, "Sufi Charisma."

71. The term "professional Muslims" was suggested to me during a conversation with Prof. John Esposito on November 16, 1995.

72. Yvonne Yazbeck Haddad and Adair T. Lummis, *Islamic Values in the United States* (New York: Oxford University Press, 1987), 58–66; Poston, *Islamic Da'wah in the West*, 38.

73. The School of Islamic and Social Sciences is located in Leesburg, Virginia. Candidates for the master's of imamate degree must complete two years of residency and a total of ninety credit hours at the school: See "Masters Program for Imams," website (last viewed April 2001); available at: http://www.siss.edu/imampro.htm.

74. *Sura* 49:13.

75. This argument is often raised in Islamic human-rights debates. For an in-depth study of Islam and human rights, see Jonas Svensson, *Women's Human Rights and Islam: A Study of Three Attempts at Accommodation*, Lund Studies in History of Religions 12 (Lund: Religionshistoriska Avdelingen, University of Lund, 2000).

76. During the early days of the Islamic community, direct attempts to abolish slavery were not made, although freeing slaves was described as atonement for many sins. According to both the Qur'an and the *Sunna*, slaves should be treated with kindness. Slavery has existed in countries with Muslim majorities up to the present.

77. Williams, *Religions of Immigrants*, 242.

78. Unpublished list made available by Paul D. Numrich, research associate at the Religion in Urban America Program, University of Illinois at Chicago (Fall 1996).

79. See, for example, *Assalamu 'Alaikum Chicago Muslims* (March 1997), 8–9. The list also included the addresses of five other "Friday prayer places." In 1996, a map published by the MSA at the University of Illinois at Chicago/Springfield, ISNA, and FAMTech Consultants listed twenty-four mosques in the Chicago area: *Islamic Centers in U.S.A.: Roadmap 1996–97*, FAMRTech Consultants (n.d.).

80. Patrick D. Gaffney, *The Prophet's Pulpit: Islamic Preaching in Contemporary Egypt* (Berkeley: University of California Press, 1994), 13.

81. For an enlightening article on mosque architecture in the United States, see Omar Khalidi, "Approaches to Mosque Design in North America," in Haddad and Esposito, *Muslims on the Americanization Path?*

82. Saara Behlim, *The Islamic Cultural Center of Greater Chicago: A Historical Perspective* (Chicago: Islamic Cultural Center of Greater Chicago, 1994).

83. See Atique Mahmood, "Islamic Foundation Villa Park: 22 Years of Service to Islam and the Muslim Community," *Muslim Journal*, May 3, 1996; "Fulfilling the Muslim Community's Needs: Islamic Foundation of Villa Park Hold Ground-Breaking Ceremony for New Project," *Unity Times International*, May–June 1995; Islamic Foundation, *Islamic Foundation: The Mosque and the Community Project* (pamphlet, 1995); "Introduction, Islamic Foundation," website (last viewed April 2001); available at: http://www.islamicfoundationvp.org/intro.html.

84. The new mosque opened its doors in 1998: see "Introduction, Islamic Foundation."

85. This factor has also been noted in earlier studies on Muslims in the United States: see, for example, Susan Slymovics, "The Muslim World Day Parade and 'Storefront' Mosques of New York City," in Metcalf, *Making Muslim Space*, 209.

86. Behlim, *Islamic Cultural Center of Greater Chicago*. A detailed account of the history of the ICCC can also be found at "History of ICC," website (last viewed August 2002); available at: http://iccchicago.homestead.com/ files/history/h01.html.

87. "The Islamic Cultural Center of Greater Chicago," *Muslim Journal*, November 4, 1988.

88. In one of the first studies of Muslim Americans, Abdo Elkholy mentions that in the 1960s the mosque had become a place where Muslim youth participated in social activities such as dating and mixed dancing to rock music: Abdo A. Elkholy, *The Arab Moslems in the United States* (New Haven, Conn.: College and University Press Publishers, 1966), 33. During my fieldwork in Chicago I never saw such activities in any of the mosques. The only exception may be the ICCC, and only to the extent of folk dancing.

89. *Islam in North America* gives 1982 as the founding year; Cainkar, *Palestinian Women*, 212, gives 1980 as the founding year); and Husain and Vogelaar, "Activities," 240, gives 1983 as the founding year. Also interviews with MF board members on August 24, 1995 (taped), and June 7, 1997. The last informant gave 1981 as the founding year.

90. Cainkar, *Palestinian Women*, 212.

91. Stephen Franklin, "Area Muslims Fight 'False Stereotypes,'" *Chicago Tribune*, September 3, 1993.

92. By the late 1990s, the MF's board consisted of twenty-one members and was based on a rotating membership in which each member was elected for a three-year term, with seven people coming up for election each year. People voting in the elections had to be members of the mosque for at least six months. Elections could be annulled if the elected official was not an MF member or if it could be confirmed that he or she had behaved in a manner that was inconsistent with Islamic norms—for example, by committing theft or adultery: interview with MF member (taped), June 7, 1997.

93. Steven Emerson, "Regarding Terrorism and the Middle East Peace Process," prepared testimony before the Senate Foreign Relations Committee, Subcommittee on Near East and South Asia, March 19, 1996; see also idem, "The Other Fundamentalists," *New Republic*, June 12, 1995. The allegations have been repeated by sources in Israel's Shin Bet secret police: Hundley, "Two Chicagoans Aided Militants."

94. Emerson is known for claiming that Middle Eastern terrorist organizations are supported and trained by parts of the Muslim-American community: see, for example, Steven Emerson, "A Terrorist Network in America?" *New York Times*, April 7, 1993. He has frequently served as a witness on national and international terrorist matters in congressional hearings. Vigorous protests against Emerson are frequently raised by Islamic organi-

zations such as CAIR: Ibrahim Hooper, "Self-Proclaimed Terrorist Expert Attacks Muslims," letter to the editor, Washington Times, May 12, 1995). Emerson also associates CAIR with Middle Eastern terrorism: Steven Emerson, "A Textbook Case of the Dangers of Radical U.S. Groups," letter to the editor, Washington Times, July 1, 1995. Emerson's work has also been criticized by non-Muslims, in particular because of his obvious pro-Zionist tendencies: see Jane Hunter, "Steven Emerson: A Journalist Who Knows How to Take a Leak," Extra (October–November 1992); Greg Noakes, "Muslims and the American Press," in Haddad and Esposito, Muslims on the Americanization Path? 289–90. Emerson was particularly criticized after his documentary Jihad in America aired on PBS on November 21, 1994; it included perspectives on claimed terrorist activities supported by Muslim organizations inside the United States. The documentary met public protest by Muslim Americans, fostering demonstrations in Washington, D.C., and other cities such as Alexandria, Virginia; Dallas; and Detroit: see Shawn M. Terry, "Muslims Try to Stop TV Show on Militants; PBS Says Program Targets Small Extremist Groups," Dallas Morning News, November 12, 1994; "Vandals Attack Muslim School due to PBS Documentary" (e-mail), MSANEWS, November 30, 1994; "Detroit Area Arabs and Muslims Angered over Broadcast Jihad in America," PR Newswire, November 18, 1994. In Chicago, press attention was once again aimed at alleged ties to Hamas: CNN, "Domestic News" (television broadcast), November 22, 1994.

95. The following is based on my interview with a former chairman and director of the DTIC (taped), February 25, 1997.

96. According to other sources, organized Muslim prayer actually took place in the Loop area before 1976. In 1974, the Chicago Sun-Times reporter Roy Larson mentioned that prayer took place in "an ultramodern Loop office": Larson, "Feasting . . . Fasting."

97. NAIT, established in 1971, describes itself as a trust that "provides protection and safeguarding for the assets of ISNA/MSA and other communities by holding their assets and real estate in 'waqf.' It also . . . supports and subsidizes projects beneficial to the cause of Islam and Muslims": "NAIT," website (last viewed August 2002); available at: http://www.nait.net/nait.html. According to flyers distributed at the DTIC, NAIT had promised a loan of no less than 25 percent of the money collected: "Building Update" (DTIC flyer, October 4, 1996); "Agreement" DTIC flyer, September 18, 1996). No indication of the price of the building was given.

98. Before the Kedzie building was purchased, people engaged in the MCC shared their religious activities with the Bosnian community. The split between the two ethnic groups after that period was, according to prominent members of the MCC, grounded in a dispute similar to the one revealed in the establishment of the Mosque Foundation. Whereas the Bosnian community wanted a center where members could carry out ethno-cultural traditions such as dancing, the South Asians found such activities unsuitable for an Islamic center. Therefore, the Bosnians continued

autonomously and later built their own center (the ICCC), while the South Asians established their center in the Kedzie building: *MCC 25th Anniversary Video*.

99. Interview with the chairman of MCC (taped), January 19, 1997.

100. In 1996, the MCC had 465 family members (a total of 930 people), 85 single members, 13 life members, 8 student members, and 6 senior members: *27th Annual Report of the Muslim Community Center Inc., Presented to the General Assembly on January 21, 1996* (Chicago: Muslim Community Center, 1996), 3.

101. The MCC publishes a monthly newsletter, *The Message*, that contains articles, summaries of *khutbas*, and matrimonials.

102. *Islam in North America*, 7.

103. *27th Annual Report*, 1.

104. Imam Bukhari (A.D. 810–870) is particularly well known for his collection of *ahadith*, the *Sahih*.

105. Interview with member of the MCC, June 30, 1997.

106. Interview with member of the MF, June 7, 1997.

107. *The Council of Islamic Organizations of Greater Chicago* (Chicago: Council of Islamic Organizations of Greater Chicago, 1995).

108. Interview with a former board member of the Council of Islamic Organizations of Greater Chicago (taped), August 10, 1995.

109. According to a former producer of the Council of Islamic Organizations of Greater Chicago's TV program, March 22, 1997.

110. *'Id al-Adha* falls in the Islamic month *Dhul-Hijjah* by the end of the *hajj*.

111. Interview with Chicago *'alim*, May 20, 1997.

112. Interview (taped), January 30, 1996.

113. For example, "Stranger in a *Strange* Land," *Islamic Renaissance*, vol. 3 (1995), 17–18.

114. Interview, November 14, 1996.

115. This assumption was supported by a recent survey of mosques in America stating that, whereas in 52 percent of the mosques women prayed behind a curtain or in a separate room in 1994, the proportion had increased to 66 percent in 2001: see Bagby, *The Mosque in America*, 11.

116. Richard T. Antoun, *Muslim Preacher in the Modern World: A Jordanian Case Study in Comparative Perspective* (Princeton, N.J.: Princeton University Press, 1989); Gaffney, *Prophet's Pulpit*.

117. See, for example, Skovgaard-Petersen, *Defining Islam*.

118. *Sura* 7:156.

119. Interview (taped), February 25, 1997.

120. Benedict Anderson defines "truth-languages" as languages that, to the believer and community of believers, are "emanations of reality, not randomly fabricated representations of it. . . . Ontological reality is [to the believer] apprehensible only through a single, privileged system of

re-presentation: the truth-language of Church Latin, Qur'anic Arabic, or Examination Chinese": Benedict Anderson, *Imagined Communities* (New York: Verso, 1991), 14.

121. His booklets include Yakub A. Patel, *Reflections on Change—An Islamic Perspective* (Chicago: Downtown Islamic Center, 1984); idem, *Muhammad (s) a Model of Human Excellence* (Chicago: Downtown Islamic Center, 1986); idem, *Islam: The Natural Way of Life* (Chicago: Downtown Islamic Center, n.d.).

122. Interview (taped), February 25, 1997.

123. Gaffney, *Prophet's Pulpit*, 34.

124. The following account is based on observations during the spring of 1997. It is not based on tape recordings, but it attempts, through its style, to highlight the narratives and narrative styles that were a vital part of these women's meetings.

125. *Umm* means "mother" in Arabic. In the Middle East (and among some groups of Muslim Americans who do not come from that part of the world), it is customary for a woman to take the name of her first-born male child. She is thus called "the mother (*Umm*) of [the child's name]," whereas the father is called "father (*Abu*) of [the child's name]."

126. Statement from a member of the group, March 9, 1996.

127. Particularly audiotapes with Imam Siraj Wahaj (New York) and Imam Hamza Yusuf (California) are distributed. Both *imams* are popular speakers and recognized for their knowledge of Islam. Their fame further derives from their great fluency in the Qur'an, the *hadith*, and the Arabic language, even though they are converts. During the sessions I attended, Umm Khadija mentioned only one Muslim scholar by name: Sayyed Qutb of Egypt. Qutb, a prominent ideologist of the Ikhwan al-Muslimun, was executed by the Egyptian government in 1966.

128. The sixth verse in *Surat al-Fatiha*, the first *sura* of the Qur'an.

129. Abu Bakr was one of the Prophet's closest friends and one of the first converts to Islam. He became the first caliph after the Prophet's death (A.D. 632–34).

130. Abu Jahl (father of ignorance) was the mock name given by the first Muslim community to 'Amr ibn Hisham, one of the leaders of Mecca. Abu Jahl was one of the Prophet's hardest and most passionate adversaries.

131. Cainkar, *Palestinian Women*; Arjun Appadurai, *Modernity at Large: Cultural Dimensions of Globalization* (Minneapolis: University of Minnesota Press, 1990), 19; Rachel Bloul, "Engendering Muslim Identities: Deterritorialization and the Ethnicization in France," in Metcalf, *Making Muslim Space*, 235.

Glossary of Arabic Words and Phrases

'Abd	Slave or servant (pl. *'ibad*); servant of God (pl. *'abid*)
al-Akhira	Judgment in the hereafter
Allah	The Arabic name for God
Allahu akbar	"God is greater!"
'Alim (pl. *'ulama'*)	Islamic scholar
Amir (m.)/*amira* (f.)	Leader
al-Asma' al-husna	The ninety-nine beautiful names of God
Astaghfir Allah	"May God forgive!"
Awra	Those parts of the human body that must be covered according to Islamic tradition
Aya (Ar. pl. *ayat*)	Verse in the Qur'an
Bay'a	The pledging of allegiance (to a Sufi *shaykh*)
Bismi Allah al-Rahman al-Rahim	"In the name of God, the Beneficent, the Merciful" (sentence that introduces every *sura* in the Qur'an except *sura 9*)
Dars al-Qur'an	Lesson presenting the teaching of the Qur'an
Da'wa	The act of proselytizing or informing others about Islam
Dhabiha (*zabiha*)	Food considered *halal*
Dhikr	Remembrance of Allah, the central ritual of the Sufis
Du'a	Personal prayer to God

(Salat) al-Fajr	Ritual prayer prescribed for the period from dawn until just before sunrise
Fatwa (Ar. pl. fatawa)	Legislative opinion according to Islamic law
Fiqh	Islamic jurisprudence
Fitna	Confusion, chaos
Hadith (Ar. pl. ahadith)	The narrated tradition of the Prophet Muhammad
Hafiz (m.)/hafiza (f.) (Ar. pl. huffaz)	A person who has learned the Qur'an by heart
Hajj	The fourth pillar of Islam; the great pilgrimage
Halal	That which is permitted or legitimate according to Islam
Halaqa	Study circle
Al-hamdu li-llah	"Thanks be to God!"
Haram	That which is prohibited or forbidden according to Islam
Hasana (pl. hasanat)	God's positive reward for the good deeds of humans
Hijab (Ar. pl. hujub)	The head covering some Muslim women wear (often explained according to Qur'an 24:31 or 33:59)
Hijabi (Ar. pl. muhajjabat)	A woman who wears the hijab
Hizb al-Tahrir	Liberation Party
'Id al-Adha	The festival marking Abraham's sacrifice, which takes place by the end of the hajj
'Id al-Fitr	The festival marking the end of Ramadan
Iftar	The meal eaten to break the fast during Ramadan
Ikhwan al-Muslimun	Islamic reform movement that originated in Egypt

Imam	The leader of prayer, and eventually the leader of Islamic center affairs
Iman	Faith
In sha'a Allah	"God willing!"
Jahannam	Hell
Jahiliyya	The time of ignorance
Jalabiyya	Long, loose shirt-like robe worn by some Muslim men
Jama'at-i Islami	Islamic reform movement that originated in Pakistan
Janna	Paradise
Jihad	Internal religious struggle, holy war
Jilbab	A long gown worn by some Muslim women (often explained according to Qur'an 33.59)
(Salat) al-Jum'a	Ritual prayer in congregation
Ka'ba	Islam's central house of worship, located in Mecca
Khalifa	The vice-regent of God, or caliph
Khatib (Ar. pl. *khutaba'*)	The person who delivers the sermon
Khilafa	The institutionalized government of the *umma*; the caliphate
Khutba (Ar. pl. *khutab*)	Sermon
Kufr	Disbelief (in Islam)
Kuttab	School for the memorization of the Qur'an
La ilaha illa Allah	"There is no God but God!"
La ilaha illa Allah wa Muhammad Rasul Allah	The content of the Islamic proclamation of faith; the *Shahada*; "There is no God but God, and Muhammad is his messenger."
al-Latif	The Gentle; one of the beautiful names of God

Ma sha'a Allah	"Whatever God wants!"
Madhhab (Ar. pl. *madhahib*)	School of Islamic law
Madrasa	Academy for the study of Islamic theology
Mahdi	The person sent by God before the end of all time, the messiah
Markaz	Center
Masjid (Ar. pl. *masajid*)	Mosque
Mawlid al-Nabi	Birthday of the Prophet Muhammad
Medina	City
Mubarak	"May it be blessed!"
Mullah	Islamic scholar
Mu'min (pl. *Mu'minun*)	(Male) believer
Murid	Novice
Naqshbandiyya-Haqqaniyya	The most prominent Sufi order in the United States
Nar	(Hell)fire
Qasida (Ar. pl. *Qasa'id*)	Special style of poetry
al-Qur'an	The Holy Scripture of Islam
Quraysh	The tribe from which the Prophet Muhammad originated
Rabitat al-'Alam al-Islamiyya	The Muslim World League
al-Rahman	The Merciful; one of the ninety-nine names of God
Ramadan	The Islamic month of fasting
Salam	Peace
Al-salam 'alaykum (*wa rahmat Ullah*)	"Peace (and God's mercy) be with you"; the Islamic greeting
Salat	Ritual prayer
Salla Allahu 'alyhi wa sallam	"May God's peace be with him!"
Shahada	The proclamation of the Islamic attestation of faith, the first pillar of Islam, marking conversion

Shari'a	Islamic law
Shaykh	Superior, authoritative person or preacher within the Muslim community; often used as the title for the person leading a Sufi *tariqa*
Shirk	Belief in more than one God, understood in Islam as a major blasphemy
Shura	Council, leadership
Silsila	Chain of transmission of knowledge
Sira	The life and biography of the Prophet Muhammad
Siyasa	Politics
Subhana Allah	"May God be praised!"
Subhanahu wa ta'ala	"Praised and glorified is He [God]!"
Sunna	The deeds and sayings of the Prophet Muhammad
Sura (Ar. pl. *suwar*)	Chapter of the Qur'an
Tablighi Jama'at	Islamic movement that originated on the South Asian subcontinent
Tafsir	Qur'anic interpretation
Taghut	Idol/idolatry
Tajwid	Intoned recitation of the Qur'an
Takbir	"Give praise!"; uttered before the exclamation *"Allahu Akbar"*
Tarawih	Special prayer during the month of Ramadan; includes the reading of the entire Qur'an
Tariqa (pl. *turuq*)	Sufi order
Tasawwuf	Sufism; the mystical dimension and practice of Islam
Tasbiha	Muslim "rosary"; known in the Middle East as *mishaba*. The Arabic term means "glorification of God," "hymn," and "praise."

Topi/kufi	A small, round, soft hat worn by some Muslim men
Umma	The community of Muslims
'Umra	The little pilgrimage
Wahy	Revelation
Wazir	Vizier
Wudu'	Ablution
Zakat	Tithing, alms-giving; the third pillar of Islam

Index

Association of Muslim Social Scientists, 90
Authority (religious authority), 11–12. See Mosque; Muslim-American community; Muslim full-time schools; Muslim Students' Association; Professional Muslims; Women's study groups
Awra (those parts of the human body that must be covered according to Islamic tradition), 185, 227
Aya (Ar. pl. ayat; verse in the Qur'an), 54, 76, 149, 173, 227
Ayat al-Kursi, 149
al-Azhar University, 165

Ba-Yunus, Ilyas, 198–99n41
Badawi, Jamal, 216n15
Bait ul-Salaam, 97, 98, 99
Bakhtiar, Laleh, 148, 149–53
Banderas, Antonio, 4
al-Banna, Hassan, 5
Bay'a (initiation), 147, 151, 227
Benaat Chicago (Daughters of Chicago), 42
Betterjee, Sobhi, 216n15
Bible, 159, 160
Black P Stone Nation, 27
Bosnian American Cultural Association, 21, 23, 164
Bosnians (Bosnian Americans): in Chicago, 21, 164
Bukhari, Abu Abdullah Muhammad, 167
Bush, George W., 7, 198n38

Cainkar, Louise, 22, 165, 198n40, 206n22, 207n31
Center for Muslim-Christian Understanding (Georgetown), 197n32
Center for Policy and Future Studies (EWU), 89
Central Intelligence Agency (CIA), 145
Chicago Fiqh Council, 168
Chicago's Muslim community: colleges established by, 85, 86–92, 133–34; federal surveillance of, 24–25; full-time schools established by, 61–78

(see also Muslim full-time schools); Hafiz schools established by, 78–80, 209n63 (see also Hafiz school); history of, 16–29; mosques established by, 23–24, 163–67 (see also Mosque); Muslim Students' Associations established by, 93–135 (see also Muslim Students' Association); previous research on, 198n40; Shi'ites within, 25–26; size of, 198n41; weekend and Sunday Schools in, 35–41 (see also Muslim weekend and Sunday schools); women's study groups within, 176–86 (see also Women's study groups)
Chick Publications, 217n23
Children. See Muslim children
Children of Beituniya Society, 20
Christianity, 17, 44, 105, 118, 152, 153, 158, 160
Christians, 4, 20, 44, 50, 52, 117, 144, 158, 159, 207n28, 211n12; colleges and universities, 85; fundamentalists, 142–43, 144, 154; missionaries, 17, 143, 144
Christmas, 47
Citizens Advocating Responsible Education (CARE), 25
Class (social), 12, 31, 59, 118, 137, 157, 161, 163, 175, 187
Clinton, William J., 7, 9
College Bowl, 93
College Preparatory School of America, 62, 208n41
Columbian Exposition in Chicago, 16–18
Committee of the Judiciary, 9
Computer technology, 93, 104, 139
Conference for Improved Muslim–Christian Relations, 88, 210–11n9
Converts (to Islam), 44, 76, 77–78, 116–18, 140, 141, 159, 169–70, 177, 182–83, 186
Council for a Parliament of the World's Religions, 25, 63, 143, 198n33, 210–11n9
Council for Islamic Organizations of Greater Chicago, 166, 168, 187
Council of Islamic Education, 113n11